Data Science for De

Enhance your leadership skills with data science and AI expertise

Jon Howells

<packt>

Data Science for Decision Makers

Copyright © 2024 Packt Publishing

All rights reserved. No part of this book may be reproduced, stored in a retrieval system, or transmitted in any form or by any means, without the prior written permission of the publisher, except in the case of brief quotations embedded in critical articles or reviews.

Every effort has been made in the preparation of this book to ensure the accuracy of the information presented. However, the information contained in this book is sold without warranty, either express or implied. Neither the author, nor Packt Publishing or its dealers and distributors, will be held liable for any damages caused or alleged to have been caused directly or indirectly by this book.

Packt Publishing has endeavored to provide trademark information about all of the companies and products mentioned in this book by the appropriate use of capitals. However, Packt Publishing cannot guarantee the accuracy of this information.

Group Product Manager: Ali Abidi
Publishing Product Manager: Tejashwini R
Book Project Manager: Hemangi Lotlikar
Content Development Editor: Joseph Sunil
Technical Editor: Rahul Limbachiya
Copy Editor: Safis Editing
Proofreader: Joseph Sunil
Indexer: Rekha Nair
Production Designer: Ponraj Dhandapani
DevRel Marketing Coordinator: Vinishka Kalra

First published: June 2024

Production reference: 1190624

Published by Packt Publishing Ltd.

Grosvenor House
11 St Paul's Square
Birmingham
B3 1RB, UK

ISBN 978-1-83763-729-4

www.packtpub.com

To my mother and father, Caroline and Robert, for instilling in me the values of education and constant curiosity. To my partner, Yeshica, for your unwavering support, and to my sister, Felicity, for your keen eye in reviewing and shaping this book.

– Jon Howells

Contributors

About the author

Jon Howells, director of AI consultancy QualifAI, is an experienced professional in data science and machine learning, with over a decade of experience in the consumer goods, market research, and public sectors. He has worked within consultancies including KPMG and Capgemini and with multinational clients such as Unilever and Permira, as well as public sector bodies such as the UK Home Office and the US **Food and Drug Administration (FDA)**.

With an MSc in computational statistics and machine learning from UCL, Jon specializes in applying **large language models** (**LLMs**) to consumer-focused businesses, leveraging them for consumer research, personalized content generation, and enhanced customer support. His expertise helps businesses better understand and engage with their customers, driving innovation and unlocking the potential of data-driven decision-making.

About the reviewer

As a principal architect at T-Mobile, **Tanmaya Gaur** has more than 10 years of web development experience and a passion for delivering technical and architectural leadership for key technology initiatives and business capabilities. In the latest chapter of his professional career, he has been instrumental in shaping the architecture of T-Mobile's primary CRM solution, which is built using modular micro-frontend architecture and enhances the digital experience for their care representatives and customers.

His expertise in web, infrastructure, and microservices enables him to design and deliver scalable solutions that are performant, secure, and resilient. He works closely with other business and IT partner teams in a highly collaborative environment and is committed to driving the best customer experience across mobile, desktop, point-of-sale, and other emerging devices.

Table of Contents

Preface xiii

Part 1: Understanding Data Science and Its Foundations

1

Introducing Data Science 3

Data science, AI, and ML – what's the difference?	4	Conditional probability	12
The mathematical and statistical underpinnings of data science	5	**Describing our samples**	**13**
		Measures of central tendency	13
Statistics and data science	**6**	Measures of dispersion	14
What is statistics?	6	Degrees of freedom	16
Descriptive and inferential statistics	**7**	Correlation, causation, and covariance	16
Sampling strategies	9	The shape of data	18
Probability	**11**	**Probability distributions**	**18**
Probability distribution	12	Discrete probability distributions	18
		Continuous probability distributions	19
		Summary	**20**

2

Characterizing and Collecting Data 21

What are the key criteria to consider when evaluating datasets?	22	Data variety	23
		Data quality	23
Data quantity	22	**First-, second-, and third-party data**	**24**
Data velocity	22		

First-party data – the treasure trove within	25	Storing and processing data	30
Second-party data – building bridges through collaboration	25	Cloud, on-premises, and hybrid solutions – navigating the data storage and analysis landscape	36
Third-party data – broadening horizons with external expertise	25	Cloud computing – scalable services in the cloud	36

Structured, unstructured, and semi-structured data — 26
On-premises – maintaining control within your walls — 37
Structured data — 26
Hybrid – the best of both worlds? — 37
Unstructured data — 27
Data processing — 38
Semi-structured data — 28
Summary — 39

Methods for collecting data — 29

3

Exploratory Data Analysis — 41

Getting started with Google Colab — 41
Histograms — 48
What is Google Colab? — 42
Density curves — 49
A step-by-step guide to setting up Google Colab — 42
Boxplots — 50
Heatmaps — 51
Understanding the data you have — 43
Dimensionality reduction — 52
EDA techniques and tools — 43
Correlation analysis — 53
Descriptive statistics — 43
Outlier detection — 55
Data visualization — 45
Summary — 57

4

The Significance of Significance — 59

The idea of testing hypotheses — 60
Significance tests for a population proportion – making informed decisions about proportions — 66
What is a hypothesis? — 60
How does hypothesis testing work? — 60
Formulating null and alternative hypotheses — 61
The z-test – comparing a sample proportion to a population proportion — 68
Determining the significance level — 62
Z-test example made easy — 70
Understanding errors — 63
Significance tests for a population average (mean) — 70
Getting to grips with p-values — 65

Writing hypotheses for a significance test about a mean	71	Using a table to estimate the p-value from the t-statistic	72
Conditions for a t-test about a mean	71	Comparing the p-value from the t-statistic to the significance level	72
When to use z or t statistics in significance tests	71	One-tailed and two-tailed tests	72
Example – calculating the t-statistic for a test about a mean	71	**Walking through a case study**	**72**
		Summary	**74**

5

Understanding Regression 75

How can I benefit from understanding regression?	75	Interpreting the slope of a regression line	82
Introduction to trend lines	76	Interpreting the intercept of a regression line	83
Fitting a trend line to data	77	Understanding residuals	84
Estimating the line of best fit	79	Evaluating the goodness of fit in least-squares regression	86
Calculating the equations of the lines of best fit	79	Summary	87

Part 2: Machine Learning – Concepts, Applications, and Pitfalls

6

Introducing Machine Learning 91

From statistics to machine learning	**91**	Healthcare diagnostics and treatment	94
What is machine learning?	92	**The different types of machine learning**	**94**
How does machine learning relate to statistics?	92	Supervised learning	95
Why is machine learning important?	**93**	Unsupervised learning	95
Customer personalization and segmentation	93	Semi-supervised learning	95
Fraud detection and security	93	Reinforcement learning	95
Supply chain and inventory optimization	93	Transfer learning	96
Predictive maintenance	94	**Popular machine learning algorithms**	**97**

Linear regression	97	**Risks and limitations of machine learning**	**106**
Logistic regression	98	Overfitting and underfitting	107
Decision trees	99	Bias and variance	107
Random forests	99	Balanced dataset	107
Support vector machines	100	Models are approximations of reality	108
k-nearest neighbors	101		
Neural networks	102	**Machine learning on unstructured data**	**108**
The machine learning process	**103**	Natural language processing (NLP)	108
Training a supervised machine learning model	103	Computer vision	108
Validation of a supervised machine learning model	103	**Deep learning and artificial intelligence**	**109**
Testing a supervised machine learning model	104	Artificial intelligence	109
Evaluating machine learning models	104	Deep learning	109
		Summary	**110**

7

Supervised Machine Learning — 111

Defining supervised learning	**111**	**Characteristics of regression and classification algorithms**	**117**
Applications of supervised learning	112	Regression algorithms	117
The two types of supervised learning	112	Classification algorithms	119
Key factors in supervised learning	113	Key considerations in supervised learning	121
Steps within supervised learning	**115**	Evaluation metrics	121
Data preparation – laying the foundation	115	**Applications of supervised learning**	**122**
Algorithm selection – choosing the right tool	115	Consumer goods	122
Model training – learning from data	116	Retail	122
Model evaluation – assessing performance	116	Manufacturing	123
Prediction and deployment – putting the model to work	116	**Summary**	**123**

8

Unsupervised Machine Learning — 125

Defining UL — 125
Practical examples of UL — 126

Steps in UL — 126
Step 1 – Data collection — 127
Step 2 – Data preprocessing — 127
Step 3 – Choosing the right model — 127
Step 4 – Training the model — 128
Step 5 – Interpretation and evaluation — 128
In summary — 128

Clustering – unveiling hidden patterns in your data — 128
What is clustering? — 128
How does clustering work? — 129
k-means clustering — 130
Practical applications of clustering — 131
Evaluation metrics for clustering — 132
In summary — 132

Association rule learning — 133
What is association rule learning? — 133
The Apriori algorithm – a practical example — 133
Evaluation metrics — 134
In summary — 134

Applications of UL — 134
Market segmentation — 134
Anomaly detection — 134
Feature extraction — 135

Summary — 135

9

Interpreting and Evaluating Machine Learning Models — 137

How do I know whether this model will be accurate? — 137
Evaluating on test (holdout) data — 138

Understanding evaluation metrics — 138
Evaluating regression models — 138
R-squared — 139
Root mean squared error — 140
Mean absolute error — 142
When and how to use each metric — 143
Practical evaluation strategies — 144
Summarizing the evaluation of regression models — 145

Evaluating classification models — 145
Classification model evaluation metrics — 147
Precision, recall, and F1-Score — 147
Recall — 149
F1-score — 150

Methods for explaining machine learning models — 152
Making sense of regression models – the power of coefficients — 152
Decoding classification models – unveiling feature importance — 152
Beyond specific models – universal insights using SHAP values — 153

Summary — 154

10

Common Pitfalls in Machine Learning — 157

Understanding the complexity	158	Underfitting – when your model is too simplistic	163
Dirty data, damaged models – how data quantity and quality impact ML	158	Spotting the problem	163
		Conclusion	167
The importance of adequate training data	159	**Training-serving skew and model drift**	**167**
Dealing with poor data quality	160	Training-serving skew	167
Conclusion	161	Model drift	168
Overcoming overfitting and underfitting	**162**	Key takeaways	168
Navigating training-serving skew and model drift	162	**Bias and fairness**	**169**
Ensuring fairness	162	Understanding bias	169
Mastering overfitting and underfitting for optimal model performance	**163**	Understanding fairness	169
		Mitigating bias and ensuring fairness	169
		Key takeaways	170
Overfitting – when your model is too specific	163	**Summary**	**170**

Part 3: Leading Successful Data Science Projects and Teams

11

The Structure of a Data Science Project — 173

The various types of data science projects	**174**	**Developing a data product**	**182**
		Data preparation and exploratory analysis	182
Data products	174	Model design and development	183
Reports and analytics	175	Evaluation and testing	183
Research and methodology	176	**Deploying and monitoring a data product**	**184**
The stages of a data product	**177**		
Identifying use cases	178	**General best practices for data product development**	**185**
Evaluating use cases	179		
Planning the data product	180	**Evaluating impact**	**186**

Predictive maintenance in manufacturing	187	Predictive maintenance in energy	188
Fraud detection in banking	187	Workforce optimization in quick service restaurants	189
Customer churn prediction in telecom	187	Chatbot-assisted customer support	189
Demand forecasting in retail	188	**Summary**	**190**
Personalized recommendations in e-commerce	188		

12

The Data Science Team — 191

Assembling your data science team – key roles and considerations	**192**	Practical applications of the hub and spoke model	199
Data scientists	192	Building a hub and spoke model	200
Machine learning engineers	192	**The art of recruitment**	**200**
Data engineers	193	Where to find technical talent	201
MLOps engineers	193	**How high-performing data science teams operate**	**202**
Analytics engineers	194	Cross-functional collaboration is essential	203
Software engineers (full stack, frontend, backend)	194	Diversity of perspectives drives innovation	203
Product managers	195	Start with the right problem to solve	203
Business analysts	195	Invest in tooling, infrastructure, and workflow	203
Data storytellers/visualization experts	196	Continuous adaption and learning are a must	203
Considerations when assembling your team	196	Focus ruthlessly on outcomes over activity	203
Data science teams within larger organizations	197		
The hub and spoke model	**198**	**Summary**	**204**
What is the hub and spoke model?	198		

13

Managing the Data Science Team — 205

Day-to-day management of a data science team	**206**	Communicating effectively in data science and artificial intelligence	206
Enabling rapid experimentation and innovation	206	Fostering a culture of curiosity and continuous learning	207
Managing inherent uncertainty	206	Embracing peer review and collaboration	207
Balancing research and application	206	**Common challenges in managing a data science team**	**207**

Challenge 1 – recruiting and retaining top talent 207
Challenge 2 – aligning projects with business goals 209
Challenge 3 – managing inherent uncertainty 210
Challenge 4 – scaling and operationalizing models 211
Challenge 5 – deploying robust, reliable, fair models ethically 212

Empowering and motivating your data science team 213

Working with other teams and external stakeholders and empowering them to use data 214

Summary 215

14

Continuing Your Journey as a Data Science Leader 217

Navigating the landscape of emerging technologies 217
Specializing in an industry 218
Specializing in a field 220
Embracing continuous learning 222
Online courses 222
Cloud certifications 223
Technical tutorials and documentation 224
Learning plan framework 225

Staying up to date with current DS/ML/AI news and trends 225

Promoting data-driven thinking within your organization 227
Host internal learning sessions 227
Collaborate on cross-functional projects 228
Share success stories and lessons learned 228
Mentor and upskill colleagues 228
Establish a data science community of practice 228

Networking beyond your organization 229
Attend industry conferences and events 229
Join online communities and forums 229
Engage with local meetups and user groups 230
Collaborate on side projects or research 230
Offer mentorship or seek mentors 230

Summary 230

Index 233

Other Books You May Enjoy 246

Preface

Data science, machine learning, and **artificial intelligence** (**AI**) are transforming the business landscape.

Organizations in every industry are harnessing these powerful tools to uncover insights, make predictions, and gain a competitive edge. This trend has only accelerated with the rise in large language models and Generative AI.

But for decision makers without a data science background, or those stepping up from being a data scientist to leading data teams, there are a myriad of challenges. It can be challenging to understand underlying concepts of statistics, machine learning, and AI; manage data teams effectively; and, most importantly, translate complex models into tangible business outcomes – business outcomes that deliver real, bottom-line value to an organization, not just vanity metrics and shiny demos.

This book is your guide. In *Data Science for Decision Makers*, you'll gain the essential knowledge and skills to lead in the age of AI. Through clear explanations and practical examples, you'll learn how to interpret machine learning models, identify valuable use cases, and drive measurable results. Step by step, you'll learn the foundations of statistics and machine learning. You'll discover how to plan and execute successful data science initiatives from start to finish.

Along the way, you'll pick up best practices for building and empowering high-performing teams. Most importantly, you'll learn how to bridge the gap between the technical world of data science and the business needs of your organization. Whether you're an executive, a manager, or a data scientist moving into leadership, this book will help you leverage data-driven insights to inform your decisions and propel your company forward.

Who this book is for

Are you an executive seeking to harness the power of data science and AI? A manager eager to lead data-driven teams to success? Or perhaps a data scientist ready to step into a leadership role? If so, this book is for you.

Data Science for Decision Makers is designed for leaders who want to leverage data insights effectively. You don't need a formal background in statistics or machine learning. What you do need is a desire to understand these concepts, ask the right questions, and make informed decisions.

If you work with data scientists and machine learning engineers, this book will help you interpret their models with confidence. You'll learn how to recognize valuable opportunities for AI and plan projects that deliver real business value.

Executives will gain a solid foundation in data science methods. Managers will discover how to build and guide high-performing teams. Data scientists will develop the skills to become influential leaders. Wherever you are in your career, this book will help you succeed in the age of AI.

What this book covers

This book is structured into three parts. Firstly, we cover data science and its foundations in statistics. Then, we cover machine learning as it relates to data science, including core machine learning concepts, applications, and pitfalls to avoid. Finally, we cover how to lead successful data science projects and teams. If you are already familiar with the foundations of data science and the core statistical concepts covered in *Part 1*, you may wish to skip ahead to *Part 2* or refresh your knowledge.

Part 1: Understanding Data Science and Its Foundations

Chapter 1, *Introducing Data Science*, will provide you with a foundational understanding of data science, its relationship to AI and machine learning, and key statistical concepts. It explores descriptive and inferential statistics, probability, and data distributions, establishing a common language for readers.

Chapter 2, *Characterizing and Collecting Data*, will give you the knowledge of how to distinguish between different types of data, including first-, second-, and third-party data, as well as structured, unstructured, and semi-structured data. It explores technologies and methods for collecting, storing, and processing data, and provides guidance on navigating the landscape of data-focused solutions, including cloud, on-premises, and hybrid solutions.

Chapter 3, *Exploratory Data Analysis*, introduces the process of **exploratory data analysis** (**EDA**) and its importance in understanding data, developing hypotheses, and building better models. The chapter provides hands-on code examples in Python to reinforce the concepts, with step-by-step explanations suitable for readers with no prior experience in Python.

Chapter 4, *The Significance of Significance*, explores the concept of statistical significance and its importance in making data-driven decisions. It covers hypothesis testing, also known as significance testing, and provides practical examples to illustrate its application in business scenarios, such as reducing customer churn and evaluating machine learning model improvements.

Chapter 5, *Understanding Regression*, introduces regression as a powerful statistical tool for uncovering patterns and relationships within data. It explores various use cases for regression in a business context. The chapter begins with the foundational concept of trend lines before delving into the complexities of regression analysis.

Part 2: Machine Learning – Concepts, Applications, and Pitfalls

Chapter 6, *Introducing Machine Learning*, provides an overview of machine learning and its importance in data-driven decision-making. It covers the progression from traditional statistics to machine learning, the various types of machine learning techniques, and the process of training, validating, and testing models.

Chapter 7, Supervised Machine Learning, focuses on one of the most utilized and beneficial subfields of machine learning. It discusses the steps involved in training and deploying supervised machine learning models and core supervised learning algorithms, as well as factors to consider when training and evaluating these models and their applications.

Chapter 8, Unsupervised Machine Learning, explores the field of unsupervised learning, where algorithms discover hidden patterns and insights from unlabeled data. The chapter covers practical examples of unsupervised learning, the key steps involved, and techniques such as clustering, anomaly detection, dimensionality reduction, and association rule learning. It emphasizes the distinct nature of unsupervised learning compared to supervised learning and highlights its potential for uncovering valuable information in data without prior training.

Chapter 9, Interpreting and Evaluating Machine Learning Models, equips readers with the skills needed to assess the accuracy and reliability of machine learning models. You will learn how to use evaluation metrics to measure model performance and understand the importance of using holdout (test) data for unbiased evaluation. The chapter provides insights into the differences between evaluation metrics for regression and classification models, enabling readers to effectively interpret and validate the quality of machine learning models, ensuring their successful implementation in real-world scenarios.

Chapter 10, Common Pitfalls in Machine Learning, provides readers with the knowledge to identify and address common challenges in developing and deploying machine learning models. It covers issues such as inadequate or poor-quality training data, overfitting and underfitting, training-serving skew, model drift, and bias and fairness. You will learn practical strategies to mitigate these pitfalls, ensuring your models are reliable, accurate, and equitable, ultimately leading to better business decisions and outcomes.

Part 3: Leading Successful Data Science Projects and Teams

Chapter 11, The Structure of a Data Science Project, provides a comprehensive framework for planning and executing data science projects, focusing on delivering impactful data products. You will learn how to identify, evaluate, and prioritize use cases that align with your organization's goals and have the potential to drive real business value. The chapter covers the key stages of data product development, from data preparation to model design, evaluation, and deployment. You will also learn how to evaluate the business impact of your data products by selecting relevant metrics and KPIs, enabling you to demonstrate the tangible value and ROI of your initiatives and secure ongoing support for your projects.

Chapter 12, The Data Science Team, looks at the art and science of assembling a high-performing data science team. You will learn about the key roles that make up a successful team, including data scientists, machine learning engineers, and data engineers, along with the skills and expertise each role brings to the table. The chapter explores different operating models for structuring data science teams within larger organizations.

Chapter 13, *Managing the Data Science Team*, explores the unique challenges and best practices for leading data science teams effectively. It covers strategies for enabling rapid experimentation, managing uncertainty, balancing research and production work, communicating effectively, fostering continuous learning, and promoting collaboration. The chapter also discusses common challenges such as aligning projects with business goals, scaling and deploying models, ensuring fairness and ethics, and driving the adoption of data science solutions.

Chapter 14, *Continuing Your Journey as a Data Science Leader*, provides guidance on navigating the rapidly evolving landscape of data science, machine learning, and AI. It explores strategies for staying current with emerging technologies, specializing in specific industries or fields, and embracing continuous learning. The chapter also discusses the importance of staying informed about the latest trends and news and how data science leaders can promote data-driven thinking within their organizations.

To get the most out of this book, some familiarity with basic mathematical concepts such as algebra, probability, and statistics is helpful but not required. The real prerequisites are curiosity, a willingness to learn, and a drive to use data for the good of your organization. If you bring those qualities, this book will supply the knowledge and practical skills you need. Step by step, you'll learn to wield the tools of data science and AI with clarity, confidence, and purpose.

Software/hardware covered in the book	Operating system requirements
Python (Google Colab)	Windows, macOS, or Linux A Google account (to access Google Colab) A modern web browser (Google Chrome, Mozilla Firefox, Microsoft Edge, or Apple Safari)

Setup instructions will be provided in the chapters where there are code exercises.

Conventions used

There are a number of text conventions used throughout this book.

`Code in text`: Indicates code words in text, database table names, folder names, filenames, file extensions, pathnames, dummy URLs, user input, and Twitter handles. Here is an example: "Click on the cell to activate it, type **print**("**Hello, world!**"), and then click the play button to run the code."

A block of code is set as follows:

```
# Calculate median (middle value)
median_sales = sales_data_year1.median()
print(f"The median monthly sales, a typical sales month, is
    {round(median_sales)} units.")
```

When we wish to draw your attention to a particular part of a code block, the relevant lines or items are set in bold:

```
# Calculate standard deviation (measure of the amount of variation)
std_dev_sales = sales_data_year1.std()
print(f"The standard deviation,
    showing the typical variation from the mean sales,
    is {round(std_dev_sales)} units.")
```

Bold: Indicates a new term, an important word, or words that you see onscreen. For instance, words in menus or dialog boxes appear in **bold**. Here is an example: "Click **File**, then choose **New Notebook** from the dropdown."

> Tips or important notes
> Appear like this.

Get in touch

Feedback from our readers is always welcome.

General feedback: If you have questions about any aspect of this book, email us at customercare@packtpub.com and mention the book title in the subject of your message.

Errata: Although we have taken every care to ensure the accuracy of our content, mistakes do happen. If you have found a mistake in this book, we would be grateful if you would report this to us. Please visit www.packtpub.com/support/errata and fill in the form.

Piracy: If you come across any illegal copies of our works in any form on the internet, we would be grateful if you would provide us with the location address or website name. Please contact us at copyright@packt.com with a link to the material.

If you are interested in becoming an author: If there is a topic that you have expertise in and you are interested in either writing or contributing to a book, please visit authors.packtpub.com.

Share Your Thoughts

Once you've read *Data Science for Decision Makers*, we'd love to hear your thoughts! Scan the QR code below to go straight to the Amazon review page for this book and share your feedback.

https://packt.link/r/1-837-63729-6

Your review is important to us and the tech community and will help us make sure we're delivering excellent quality content.

Download a free PDF copy of this book

Thanks for purchasing this book!

Do you like to read on the go but are unable to carry your print books everywhere?

Is your eBook purchase not compatible with the device of your choice?

Don't worry, now with every Packt book you get a DRM-free PDF version of that book at no cost.

Read anywhere, any place, on any device. Search, copy, and paste code from your favorite technical books directly into your application.

The perks don't stop there, you can get exclusive access to discounts, newsletters, and great free content in your inbox daily

Follow these simple steps to get the benefits:

1. Scan the QR code or visit the link below

   https://packt.link/free-ebook/9781837637294

2. Submit your proof of purchase
3. That's it! We'll send your free PDF and other benefits to your email directly

Part 1: Understanding Data Science and Its Foundations

This part covers the foundations of data science, including key statistical concepts, data types, collection methods, exploratory data analysis, statistical significance, and regression. This part has the following chapters:

- *Chapter 1, Introducing Data Science*
- *Chapter 2, Characterizing and Collecting Data*
- *Chapter 3, Exploratory Data Analysis*
- *Chapter 4, The Significance of Significance*
- *Chapter 5, Understanding Regression*

1
Introducing Data Science

Data science is not a new term; in fact, it was coined in the 1960s by Peter Naur, a Danish computer science pioneer who used the term data science to describe the process of working with data in various fields, including mathematics, statistics, and computer science.

Later, the modern use of data science began to take shape in the 1990s and early 2000s, and data scientist, as a profession, became more and more common across different industries.

With the exponential rise in artificial intelligence, one may think that data science is less relevant.

However, the scientific approach to understanding data, which defines data science, is the bedrock upon which successful machine learning and artificial intelligence-based solutions can be built.

Within this book, we will explore these different terms, provide a solid foundation in core statistical and machine learning theory, and concepts that can be applied to statistical, machine learning and artificial intelligence-based models alike, and walk through how to lead data science teams and projects to successful outcomes.

This first chapter introduces the reader to how statistics and data science are intertwined, and some fundamental concepts in statistics which can help you in working with data.

We will explore the differences between data science, artificial intelligence, and machine learning, explain the relationship between statistics and data science, explain the concepts of descriptive and inferential statistics, as well as probability, and basic methods to understand the shape (distribution) of data.

While some readers may find this chapter covering basic, foundational knowledge, the aim is to provide all readers, especially those from less technical backgrounds, with a solid understanding of these concepts before diving deeper into the world of data science. For more experienced readers, this chapter serves as a quick refresher and helps establish a common language that will be used throughout the book.

In this next section, let's look at these terms of data science, artificial intelligence, and machine learning, how they are related, and how they differ.

This chapter covers the following topics:

- Data science, AI, and ML – what's the difference?
- Statistics and data science
- Descriptive and inferential statistics
- Probability
- Describing our samples
- Probability distributions

Data science, AI, and ML – what's the difference?

You may have heard the terms data science, AI, and ML used interchangeably, but they are distinct concepts with unique characteristics.

AI is a broad field that focuses on developing computer systems that can perform tasks that typically require human intelligence, such as visual perception, speech recognition, decision-making, and language translation. ML is a subset of AI that involves training computer systems to learn from data and improve their performance on a specific task without being explicitly programmed.

ML algorithms enable computer systems to learn from data and identify patterns, which can then be used to make predictions or decisions. While all ML falls under the umbrella of AI, not all AI encompasses ML, as some AI systems may rely on rule-based or symbolic reasoning approaches.

Deep learning is a specific type of ML that utilizes artificial neural networks with multiple layers to extract higher-level features from raw data. This technique is highly effective for tasks such as image and speech recognition.

Data science is a multidisciplinary field that involves extracting and analyzing relevant insights from data. It focuses on discovering hidden patterns and relationships in data to derive meaningful conclusions. A data scientist leverages ML algorithms to make predictions and inform decision-making.

All these fields are grounded in the foundations of mathematics, probability theory, and statistics. Understanding these core concepts is essential for anyone interested in pursuing a career or leading initiatives in data science, AI, or ML.

The following is an attempt to visualize the relationship between these fields:

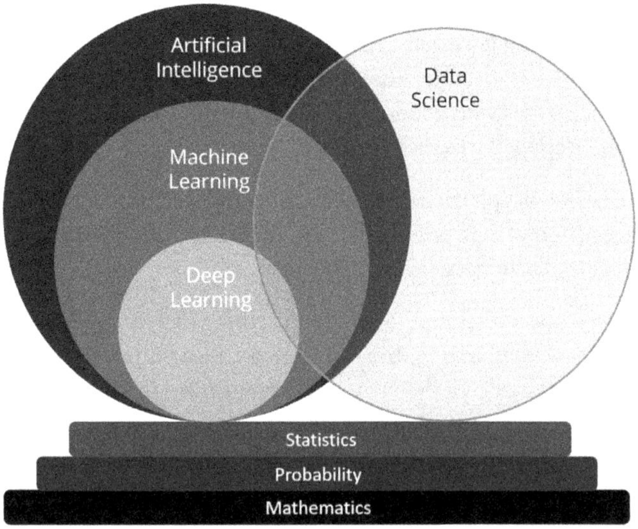

Figure 1.1: A visual representation of the relationship between data science, ML, and AI

Here, deep learning is a subset of machine learning, and artificial intelligence is a broader field which includes machine learning and other methods to perform intelligent tasks.

Data science, as a practice, overlaps with all these fields, as it can make use of whichever methods are most appropriate to extract insight, predictions, and recommendations from data.

All these fields are built upon the foundation of mathematics, probability, and statistics. For this reason, in the next section, we will investigate these mathematical and statistical underpinnings of data science.

The mathematical and statistical underpinnings of data science

This book is aimed at the business-focused decision maker, **not** the technical expert, so you might be wondering why are we starting by talking about mathematics.

Well, at its core, data science is based on mathematical and statistical foundations, so even if you aren't working as a data scientist or ML/AI engineer, having a basic understanding of the important mathematical and statistical concepts that are used within data science is one of the most important tools you can have at your disposal when working with data scientists or leading data science, ML, or AI initiatives, whether that's interpreting the models and results that data scientists and ML engineers bring your way, better understanding the limitations of certain data and models, and being able to evaluate which business use cases may or may not be appropriate for data science.

Research has found that 87% of data science projects never make it into production. In other words, only around one in ten projects get to the stage where they can provide bottom-line value for a company.

These results seem poor at first glance, but there is a silver lining. In many cases, the missing piece of the puzzle is strong executive leadership, knowing which use cases are appropriate for data science, providing the data science teams with good-quality, relevant data, and framing the use cases in a way where data science can be applied successfully.

Knowing some of the core concepts around mathematics and statistics for data science will not only give you a better appreciation of data science but also the compass to plan and navigate data science projects from the outset to reach more successful results.

Within this book, we won't be attempting to provide anything like a comprehensive foundation into mathematics required for AI and ML as this would require an entire degree to achieve. However, within this chapter, we will provide you with an understanding of the fundamentals.

Statistics and data science

The British mathematician Karl Pearson once stated, *"Statistics is the grammar of science."*

If you're starting your journey of leading data science, ML, or AI initiatives within your organization, or just working with data scientists and ML engineers, having a foundation in statistical knowledge is essential.

Having a foundation in statistical knowledge is crucial for individuals embarking on a journey into leading projects or teams within the field of data science. It enables them to gain a competitive advantage in extracting valuable insights from data. Statistics plays a vital role as it offers various tools and techniques to identify patterns and uncover deeper insights from the available data. A good grasp of statistics allows individuals to think critically, approach problem-solving creatively, and make data-driven decisions. In this section, we aim to cover essential statistical topics that are relevant to data science.

What is statistics?

Before going further, it will be helpful to define what we mean by **statistics** as the term can be used in several different ways. It can be used to do the following:

- Indicate the whole discipline of statistics
- Refer to the methods that are used to collect, process, and interpret quantitative data
- Refer to collections of gathered data
- Refer to calculated figures (such as the mean) that are used to interpret the data that's been gathered

In this case, we define statistics using the second definition – the methods that are used to collect, process, and interpret quantitative data.

Today, few industries are untouched by statistical thinking. For example, within market research, statistics is used when sampling surveys and comparing results between groups to understand which insights are statistically significant; within life sciences, statistics is used to measure and evaluate the efficacy of pharmaceuticals; and within financial services, statistics is used to model and understand risk.

I'm sure you're familiar with many of these and other applications of statistics, and you may have studied statistics before at school, college, or in your professional career, and much of what follows in this chapter may not be brand new information. Even if this is the case, it can be useful to have a refresher as unfortunately, it's not possible to pause a career to complete a statistics course.

When you're leading data science, ML, or AI initiatives, understanding statistics is an essential skill, whether you're working with simple statistical models or understanding the data being used or a model's performance when you're training and evaluating deep learning AI models.

With this in mind, let's dive into some of the core concepts within probability and statistics.

Descriptive and inferential statistics

It's important to understand that there are two different types of statistics: descriptive statistics (methods used to summarize or describe observations) and inferential statistics (using those observations as a basis for making estimates or predictions) – that is, inferences about a situation that has not been investigated yet.

Look at the following two example statements. Which of them is a "descriptive" statistic and which is "inferential?"

- Based on our forecasting, we expect sales revenue next year to increase by 35%.
- Our average rating within our customer base was 8 out of 10.

The first statement is inferential as it goes beyond what has been observed in the past to make inferences about the future, while the second statement is descriptive as it summarizes historical observations.

Within data science, often, data is first explored with descriptive statistics as part of what is known as **exploratory data analysis** (**EDA**), attempting to profile and understand the data. Following this, statistical or ML models trained on a set of data (known as model training) can be used to make inferences on unseen data (known as model inference or execution). We will revisit this topic later in this book when we cover the basics of ML.

The distinction between descriptive and inferential statistics depends on the differences between **samples** and **populations**, two more important terms within statistics.

In statistical terminology, **population** not only refers to populations of people, but it may also equally refer to populations of transactions, products, or retail stores. The main point is that "population" refers to every example within a studied group. It may not be the case that a data scientist is interested in every attribute of a population – it may be that they are only interested in the sales revenues of retail stores or the price of products.

However, even if a data scientist is interested in one characteristic of a population, they will likely not have the luxury to study all members of it. Usually, they will have to study a sample – a relatively small selection – from within a population. This is often due to the limitations of time and expense, or the availability of data, where only a sample of the data is available.

In this case, descriptive statistics can be used to summarize the sampled data, and it is with inference that a data scientist can attempt to go beyond the available data to generalize information to the entire population.

So, to summarize, descriptive statistics involves summarizing a sample, whereas inferential statistics is concerned with generalizing a sample to make inferences about the entire population.

How accurate are these generalizations from the sample to the population? This is a large part of what statistics are about: measuring uncertainty and errors. It is useful, when working with the results from statistical models or even ML models, to be comfortable with the idea of uncertainty and how to measure it, not to shy away from it. Sometimes, business stakeholders may not want to see the margins of error, along with the outputs of simple statistical techniques, as they want to know things with complete certainty. Otherwise, any degree of uncertainty shown alongside results might be blown out of proportion.

However, we can rarely observe an entire population when making inferences, or have a model generalize to every possible edge case, to have absolute certainty in any result.

However, we can do a lot better than human intuition, and it is better to take a more scientific stance to understand and measure the margin of error and uncertainty with our inferences and predictions. Unconsciously, we make decisions every day with partial information and some uncertainty. For example, if you've ever booked a hotel, you may have looked at a sample of hotels and read a sample of customer reviews but had to decide on which hotel to book based on this sample. You may have seen a hotel with one five-star review and another with 1,000 reviews averaging 4.8 stars. Although the first hotel had a higher average rating, which hotel would you book? Probably the latter, because you could infer that the margin of error in the rating was less, but importantly there is still some margin of error as not every customer may have given a review.

In the data science, ML, and AI worlds, this ability to investigate and understand uncertainty when working with data science and have criteria around what margin of error would be acceptable for your business use case is critical to knowing when to proceed with deploying a model to production.

Sampling strategies

In data science, sampling is the process of selecting a subset of data from a larger population. Sampling can be a powerful tool for decision-makers to draw inferences and make predictions about the population, but it is important to choose the right sampling strategy to ensure the validity and reliability of the results.

Random sampling

Random sampling is the most common and straightforward sampling strategy. In this method, each member of the population has an equal chance of being selected for the sample. This can be done through a variety of techniques, such as simple random sampling, stratified random sampling, or cluster sampling.

Simple random sampling involves randomly selecting individuals from the population without any restrictions or stratification. Stratified random sampling involves dividing the population into strata or subgroups based on certain characteristics and then randomly selecting individuals from each stratum. Cluster sampling involves dividing the population into clusters and randomly selecting entire clusters to be included in the sample.

Random sampling can be useful when the population is large and homogenous, meaning that all members have similar characteristics. However, it may not be the best strategy when the population is diverse and there are significant differences between subgroups.

Convenience sampling

Convenience sampling involves selecting individuals from the population who are easily accessible or available. This can include individuals who are in a convenient location, such as in the same office or building, or individuals who are readily available to participate in the study.

While convenience sampling can be a quick and easy way to gather data, it is not the most reliable strategy. The sample may not be representative of the population as it may exclude certain subgroups or over-represent others.

Stratified sampling

Stratified sampling involves dividing the population into subgroups based on certain characteristics and then selecting individuals from each subgroup to be included in the sample. This strategy can be useful when the population is diverse and there are significant differences between subgroups.

In stratified sampling, the size of the sample is proportional to the size of each subgroup in the population. This ensures that each subgroup is adequately represented in the sample, and the results can be extrapolated to the population with greater accuracy.

Cluster sampling

Cluster sampling involves dividing the population into clusters and randomly selecting entire clusters to be included in the sample. This strategy can be useful when the population is geographically dispersed or when it is easier to access clusters than individuals.

Cluster sampling involves dividing the population into clusters, which are typically based on geographic proximity or other shared characteristics. From these clusters, a random sample of clusters is selected, and all members within the selected clusters are included in the sample. This strategy can be useful when the population is geographically dispersed or when it is more feasible to access and survey entire clusters rather than individual participants.

Cluster sampling is often more cost-effective and efficient than other sampling methods, especially when dealing with large, spread-out populations. However, it may lead to higher sampling error compared to simple random sampling if the clusters are not representative of the entire population:

Stratified Sampling

Individuals are selected randomly from two homogeneous strata, based on the size of each strata

Cluster Sampling

Clusters are randomly selected

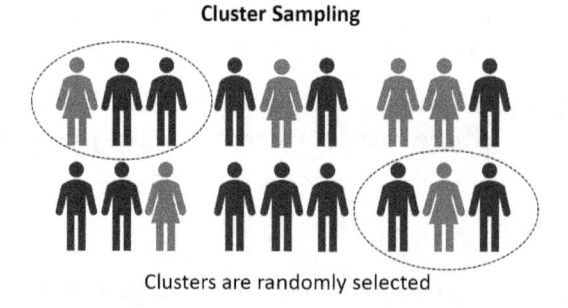

Figure 1.2: Stratified random sampling and cluster sampling

Sampling is an important tool for decision-makers to draw inferences and make predictions about a population. The choice of sampling strategy will depend on the characteristics of the population and the research question being asked. Random sampling, stratified sampling, and cluster sampling are all useful strategies, but it is important to consider the potential biases and limitations of each method. By selecting the appropriate sampling strategy, decision-makers can ensure that their results are reliable and valid and can make better-informed decisions based on the data.

Random variables

What do we do with the members of a sample once we have them?

This is where the concept of random variables comes in.

In data science, a random variable is a variable whose value is determined by chance. Random variables are often used to model uncertain events or outcomes, and they play a crucial role in statistical analysis, ML, and decision-making.

Random variables are mathematical functions that are utilized to assign a numerical value to each potential outcome of a random process. For example, when flipping a coin, the value of 0 can be assigned to tails and 1 to heads, effectively causing the random variable, X, to adopt the values of 0 or 1:

$$X = \begin{cases} 1, \text{if heads} \\ 0, \text{if tails} \end{cases}$$

There are two types of random variables: discrete and continuous. Discrete random variables can only take on a finite or countable number of values, while continuous random variables can take on any value within a specified range.

For example, the outcome of rolling a six-sided die is a discrete random variable as it can only take on the values 1, 2, 3, 4, 5, or 6. On the other hand, the height of a person is a continuous random variable as it can take on any value within a certain range.

Random variables are often used in the context of sampling strategies as they provide a way to model and analyze uncertain outcomes in a sample.

For example, suppose a decision maker wants to estimate the average height of students at a university. One possible sampling strategy would be simple random sampling, in which a random sample of students is selected from the population of all students at the university.

Probability distribution

The probability distribution of a random variable describes the likelihood of each possible value of the variable. For a discrete random variable, the probability distribution is typically represented by a **probability mass function** (**PMF**), which gives the probability of each possible value. For a continuous random variable, the probability distribution is typically represented by a **probability density function** (**PDF**), which gives the probability density at each point in the range.

Probability

Probability is a way to measure how likely something is to happen. As mentioned previously, in data science, ML, and decision-making, we often deal with uncertain events or outcomes. Probability helps us understand and quantify that uncertainty.

For example, when we flip a coin, we don't know whether it will land heads or tails. The probability of it landing heads is 50%, and the probability of it landing tails is also 50%.

Probability distribution

A probability distribution is a way to show the likelihood of each possible outcome. For example, when we roll a six-sided die, the probability of getting each number is the same – 1/6. This means that the probability distribution is equal for each outcome.

Conditional probability

Conditional probability is the likelihood of an event or outcome happening, given that another event or outcome has already occurred. For example, if we know that a person is over six feet tall, the conditional probability of them being a basketball player is higher than the probability of a randomly selected person being a basketball player.

Let's say there were two different events, A and B, which had some probability of occurring, within what is known as a sample space, S, of all possible events occurring.

For example, A could be the event that a consumer purchases a particular brand's product, and B could be the event that a consumer has visited the brand's website. In the following diagram, the probability of event A, $P(A)$, and the probability of event B, $P(B)$, are represented by the shaded areas in the following Venn diagram. The probability of **both** A **and** B occurring is represented by the shaded area where A and B overlap. In mathematical notation, this is written as $P(A \cap B)$, which means the probability of the **intersection** of A and B. This intersection simply means both A and B occur:

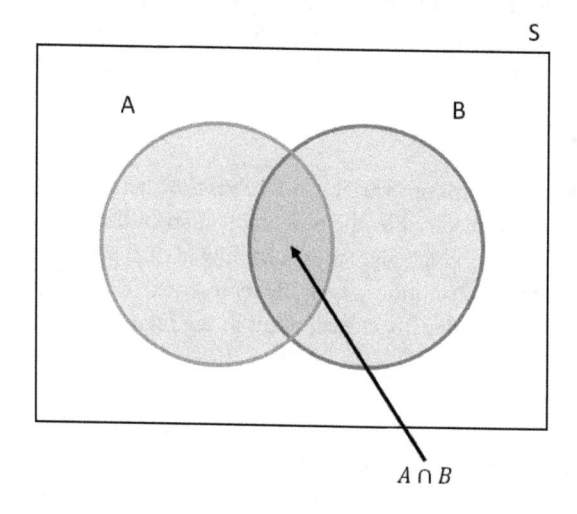

Figure 1.3: A Venn diagram visualizing the probability of two events (A and B) occurring in a sample space (S)

The conditional probability of A occurring, **given** that B has occurred, can be calculated as follows:

In our example, this would be the probability of a consumer purchasing a brand's product, **given** they have visited the brand's website. By understanding the probabilities of different events and how they are related, we can calculate things such as conditional probabilities, which can help us understand the chance of events happening based on our data.

Describing our samples

Now that we understand the concepts of populations, samples, and random variables, what tools can we use to describe and understand our data sample?

Measures of central tendency

The expected value is a statistical measure that represents the average value of a random variable, weighted by its probability of occurrence. It provides a way to estimate the central tendency of a probability distribution and is useful for decision-making and predicting uncertain events or outcomes.

Measures of central tendency, including mean, median, and mode, are statistical measures that describe the central or typical value of a dataset.

The mean is the arithmetic average of a dataset, calculated by adding up all the values and dividing them by the number of values. It is a common measure of central tendency and is sensitive to outliers (values that are significantly higher or lower than the majority of the data points, often falling far from the mean). The mean can be influenced by extreme values and may not be representative of the entire dataset if there are outliers.

The median is the middle value of a dataset, with an equal number of values above and below it. It is a robust measure of central tendency and is less sensitive to outliers than the mean. The median is useful for skewed datasets, where the mean may not accurately represent the center of the data.

The mode is the value that occurs most frequently in a dataset. It is another measure of central tendency and is useful for datasets with discrete values or when the most frequent value is of particular interest. The mode can be used for both categorical and numerical data.

The following figure shows the differences between the mean, median, and mode for two different distributions of data. Imagine that this dataset shows the range of prices of a consumer product, say bottles of wine on an online wine merchant.

For symmetrical distributions, these three measures are equal; however, for asymmetrical data, they differ. The choice of which measure to use may depend on the distribution of your data. The mean can often be skewed by extreme outliers – for example, one really expensive bottle of wine is not reflective of most of the bottles being sold on the site, so you may want to use the median to better understand the average value within your dataset, and not get scared away from buying from the store!

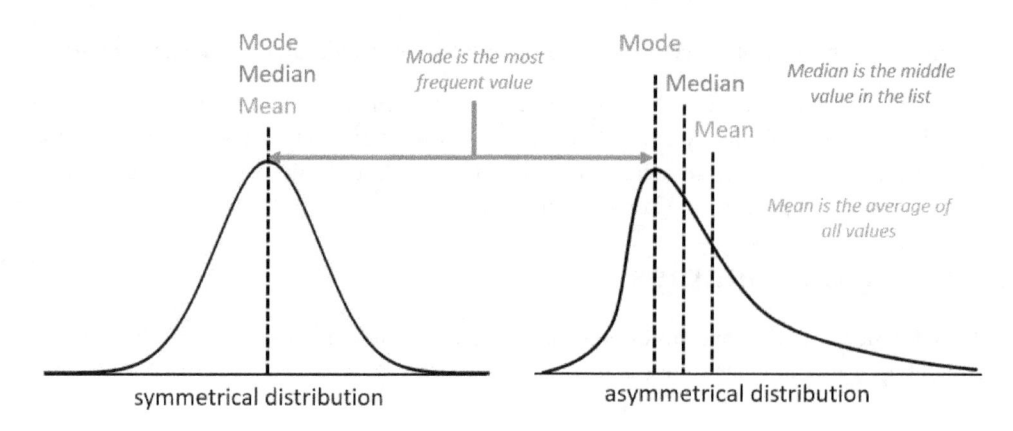

Figure 1.4: The mode, median, and mean for a symmetrical distribution and an asymmetrical distribution

Overall, the expected value and measures of central tendency are important statistical concepts that play a critical role in data science, ML, and decision-making. They provide you with a way to understand and describe the characteristics of a dataset, and they help decision-makers make better-informed decisions based on the analysis of uncertain events or outcomes.

Measures of dispersion

Measures of dispersion are statistical measures that describe how spread out or varied a dataset is. They provide us with a way to understand the variability of the data and can be used to compare datasets.

Range

The range is a simple measure of dispersion that represents the difference between the highest and lowest values in a dataset. It is easy to calculate and provides a rough estimate of the spread of the data. For example, the range of the heights of students in a class would be the difference between the tallest and shortest students.

Variance and standard deviation

Variance and standard deviation are more advanced measures of dispersion that provide a more accurate and precise estimate of the variability of the data.

Variance is a measure of how far each value in a set of data is from the mean value. It is calculated by taking the sum of the squared differences between each value and the mean, divided by the total number of values:

$$\sigma^2 = \frac{\Sigma (X - \mu)^2}{N}$$

- σ^2 = population variance
- Σ = sum of…
- X = each value
- μ = population mean
- N = number of values in the population

Standard deviation is the square root of the variance:

$$\sigma = \sqrt{\frac{\Sigma (X - \mu)^2}{N}}$$

- σ = population standard deviation
- Σ = sum of…
- X = each value
- μ = population mean
- N = number of values in the population

For example, suppose a company wants to compare the salaries of two different departments. The standard deviation of the salaries in each department can be calculated to determine the variability of the salaries within each department. The department with a higher standard deviation would have more variability in salaries than the department with a lower standard deviation.

Interquartile range

The **interquartile range** (**IQR**) is a measure of dispersion that represents the difference between the 75th and 25th percentiles of a dataset. In other words, it is the range of the middle 50% of the data. It is useful for datasets with outliers as it is less sensitive to extreme values than the range.

For example, suppose a teacher wants to compare the test scores of two different classes. One class has a few students with very high or very low scores, while the other class has a more consistent range of scores. The IQR of each class can be calculated to determine the range of scores that most students fall into.

Measures of dispersion are important statistical measures that provide insight into the variability of a dataset.

Degrees of freedom

Degrees of freedom is a fundamental concept in statistics that refers to the number of independent values or quantities that can vary in an analysis without breaking any constraints. It is essential to understand degrees of freedom when working with various statistical tests and models, such as t-tests, ANOVA, and regression analysis.

In simpler terms, degrees of freedom represents the amount of information in your data that is free to vary when estimating statistical parameters. The concept is used in hypothesis testing to determine the probability of obtaining your observed results if the null hypothesis is true.

For example, let's say you have a sample of ten observations and you want to calculate the sample mean. Once you have calculated the mean, you have nine degrees of freedom remaining (10 - 1 = 9). This is because if you know the values of nine observations and the sample mean, you can always calculate the value of the 10th observation.

The general formula for calculating degrees of freedom is as follows:

$df = n - p$

Here, we have the following:

- n is the number of observations in the sample
- p is the number of parameters estimated from the data

Degrees of freedom is used in various statistical tests to determine the critical values for test statistics and p-values. For instance, in a t-test for comparing two sample means, degrees of freedom is used to select the appropriate critical value from the t-distribution table.

Understanding degrees of freedom is crucial for data science leaders as it helps them interpret the results of statistical tests and make informed decisions based on the data. It also plays a role in determining the complexity of models and avoiding overfitting, which occurs when a model is too complex and starts to fit the noise in the data rather than the underlying patterns.

Correlation, causation, and covariance

Correlation, causation, and covariance are important concepts in data science, ML, and decision-making. They are all related to the relationship between two or more variables and can be used to make predictions and inform decision-making.

Correlation

Correlation is a measure of the strength and direction of the relationship between two variables. It is a statistical measure that ranges from -1 to 1. A correlation of 1 indicates a perfect positive correlation, a correlation of 0 indicates no correlation, and a correlation of -1 indicates a perfect negative correlation.

For example, suppose we want to understand the relationship between a person's age and their income. If we observe that as a person's age increases, their income also tends to increase, this will indicate a positive correlation between age and income.

Causation

Causation refers to the relationship between two variables in which one variable causes a change in the other variable. Causation is often inferred from correlation, but it is important to note that correlation does not necessarily imply causation.

For example, suppose we observe a correlation between the number of ice cream cones sold and the number of drownings in a city. While these two variables are correlated, it would be incorrect to assume that one causes the other. Rather, there may be a third variable, such as temperature, that causes both the increase in ice cream sales and the increase in drownings.

Covariance

Covariance is a measure of the joint variability of two variables. It measures how much two variables change together. A positive covariance indicates that the two variables tend to increase or decrease together, while a negative covariance indicates that the two variables tend to change in opposite directions.

For example, suppose we want to understand the relationship between a person's height and their weight. If we observe that as a person's height increases, their weight also tends to increase, this will indicate a positive covariance between height and weight.

Correlation, causation, and covariance are important concepts in data science. By understanding these concepts, decision-makers can better understand the relationships between variables and make better-informed decisions based on the analysis of the data.

Covariance measures how two variables change together, indicating the direction of the linear relationship between them. However, covariance values are difficult to interpret because they are affected by the scale of the variables. Correlation, on the other hand, is a standardized measure that ranges from -1 to +1, making it easier to understand and compare the strength and direction of linear relationships between variables.

It is important to note that correlation does not necessarily imply causation and that other factors may be responsible for observed relationships between variables. A strong correlation between two variables does not automatically mean that one variable causes the other as there may be hidden confounding factors influencing both variables simultaneously.

The shape of data

When working with samples of data, it is helpful to understand the "shape" of the data, or how the data is distributed. In this respect, we can consider distributions of probabilities for both continuous and discrete data. These probability distributions can be used to describe and understand your data. Probability distributions can help you identify patterns or trends in the data. For example, if your data follows a normal distribution, it suggests that most values are clustered around the mean, with fewer values at the extremes. Recognizing these patterns can help inform decision-making or further analysis.

Probability distributions

Probability distributions are mathematical functions that describe the likelihood of different outcomes in a random event or process. They help us understand the behavior of random variables and make predictions about future events. There are two main types of probability distributions: discrete distributions and continuous distributions.

Discrete probability distributions

Discrete probability distributions are used when the possible outcomes of a random event are countable or finite. Let's look at some common examples of discrete probability distributions

Bernoulli distribution

This is the simplest discrete probability distribution. It models a single trial with only two possible outcomes: success (usually denoted as 1) or failure (usually denoted as 0). For example, flipping a coin has a Bernoulli distribution with a probability of success (heads) of 0.5.

Binomial distribution

This distribution models the number of successes in a fixed number of independent trials, where each trial has the same probability of success. For example, if you flip a fair coin ten times, the number of heads you observe follows a binomial distribution with parameters of n = 10 (number of trials) and p = 0.5 (probability of success).

Negative binomial distribution

This distribution models the number of failures before a specified number of successes occurs in independent trials with the same probability of success. For instance, if you're playing a game where you need to win three times before the game ends, the number of losses before the third win follows a negative binomial distribution.

Geometric distribution

This is a special case of the negative binomial distribution where the number of successes is fixed at 1. It models the number of failures before the first success in independent trials with the same probability of success. An example would be the number of times you need to roll a die before getting a 6.

Poisson distribution

This distribution models the number of events occurring in a fixed interval of time or space, given the average rate of occurrence. It is often used to model rare events, such as the number of earthquakes in a year or the number of customers arriving at a store in an hour.

Continuous probability distributions

Continuous probability distributions are used when the possible outcomes of a random event are continuous, such as measurements or time. Let's look at some common examples of continuous probability distributions.

Normal distribution

Also known as the Gaussian distribution, this is the most well-known continuous probability distribution. It models continuous variables that have a symmetric, bell-shaped distribution, such as heights, weights, or IQ scores. Many natural phenomena follow a normal distribution.

Standard normal distribution

This is a special case of the normal distribution with a mean of zero and a standard deviation of one. It is often used to standardize variables and compare values across different normal distributions.

Student's t-distribution

This distribution is similar to the normal distribution but has heavier tails. It is used when the sample size is small (typically less than 30) or when the population standard deviation is unknown. It is often used in hypothesis testing and constructing confidence intervals.

Gamma distribution

This distribution models continuous variables that are positive and have a skewed right distribution. It is often used to model waiting times, such as the time until a machine fails or the time until a customer arrives.

Exponential distribution

This is a special case of the gamma distribution where the shape parameter is equal to 1. It models the time between events occurring at a constant rate, such as the time between customer arrivals or the time between radioactive particle decays.

Chi-squared distribution

This distribution is used for positive variables. It is often used in hypothesis testing and to estimate the confidence interval of a sample variance. It is also used in the chi-squared test for independence and goodness of fit.

F-distribution

This distribution is used for variables that are positive or non-negative. It is often used to test the equality of two variances or the significance of a regression model. It is the ratio of two chi-squared distributions.

Probability distributions allow us to understand and quantify the probabilities of different outcomes in a random event or process. By understanding the different types of probability distributions and their applications, data science leaders can better model and analyze their data, make informed decisions, and improve their predictions. Knowing which distribution to use in a given situation is crucial for accurate data analysis and decision-making.

Summary

Within this chapter, we have covered many of the core concepts within statistics to provide you with the tools to better understand and interpret data and work with the outputs of data scientists.

In the next chapter, we will cover the different types of data, data quality concerns to be aware of and manage, and different methods for collecting data, storing, and processing data.

2
Characterizing and Collecting Data

In the previous chapter, we focused on general concepts and ideas around probability and statistics, but how does this translate to the data within your organization or for your project?

In this chapter, we will cover different types of data you might find within your organization, methods for collecting and processing that data to apply the statistical techniques covered in the previous chapter, and more advanced machine learning and deep learning techniques we will cover in later chapters.

Before we dive into topics such as the different categories of data and methods for collecting, storing, and processing data, we need to ask a fundamental question:

"What data in my organization is valuable and useful?"

Initially, this might seem like a trivial and obvious question, but many data science projects start on the wrong foot by not properly evaluating the feasibility of achieving business results with the data available.

Often, decision-makers incorrectly assume that the data can be used for the identified business use case.

There is a lot of data out there and not all data is created equally, so it is worth understanding whether it fits the criteria for your business use cases.

In this chapter, you will learn about different types of data, as well as methods for collecting and processing data so that it can be prepared for data science use cases.

To give you a clearer idea of how to unlock the valuable data within, or external to, your organization, we will cover the following topics:

- The key criteria to consider when evaluating data
- The difference between first-, second-, and third-party data
- The difference between structured, unstructured, and semi-structured data
- Technologies and methods for collecting data

- Technologies and methods for storing and processing data
- How can my team navigate the landscape of data-focused solutions, including cloud, on-premises, and hybrid solutions?

To better understand how to unlock the valuable data within, or external to, your organization, let's explore the key criteria to consider when evaluating datasets.

What are the key criteria to consider when evaluating datasets?

In this section, we will understand what the key criteria are when it comes to evaluating datasets.

Data quantity

Is there sufficient data to train an accurate model or to make inferences about a wider population if you're working with a data sample? As mentioned in the previous chapter, in statistics, you must often work with a limited sample of data, and the ability of that sample to represent the wider population often depends on the size of the sample. Within machine learning, models trained on larger datasets perform much better than those trained on a small sample. There are more advanced techniques, such as data augmentation and transfer learning, that can help in this situation and will be covered later, but an initial consideration is whether there is enough data available to meet business requirements around accuracy.

Consider, for instance, a customer churn model designed to predict which customers are at risk of leaving. To effectively generalize to current and future customers, it's important to assess whether there is sufficient historical data and an adequate number of examples of customers closing their accounts.

Data velocity

Another consideration is data velocity, which is how frequently data is generated or travels. Some data may not update very frequently, such as a company's quarterly profit and loss, whereas other data may be very frequent, or even real time, such as stock prices. The solutions that data teams build need to be able to handle the frequency of the incoming data. For example, batch systems might need to process data daily or streaming systems (such as Kafka) might be required for real-time data.

The velocity or frequency of the data required also depends on the business use case. For example, a public relations issue tracker that monitors news and social media sentiment may require data every minute to detect emerging issues quickly. Another example would be predictive maintenance, where data outputs from IoT sensors within manufacturing equipment would benefit from being streamed in real time to detect issues and defects so that they can be resolved quickly.

Data variety

For some use cases, a single source of data will not be sufficient to make accurate inferences about a population or provide compelling insights to the end users. One industry where this is often the case is market research, where the data from a single survey may not provide the in-depth insights around consumer behavior the brand or company is looking for, and combining this data with additional data sources, such as product reviews, consumer social media data, or sales data, will provide the context to understand consumer behavior.

Data quality

Finally, one of the key criteria to evaluate is the quality of the data. Data quality and governance is a whole domain within itself, but some of the things you must consider are as follows:

- **Accuracy**: Data is accurate when it reflects reality. This could refer to the value of financial transactions accurately reflecting the exact amount spent, consumer survey responses reflecting the respondents' true opinions, or customer details within a CRM being accurately filled for a given customer. Data should not always be assumed to be accurate, and high data accuracy can allow models to be trained and inferences to be made that can also be trusted. The expression "garbage in, garbage out" is often used to describe this fact.

- **Completeness**: Data is "complete" when all fields required for a particular use case are present. It doesn't necessarily mean that all fields need to be complete. For example, if a company is looking to understand the average price of products from different vendors, then fields such as price, quantity, and pack size are important to complete, but other fields, such as ingredients, product descriptions, or product image URLs, are not as important for this use case.

- **Uniqueness**: Data is unique if it appears only once within a given dataset. Sometimes, duplicates are expected. For example, in a set of financial transactions, the same customer can appear many times across transactions, and this is nothing to worry about. However, in other situations, such as within a master list of customers within a CRM, each customer should be unique, and having duplicates can lead to inaccurate reporting.

- **Consistency**: Consistency is an important factor when it comes to data as it ensures that the values within a single record and across multiple datasets do not conflict with each other. For example, a postcode should always begin with the same characters that represent the locality of the address, and the date of birth for any given individual should be the same across different datasets. By ensuring consistent data, it is possible to link information from multiple sources. This can add to your dataset and increase its value by providing additional insight.

- **Timeliness**: Relevant to the data velocity criteria, the timeliness of data is also a consideration for data quality. More recent data may be required to accurately represent the current-day situation. Take, for example, a loan default model a bank may have to predict the probability of customers defaulting on loans. If this model was trained on old historical data where the macroeconomic environment was different, and interest rates were lower, then the data that's used for training may not be timely enough to make accurate inferences about current customers.

- **Validity**: Validity is a measure of how well data conforms to the expected format, type, and range. For example, a valid US postcode must be within the range of 00001 to 99950, and a valid email address must consist of an email prefix and an email domain separated by an "@" symbol. Often, tools such as regular expressions (a way of checking that data matches a certain pattern) or cross-referencing against standard datasets (such as ISO standards) can be used to ensure data is valid. Having valid data means that it can be used in harmony with other sources, and it helps to ensure that automated data processes run efficiently.

Now that we've discussed the key criteria for evaluating datasets, it's important to understand that data can come from various sources, such as first parties, second parties, and third parties. Let's look into these different types of data.

First-, second-, and third-party data

Within any mid to large-sized organization, you can find a vast swathe of different types of data that serve unique purposes and can provide valuable insights when harnessed effectively. Even if your organization does not have easily accessible or useful internal data to suit the business use cases you have identified, it is possible to look outside your organization toward external data sources. This is where the concepts of first-, second-, and third-party data are useful to understand.

The following diagram represents how your data (darker) interacts with data from external organizations (lighter) for the definitions of first-, second-, and third-party data:

- **First-party data** is data that's internal to your organization, such as customer data or employee data.
- **Second-party data** is data that's shared as part of a data-sharing partnership or agreement with another organization.
- **Third-party data** is data that's collected from external sources, such as proprietary or open source APIs:

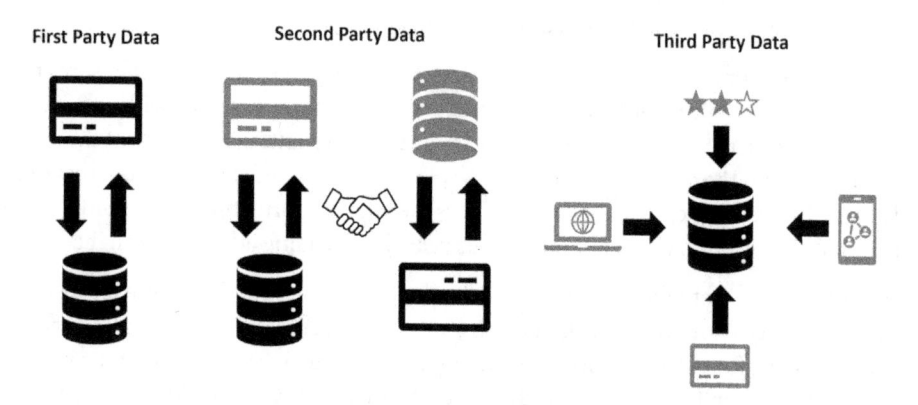

Figure 2.1: How first-, second-, and third-party data interacts with external organizations

Let's take a closer look at each.

First-party data – the treasure trove within

First, we will begin with first-party data – the data that your organization collects directly from its customers, users, or other sources. Have you ever considered the wealth of information that lies within your systems? Customer interactions, sales transactions, website analytics, and even employee records are all examples of first-party data. This data is invaluable as it provides organizations with a unique perspective on their customers, products, and services.

But why is first-party data so important? The answer lies in its accuracy, relevance, and control. Since it is collected directly from the source, it is often considered the most reliable and accurate type of data. Furthermore, this data is inherently relevant to your organization's specific needs and goals. Lastly, your organization maintains full control over its first-party data, ensuring compliance with privacy regulations and minimizing potential data breaches.

Consider, for example, the insights gained from analyzing customer purchase history or website behavior. How can these insights inform marketing strategies, product development, or even customer support? By effectively harnessing first-party data, organizations can unlock a treasure trove of insights and opportunities.

Second-party data – building bridges through collaboration

Next, we will cover second-party data, which is essentially another organization's first-party data that is shared or purchased for mutual benefit. While this may initially seem counterintuitive, sharing data can lead to fruitful collaborations and partnerships, expanding your organization's reach and knowledge base.

What makes second-party data valuable? The answer lies in its exclusivity and potential for collaboration. Second-party data can provide unique insights that are not readily available in the public domain, giving your organization a competitive edge. Furthermore, the process of sharing data can lead to collaborative opportunities and foster strategic partnerships.

Imagine, for example, a retail company collaborating with a payment processing platform to better understand customer spending habits and preferences. By sharing data, both organizations stand to benefit from enhanced insights and informed decision-making. However, it is crucial to ensure that all parties involved adhere to strict data privacy and security standards when sharing second-party data.

Third-party data – broadening horizons with external expertise

Finally, let's consider third-party data, which is collected by organizations that specialize in aggregating and selling data to other businesses. This data can offer insights into market trends, demographics, and other valuable information that may be difficult or time-consuming to collect internally.

Why should organizations consider third-party data? The answer lies in its breadth, specialization, and potential for uncovering new opportunities. Third-party data can provide access to a wide range of datasets, including industry-specific information, demographic data, and location data. These providers often possess specialized expertise in collecting and analyzing data, ensuring high-quality insights.

Picture, for example, a company in the fast-moving consumer goods industry looking to expand its product offerings. By acquiring third-party data on consumer preferences and market trends, the company can make informed decisions regarding product development and marketing strategies.

Another example might be a company looking to understand how companies are talking about their brand online, through social listening. This would involve collecting and analyzing third-party social media data from sources such as X (formerly Twitter) and Reddit.

It is important to note, however, that the quality of third-party data can vary, and organizations must carefully evaluate the reliability and accuracy of the data they purchase.

While categorizing data based on its source is essential, it's also important to understand how data can be structured differently. In the next section, we'll explore the differences between structured, unstructured, and semi-structured data.

Structured, unstructured, and semi-structured data

When working with data from data sources, how can you usefully categorize them? There are three broad categories of data: structured, unstructured, and semi-structured.

As a decision-maker, it is useful to understand the nuances and applications of structured, unstructured, and semi-structured data to make informed decisions regarding data storage, management, and analytics.

Structured data

Structured data, which is organized in a specific format such as relational databases, is easily searchable and analyzable. This type of data can include a wide range of information, such as customer names, addresses, ages, and transaction amounts, to name a few. The advantage of structured data is that it is well-defined and easier to use by data scientists and engineers, often requiring less pre-processing than other forms of data:

Structured Data

product_id	product_name	product_description	product_price	product_size	upc_number	created_date
1	Widget Pro	A high-quality widget for experts	49.99	L	12345678901	2021-05-03
2	Widget Classic	The classic widget for daily use	29.99	M	12345678902	2020-10-12
3	Widget Mini	A compact widget for portability	19.99	S	12345678903	2021-03-20
4	Widget Max	The largest widget for heavy tasks	59.99	XL	12345678904	2021-09-15

Figure 2.2: An example of structured data in a SQL table

Unstructured data

On the other hand, unstructured data, which lacks a predefined format or organization, encompasses a wide array of information, including documents, emails, social media posts, images, and videos. Value can be gained from unstructured data. For example, you can analyze e-commerce product reviews, emails, social media posts, or legal contracts to identify patterns or insights or analyze images or videos for applications such as quality control in manufacturing.

There has been a huge amount of progress in deep learning techniques and their application to natural language data via **natural language processing** (**NLP**), including **large language models** (**LLMs**) such as GPT-4. There has also been great progress in applying deep learning models to image and video data (**computer vision**). This explosion in capability means that unstructured data, while sometimes neglected by large, slow-moving organizations due to its relative complexity compared to traditional structured data, is more valuable to organizations than ever before. Other formats of unstructured data, such as audio data and sensor data, can also be analyzed through the use of deep learning models.

We will cover some of the applications of NLP and computer vision in more detail later in this book:

Unstructured Data

> This Contract (the "Agreement") is entered into as of the _____ day of _____, 20__, by and between ABC Company, a [State] corporation with its principal place of business located at [Address], (the "Company"), and John Doe, an individual residing at [Address] (the "Consultant") (collectively, the "Parties")

Figure 2.3: An example of unstructured data in the form of a legal contract

Semi-structured data

Semi-structured data bridges the gap between structured and unstructured data, offering a more flexible approach to data organization. While it does not adhere to the rigid structure of data models typically associated with relational databases, it contains tags or markers that help in organizing the data. Examples of semi-structured data include XML, JSON, or HTML files, all of which are common data standards. Web scraping can be employed to collect this type of data, such as product prices and descriptions, from multiple websites for competitive analysis. Additionally, data integration projects can benefit from the adaptability of semi-structured data when combining information from different sources or systems. IoT devices often generate semi-structured data, which can be used to monitor and optimize performance in various areas, such as energy usage, manufacturing, or transportation:

Semi-Structured Data

```
<!DOCTYPE html>
<html lang="en">
<head>
<title>ABC Corporation</title>
</head>
<body>
<main>
  <section>
   <h2>Our Products</h2>
    <p>ABC Corporation produces a number of "widgets" for use within the industrial widget using industry.</p>
   </section>
```

Figure 2.4: An example of semi-structured data in the form of an HTML web page file

To successfully navigate the world of data, decision-makers should consider some key takeaways.

First, understand the types of data your organization works with so that you can make informed decisions about data storage, management, and analytics. Second, make use of structured data for traditional business analytics while employing unstructured and semi-structured data for more complex analyses, such as NLP or computer vision. Finally, foster collaboration between data scientists, IT professionals, and business stakeholders to ensure the efficient understanding, storage, and use of the different types of data in your organization's data-driven initiatives.

By comprehending the distinctions and applications of structured, unstructured, and semi-structured data, you will be better prepared to lead your organization's data science, machine learning, or AI initiatives toward success.

Now that you have a clear understanding of the different types and structures of data, the next step is to explore the various methods for collecting data that will best serve your organization's needs.

Methods for collecting data

Imagine standing at the edge of a vast field and you wish to discover hidden treasures buried beneath the surface. You know the treasures are there, waiting to be found, but how do you go about finding them? This is the challenge that organizations face when it comes to collecting data. Data is the lifeblood of data-driven decision-making, and the process of collecting it is as crucial as the insights it can ultimately provide. But how do you collect data that is accurate, relevant, and valuable? How do you ensure the data you gather will help you make informed decisions?

As a decision-maker, understanding the methods and best practices for collecting data is essential to maximizing the potential of data science within your organization. In this section, we will explore data collection, its challenges, and its opportunities to help you establish a solid foundation for your data-driven journey.

How do you know which type of data is right for your organization? How do you ensure that the data you collect is relevant, accurate, and reliable?

The key to answering these questions lies in understanding your organization's unique needs and objectives. Begin by identifying the specific questions you want to answer, the problems you want to solve, or the decisions you want to make. For example, a retailer might want to understand customer preferences to optimize their product offerings, while a hospital might want to study patient outcomes to improve the quality of care. Once you have a clear understanding of your goals, you can determine the type of data that will best serve your needs and guide your data collection efforts.

When collecting data, it's essential to choose the right data collection method for your specific objectives. Within market research, surveys, interviews, focus groups, and observations are some of the most used methods, each with its strengths and limitations. Surveys, for instance, can provide a wealth of quantitative data from a large sample of respondents but may lack the depth and nuance of qualitative data obtained from interviews or focus groups. As you select a data collection method, consider factors such as the scale of your research, the resources available, and the level of detail you require.

You may look at collecting data from other parts of your organization or externally via methods such as data transfer services, **application programming interfaces** (**APIs**) (a way for different applications to efficiently talk to each other), or more indirect methods of collecting data, such as web scraping.

Take a moment to ponder the challenges you might face when collecting data. Is there a large enough sample to be representative of the total population? What are the potential sources of bias or error in your data collection process? How can you ensure the data you collect is representative and reliable? One of the most critical aspects of data collection is ensuring that your sample is diverse and representative of the population you are studying.

Be mindful of potential sampling biases that could skew your results, such as **nonresponse bias** or **self-selection bias**.

Nonresponse bias occurs when certain groups of people are less likely to respond to your survey or participate in your study, leading to an unrepresentative sample. **Self-selection bias** happens when individuals voluntarily choose to participate in a study, and these self-selected participants may differ from the general population in important ways.

To minimize these biases, consider using probability sampling methods such as random sampling, which we discussed in the previous chapter. Follow up with non-respondents to encourage participation and analyze differences between respondents and non-respondents. Additionally, avoid relying solely on voluntary participation and actively recruit participants from diverse backgrounds.

Once you've collected this data using the appropriate methods, the next critical step is to store and process it so that you can extract meaningful insights.

Storing and processing data

If you were to walk into a library, you would find hundreds of books lining the shelves, each containing valuable knowledge. Now, think of how difficult it would be to find the exact book you need if they were all scattered randomly on the floor. This is the challenge that businesses face when it comes to storing and processing data. Organizing, categorizing, processing, and labeling data are essential steps in turning raw information into valuable insights that can drive effective decision-making.

As a decision-maker, understanding how data is stored and processed will empower you to unlock the full potential of data science in your organization. So, how do you ensure your company's data is properly stored and processed to facilitate accurate and actionable insights? What are the best practices to make data easily accessible, interpretable, and actionable for your team? Let's dive into the world of data storage and processing to answer these questions.

Picture your company's data as a vast ocean of information, constantly growing and changing. To navigate this ocean, you need a robust and reliable storage system that can handle the volume, variety, and velocity of the data. There are numerous data storage options available, from traditional databases such as SQL and NoSQL to cloud-based storage solutions such as Amazon S3 and Google Cloud Storage. How do you choose the right option for your organization? What factors should you consider when selecting a data storage system? The answers lie in understanding your data's characteristics, your organization's unique requirements, and the storage system's capabilities:

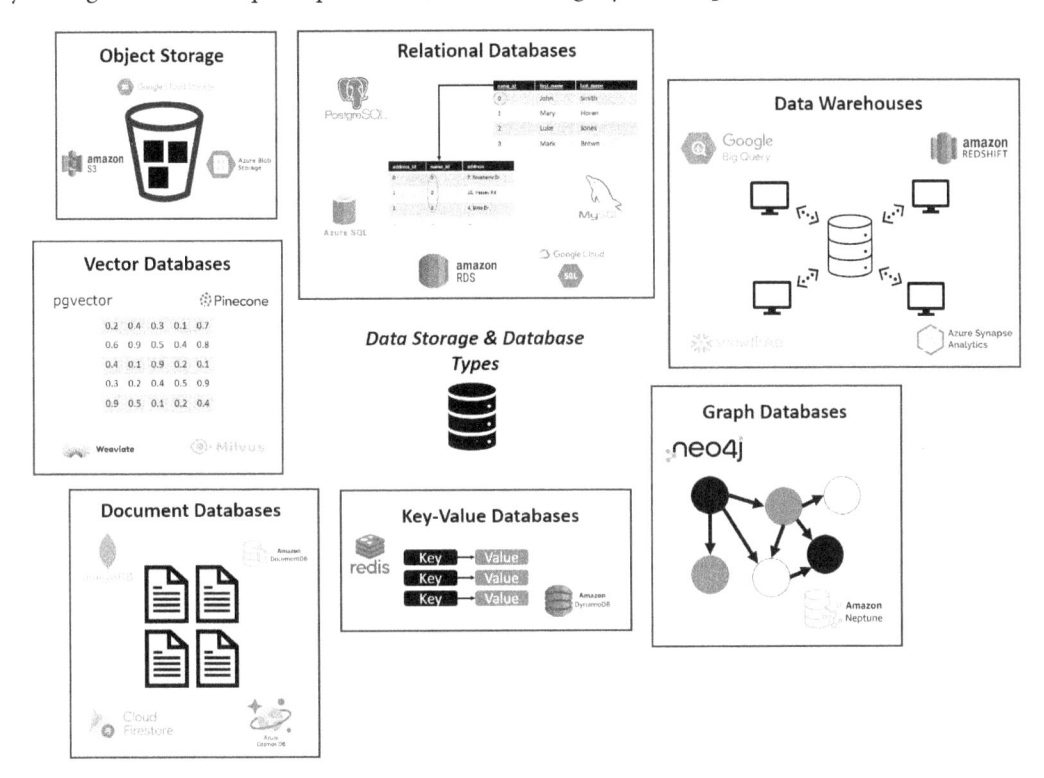

Figure 2.5: Types of data storage and databases

Relational databases

Relational databases have long been the bedrock of business data management systems thanks to their organized structure of tables, rows, and columns that facilitate efficient querying and data retrieval using SQL. They are a tried-and-true solution, with widespread adoption making it easier to find resources and talent. Their suitability for managing structured data and complex queries, coupled with their compliance with ACID principles, make them a solid choice for ensuring data integrity and consistency. However, relational databases can face challenges when it comes to scaling horizontally, particularly with large datasets, and they're not designed to handle unstructured or semi-structured data. Some well-known examples of relational databases include MySQL, PostgreSQL, and Microsoft SQL Server:

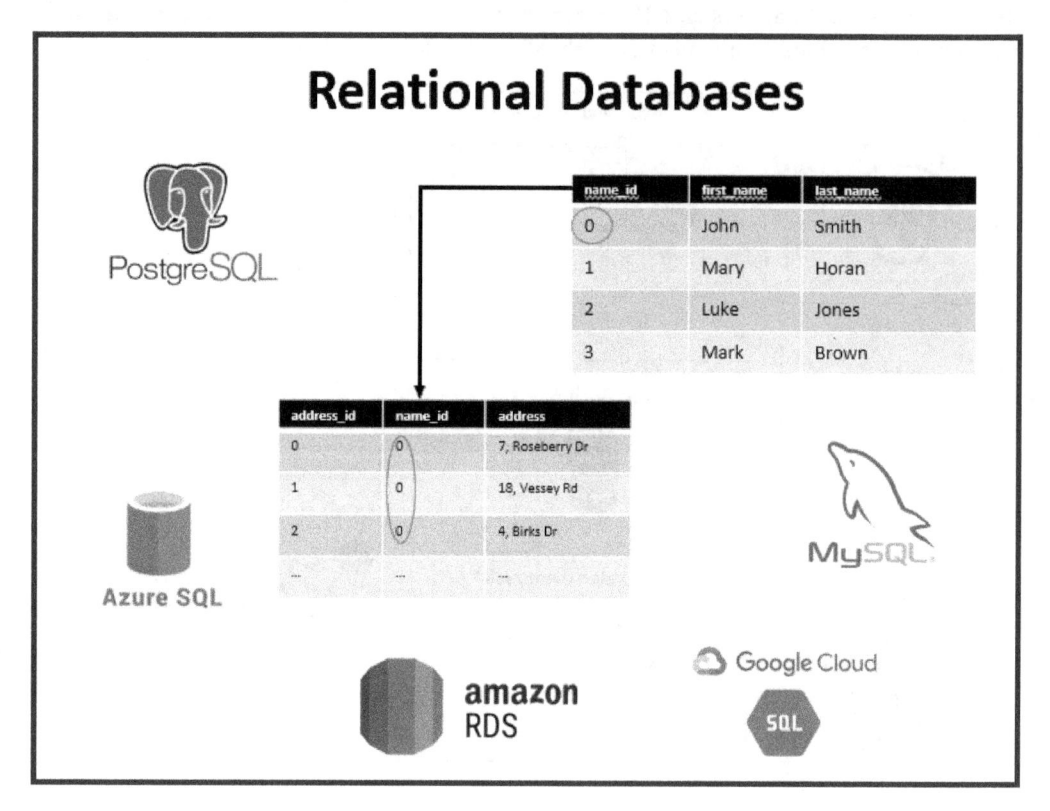

Figure 2.6: Relational databases

Object storage

In contrast, object storage offers a flexible solution for managing unstructured data, such as images, videos, and large documents. Object storage handles data as objects rather than files or blocks, allowing for easy scalability and cost-effective storage, particularly for long-term needs. Object storage shines in distributed systems and cloud-based environments, though it isn't designed for structured data management or complex queries, and its performance might lag compared to block storage. Amazon S3, Google Cloud Storage, and Microsoft Azure Blob Storage are prime examples of object storage solutions:

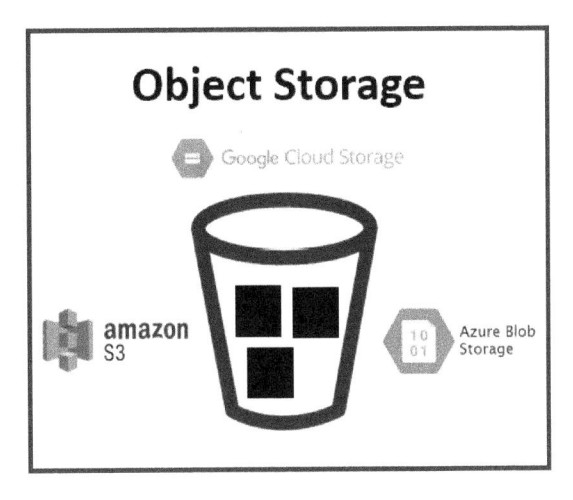

Figure 2.7: Object storage

Document databases

Document databases provide a versatile approach to storing data and handling semi-structured data and they offer a more flexible schema than relational databases. They store data as documents, supporting horizontal scaling and distributed systems. While document databases are powerful, they are less mature than their relational counterparts, and they may not be the best fit for complex relational queries. MongoDB, Couchbase, and Amazon DocumentDB are popular examples of document databases:

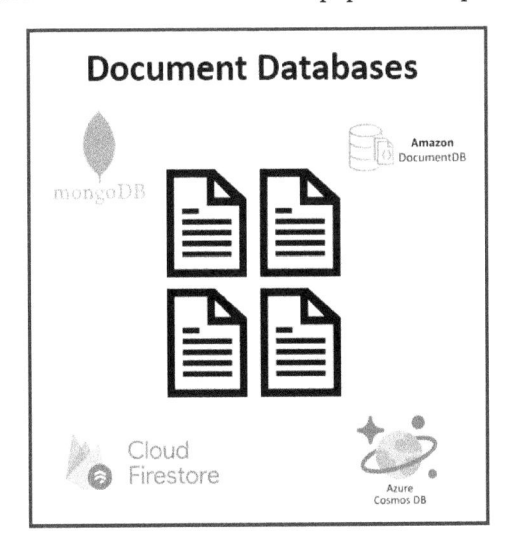

Figure 2.8: Document databases

Graph databases

For applications requiring intricate data relationships, graph databases excel in representing and querying complex connections between data entities. They employ graph structures comprising nodes, edges, and properties, making them an excellent choice for social networks, recommendation systems, and fraud detection applications. However, graph databases are less mature compared to relational databases and may not be the best option for use cases that don't require complex relationships. Some well-known graph databases include Neo4j and Amazon Neptune:

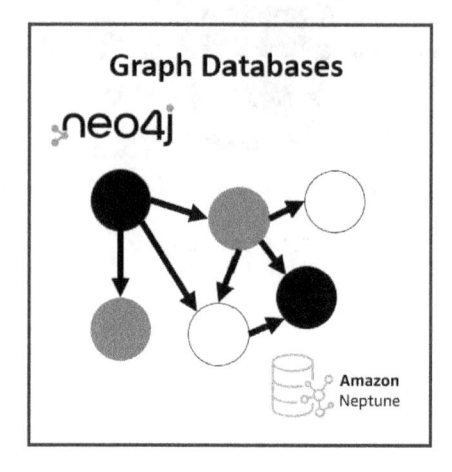

Figure 2.9: Graph databases

Key-value databases

Key-value databases focus on simplicity and speed, storing data as key-value pairs. They are best suited for use cases that require data retrieval based on a single key and don't necessitate complex querying. With fast and efficient low-latency performance, they easily scale and are ideal for caching and real-time applications. Their limitations lie in their querying capabilities and inability to handle complex relationships or data models. Redis, Amazon DynamoDB, and Riak are examples of key-value databases:

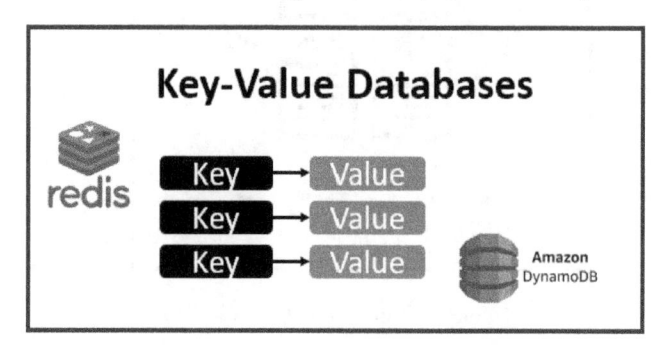

Figure 2.10: Key-value databases

Data warehouses

Data warehouses are centralized repositories that are designed to store and manage vast amounts of structured data from various sources, enabling businesses to perform complex queries, generate reports, and derive valuable insights. Unlike the **online transaction processing** (**OLTP**) relational databases mentioned earlier, which are optimized for real-time transactional processing and frequent updates, data warehouses are built for read-intensive operations and complex analytics workloads. They follow a schema-on-write approach, where data is transformed and structured before being loaded, ensuring data consistency and quality. Data warehouses are useful for supporting data-driven decision-making and are designed to handle large-scale data processing and analytics, making them an essential component of modern business intelligence and data science ecosystems. Some well-known examples of data warehouses include Google BigQuery, Amazon Redshift, Snowflake, and Azure Synapse Analytics:

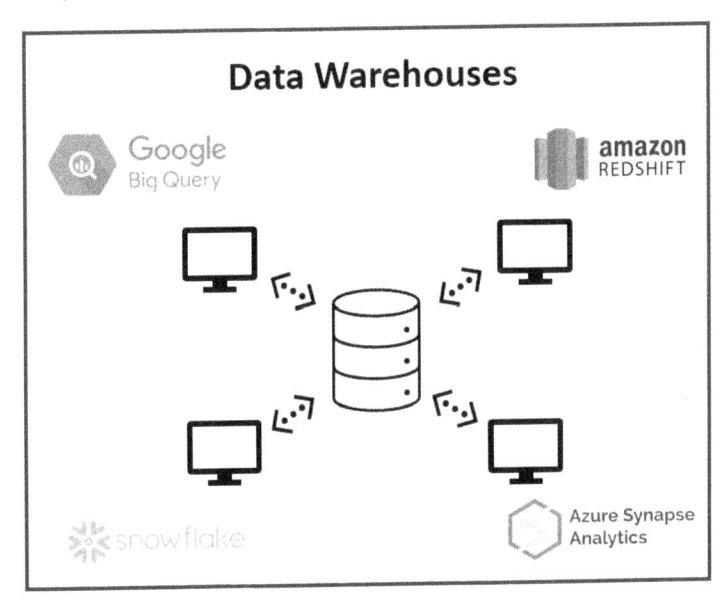

Figure 2.11: Data warehouses

Vector databases

Vector databases are a new type of database that stores data as high-dimensional vectors, which are numerical representations of data points in a multi-dimensional space. Unlike traditional databases, which handle structured data such as tables and rows, vector databases excel at managing unstructured data such as text, images, and audio. They enable fast and accurate similarity searches, making them ideal for powering advanced applications such as recommendation systems, semantic search, and question-answering. When combined with LLMs through techniques such as **retrieval-augmented generation** (**RAG**), vector databases help deliver highly relevant and contextual results by allowing the LLM to quickly access the most semantically similar information. This powerful combination is revolutionizing many NLP and information retrieval tasks. Key players in the vector database space include pgvector, Pinecone, Milvus, and Weaviate:

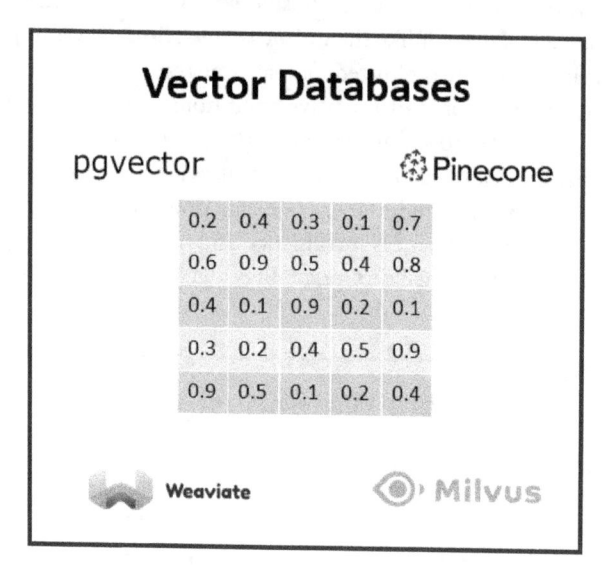

Figure 2.12: Vector databases

Understanding the various database types, their advantages and disadvantages, and their use cases will empower decision-makers to choose the most appropriate database technology for their organization's unique needs.

Cloud, on-premises, and hybrid solutions – navigating the data storage and analysis landscape

As executives and decision-makers, understanding the various options for data storage, analysis, and machine learning is critical to the success of your organization's data-driven initiatives. In this chapter, we will explore the advantages and challenges of cloud, on-premises (on-prem), and hybrid approaches, delving into their unique applications and impact on business decision-making.

Cloud computing – scalable services in the cloud

Imagine having access to virtually unlimited computing resources, scalable storage, and advanced analytics capabilities without having to invest in expensive infrastructure or manage complex hardware. This is the promise of cloud computing, a paradigm that enables organizations to store, process, and analyze data using remote servers hosted on the internet. The cloud has revolutionized the way businesses approach data science, machine learning, and artificial intelligence.

But why is cloud computing so appealing to organizations? The answer lies in its flexibility, cost-effectiveness, and ease of use. Cloud platforms offer the ability to scale resources up or down as needed, ensuring that organizations only pay for what they use. Additionally, cloud providers maintain, secure, and update their infrastructure, freeing up valuable time for your IT staff. Furthermore, the cloud enables seamless collaboration, allowing teams to access data and analytics tools from virtually anywhere.

Consider, for example, a company that wants to analyze vast amounts of customer data to improve its marketing strategies. By leveraging cloud-based machine learning tools and storage, the company can quickly and cost-effectively process and analyze the data, gaining valuable insights without incurring excessive costs or overwhelming its on-premises infrastructure. Cloud providers often have different storage and compute tiers, as well as the ability to scale up and scale down services as needed, allowing the customer to use only what they need and save cost. Many cloud providers also have out-of-the-box solutions for complex AI tasks, such as speech-to-text transcription (for example, Amazon Transcribe) or translation (for example, Amazon Translate), which can save customers time compared to building solutions in-house.

On-premises – maintaining control within your walls

Despite the numerous advantages of cloud computing, some organizations still prefer to keep their data and analytics infrastructure on-premises. On-premises solutions involve housing data storage, processing, and analysis tools within the organization's data centers or facilities.

Why would an organization choose on-premises over cloud computing? The answer lies in control, security, and customization. On-premises solutions allow organizations to maintain complete control over their infrastructure, data, and applications. This can be particularly important for companies with strict security or compliance requirements or those that handle sensitive data. Additionally, on-premises solutions offer the potential for greater customization, enabling organizations to tailor their infrastructure to their specific needs.

Imagine a financial institution that deals with sensitive customer data and must adhere to stringent regulations. In this case, an on-premises solution may be preferable as it allows the organization to maintain control over its data and ensure compliance with industry standards.

Hybrid – the best of both worlds?

For some organizations, the choice between cloud and on-premises is not black and white. Instead, they opt for a hybrid approach, which combines elements of both cloud and on-premises infrastructure. Hybrid solutions enable organizations to leverage the benefits of both paradigms, providing flexibility, scalability, and control.

Why should an organization consider a hybrid approach? The answer lies in its versatility and adaptability. Hybrid solutions allow organizations to maintain control over sensitive data on-premises while also taking advantage of the scalability and cost-effectiveness of cloud-based resources for less sensitive or resource-intensive tasks.

Envision a healthcare organization that must securely store patient records while also processing large volumes of medical research data. A hybrid approach allows the organization to keep sensitive patient data on-premises while utilizing cloud-based resources for computationally intensive research tasks, effectively balancing security and performance.

By understanding the various types of databases, their applications, and the pros and cons of cloud, on-premises, and hybrid solutions, you and your team can make informed decisions about data storage and processing that best serve your business use cases.

Collecting and storing data on the right infrastructure isn't the end of the story. Data is only useful once it has been processed, analyzed, modeled, and used for business purposes. In the next section, we will discuss data processing. Later in this book, we will look into data analytics and machine learning so that you can gain further value from your data.

Data processing

Once your data has been stored securely, the next step is processing it to extract meaningful insights. Data processing involves cleaning, transforming, and analyzing data to make it suitable for data science and decision-making. But how do you ensure that your data is processed accurately and efficiently? What tools and techniques can you use to transform raw data into valuable information?

Data processing typically involves three main stages: data preparation, data transformation, and data analysis. During the data preparation phase, your data is cleansed, and any inconsistencies, errors, or missing values are addressed. This is an important step to ensure that your subsequent analyses are based on accurate and reliable data. There are many proprietary and open source solutions to help you and your team in this process. It is also often helpful to involve subject matter experts from the business who can identify and help rectify any issues in the data.

Next, data transformation involves converting data into a suitable format for further analysis. This may involve aggregating data, normalizing variables, or encoding categorical variables, among other tasks. Consider a retail company that wants to analyze sales data to identify trends and make informed decisions. The raw sales data may include transaction-level information such as customer names, product IDs, and purchase amounts. To make sense of this data, it needs to be transformed into a format that can be easily interpreted and analyzed, such as aggregating sales by product category or calculating average purchase amounts per customer.

Finally, the data analysis and modeling stage involves using statistical and machine learning techniques to uncover patterns, relationships, and trends in the data. This will be the subject of subsequent chapters.

Summary

Navigating the landscape of data collection, storage, processing, analysis, and machine learning is no small task. However, understanding the different sources and categories of data, various databases, and the pros and cons of cloud, on-premises, and hybrid solutions will equip you to make informed decisions and better understand the data landscape within your organization.

Consider these key questions:

- What are the key criteria when evaluating data?
- What is the difference between first, second, and third-party data?
- What is the difference between structured, unstructured, and semi-structured data?
- What are the methods for collecting data?
- What are the methods for storing and processing data?
- How can you navigate the landscape of data solutions, and what are the pros and cons of each?

This knowledge will help you and your team make the right decisions about data collection and technology to best serve your business use cases and gain tangible value from your data.

Now that you have a solid understanding of the data landscape, the next step is to explore and understand the data you have gathered through **exploratory data analysis** (**EDA**). EDA allows you to summarize the main characteristics of your datasets, often using visual methods, and develop a deeper understanding of the patterns, trends, and potential issues within your data before proceeding with more advanced analysis or modeling.

EDA will help you uncover valuable insights, identify potential biases or anomalies, and communicate your findings effectively to stakeholders. This foundational knowledge will empower you to make data-driven decisions with confidence and lay the groundwork for successful machine learning and statistical modeling projects.

Let's move on to the next chapter and see how EDA can help you unlock more of the potential of your data.

3
Exploratory Data Analysis

In the previous chapter, we covered methods for characterizing and collecting data. So, now that you have collected some data, what will you do with it? Well, that is the topic of this chapter. In this chapter, we will learn about the process of **exploratory data analysis** (**EDA**).

EDA is an approach to analyzing datasets so that you can summarize their main characteristics, often with visual methods. It is used to understand data, get a context of it, develop more hypotheses, and consequently build better models and business outcomes.

In this chapter, we will get a bit more hands-on, with code examples that you can try out.

If you would rather focus on reading the content, feel free to skip the code exercises. They are completely optional and they've been written to help reinforce some of the things we'll be learning about in this book.

Also, don't worry if you have never used Python before; every exercise will be explained step by step and assumes no prior experience with Python.

This chapter covers the following topics:

- Getting started with Google Colab
- Understanding the data you have
- EDA techniques and tools

Let's dive in by learning how to set up a code environment so that you can follow the exercises laid out in this chapter.

Getting started with Google Colab

To help you gain a better understanding of the different data science techniques that will be covered in this chapter, there will be some hands-on exercises you can complete with Python.

To set everything up, we will be using **Google Colab** as it is an easy place to get started if you haven't used Python before.

What is Google Colab?

Google Colaboratory, commonly known as Google Colab, is a free cloud service that provides an environment where you can run Python code. It's like having a powerful computer right in your browser, which is particularly useful for data science tasks, including but not limited to statistics, machine learning, and **natural language processing** (NLP). You don't need to install anything, and it's available on any device with internet access.

A step-by-step guide to setting up Google Colab

Follow these steps to set up Colab with ease:

1. First, you need a Google account. If you don't already have one, you can create one here: `https://accounts.google.com/signup`.
2. Now, open your preferred web browser and go to the Google Colab website: `https://colab.research.google.com/`.
3. Click on the **Sign In** button in the top-right corner and log in with your Google account.
4. Once you've signed in, you'll see a page with a menu at the top. Click **File**, then choose **New Notebook** from the dropdown. This will open a new tab that contains your fresh notebook.
5. By default, your notebook will be named `Untitled0.ipynb`. You can change this by clicking on the name at the top of the page. A dialog box will appear where you can enter your desired name. A good idea would be to name each notebook by specifying the number and name of the chapter (for example, `Chapter 3 - Exploratory Data Analysis.ipynb`).
6. In the notebook, you'll see a cell with a play button (it looks like a right arrow). Click on the cell to activate it, type `print("Hello, world!")`, and then click the play button to run the code.
7. To save your notebook, you can click **File** in the menu and choose **Save**, or simply use the *Ctrl + S* (Windows/Linux) or *Cmd + S* (Mac) keyboard shortcut.

And that's it! You're now ready to start your journey into data science using Python on Google Colab. As you read through this book, you'll find Google Colab notebooks that have been prepared for you to practice your skills while considering real-world examples concerning data science and machine learning. Happy coding!

Now, let's get back to the topic of this chapter: **EDA**.

Understanding the data you have

Once you have gone through the process of collecting and storing data, it can be tempting to dive straight into the more interesting and exciting work of training machine learning models or building dashboards to present to your customers or stakeholders.

However, an important stage before model training or presenting results is to explore and understand the data you have, as well as its main characteristics, patterns and trends in the data, and potential anomalies or outliers.

EDA is a fundamental step in the data analysis process that involves systematically examining datasets to understand their main characteristics, identify patterns and trends, and uncover potential anomalies or outliers. EDA typically precedes more formal statistical or machine learning modeling, and its primary goal is to provide insights and context that will inform further analysis and model development.

The importance of EDA cannot be overstated. It not only helps decision-makers develop a better understanding of their data but also assists in identifying potential issues or biases in the data that could impact the accuracy and reliability of subsequent analyses. Furthermore, EDA enables the development of more meaningful visualizations and representations of data that can be easily communicated to stakeholders and team members.

Now that we understand the importance of EDA, let's explore the various tools and techniques at our disposal for performing it.

EDA techniques and tools

There are numerous EDA techniques and tools available to data scientists, analysts, and decision-makers.

Some of the most used methods for EDA are mentioned in the following subsections.

Descriptive statistics

The simplest form of EDA involves calculating the summary statistics we covered in the previous chapter, such as the mean, median, mode, standard deviation, and range, to provide an initial understanding of the data's central tendencies and dispersion.

Code example

Here, we will show you an example of how to calculate the mean, median, mode, standard deviation, and range for an example dataset showing monthly sales figures for a year.

For each code snippet, you can copy and paste it into Google Colab and press *Shift + Enter* to run them.

Exploratory Data Analysis

Open your code editor and run the following code to calculate the mean value:

```
import pandas as pd
# Define a toy dataset representing monthly sales figures for a year
sales_data_year1 = pd.Series([12000, 15000, 11000, 14000, 13000,
    15000, 16000, 17000, 16000, 15000, 14000, 18000])
# Calculate mean (average)
mean_sales_year1 = sales_data_year1.mean()
print(f"The average monthly sales across the year is
    {round(mean_sales_year1)} units.")
```

The expected output is `"The average monthly sales across the year is 14667 units."`.

Now, calculate the median (middle value):

```
median_sales_year1 = sales_data_year1.median()
print(f"The median monthly sales, a typical sales month,
    is {round(median_sales_year1)} units.")
```

The expected output is `"The median monthly sales, a typical sales month, is 15000 units."`.

Next, calculate the standard deviation (a measure of the amount of variation):

```
std_dev_sales_year1 = sales_data_year1.std()
print(f"The standard deviation,
    showing the typical variation from the mean sales,
    is {round(std_dev_sales_year1)} units.")
```

The expected output is `"The standard deviation, showing the typical variation from the mean sales, is 2015 units."`.

Now, calculate the mode (the most common value):

```
# mode() returns a Series; we want the first value
mode_sales_year1 = sales_data_year1.mode()[0]
print(f"The most common monthly sales volume is {mode_sales_year1}
    units.")
```

The expected output is `"The most common monthly sales volume is 15000 units."`.

Finally, calculate the range (the difference between the maximum and the minimum):

```
range_sales_year1 = sales_data_year1.max() - sales_data_year1.min()
print(f"The range of monthly sales volumes is {range_sales_1} units.")
```

The expected output is `"The range of monthly sales volumes is 7000 units."`.

Now, let's calculate the same statistics for another year's data:

```
# A dataset representing the following year's sales
sales_data_year2 = pd.Series([11000, 12500, 13500, 17000, 18500,
    17000, 16500, 15500, 16500, 18000, 19000, 21000])
[YOUR CODE HERE TO CALCULATE THE SUMMARY STATISTICS]
```

What can you say about the 2 years' monthly sales figures?

Before moving ahead, think about what you could conclude from these summary statistics.

Did you observe any of the differences mentioned here?

- The average sales seem to have increased from year 1 to year 2, which is good news for the business
- The median sales also increased, suggesting a general shift in sales rather than them just being influenced by a few high sales months
- The standard deviation is higher in year 2, indicating that sales were more variable or dispersed that year
- The most common monthly sales volume changed from year 1 to year 2, indicating a shift in sales performance
- The range of sales volumes has also increased, showing that the spread in sales volumes is larger in year 2

Another useful descriptive statistic that is useful when profiling data is the proportion of missing or null data. For example, if you had a dataset of customers from a **customer relationship management (CRM)** system, you might want to know the proportion of customers who had empty "Company Name" or "Job Title" fields. This can help you understand where there are gaps in data that can be filled with better data collection or annotation, or that should be treated with care when used as features when training machine learning or statistical models.

Data visualization

Beyond descriptive statistics, a useful way to explore data is by visualizing it. The use of graphical representations such as histograms, boxplots, scatter plots, and heatmaps can help identify patterns, trends, and outliers in data.

These visualizations can easily be created using dedicated dashboard software such as Microsoft's PowerBI and Tableau or Python data visualization packages such as `matplotlib` and `plotly`.

Code example

Following our previous calculation of summary statistics, we can also visualize the sales data for better insights. The matplotlib library in Python provides an excellent platform for us to create different types of data visualizations. Here, we will use a bar plot to represent the sales for each month and line charts to indicate the mean and median sales.

Open your code editor and run the following code. This builds upon the code provided in the previous exercise, so make sure you complete that exercise first, in the same notebook, before running this code:

```python
import matplotlib.pyplot as plt
# Define the months
months = range(1, 13)
month_labels = ["Jan", "Feb", "Mar", "Apr", "May", "Jun", "Jul",
    "Aug", "Sep", "Oct", "Nov", "Dec"]
# Define a figure to hold the subplots
fig, axs = plt.subplots(2, figsize=(10, 10))
# Add data for Year 1
axs[0].bar(months, sales_data_year1)
axs[0].plot([1, 12], [mean_sales_year1, mean_sales_year1],
    color='red', label='Mean')   # Mean line
axs[0].plot([1, 12], [median_sales_year1, median_sales_year1],
    color='blue', label='Median')   # Median line
axs[0].set_xticks(months)   # Add ticks for every month
axs[0].set_xticklabels(month_labels)   # Label the ticks
axs[0].set_xlabel('Month')   # Add x-axis title
axs[0].set_ylabel('Units Sold')   # Add y-axis title
axs[0].legend()
axs[0].set_title("Year 1 sales data")

# Add data for Year 2
axs[1].bar(months, sales_data_year2)
axs[1].plot([1, 12], [mean_sales_year2, mean_sales_year2],
    color='red', label='Mean')   # Mean line
axs[1].plot([1, 12], [median_sales_year2, median_sales_year2],
    color='blue', label='Median')   # Median line
axs[1].set_xticks(months)   # Add ticks for every month
axs[1].set_xticklabels(month_labels)   # Label the ticks
axs[1].set_xlabel('Month')   # Add x-axis title
axs[1].set_ylabel('Units Sold')   # Add y-axis title
axs[1].legend()
axs[1].set_title("Year 2 sales data")
# Show the plot
plt.tight_layout()
plt.show()
```

The charts should look like this:

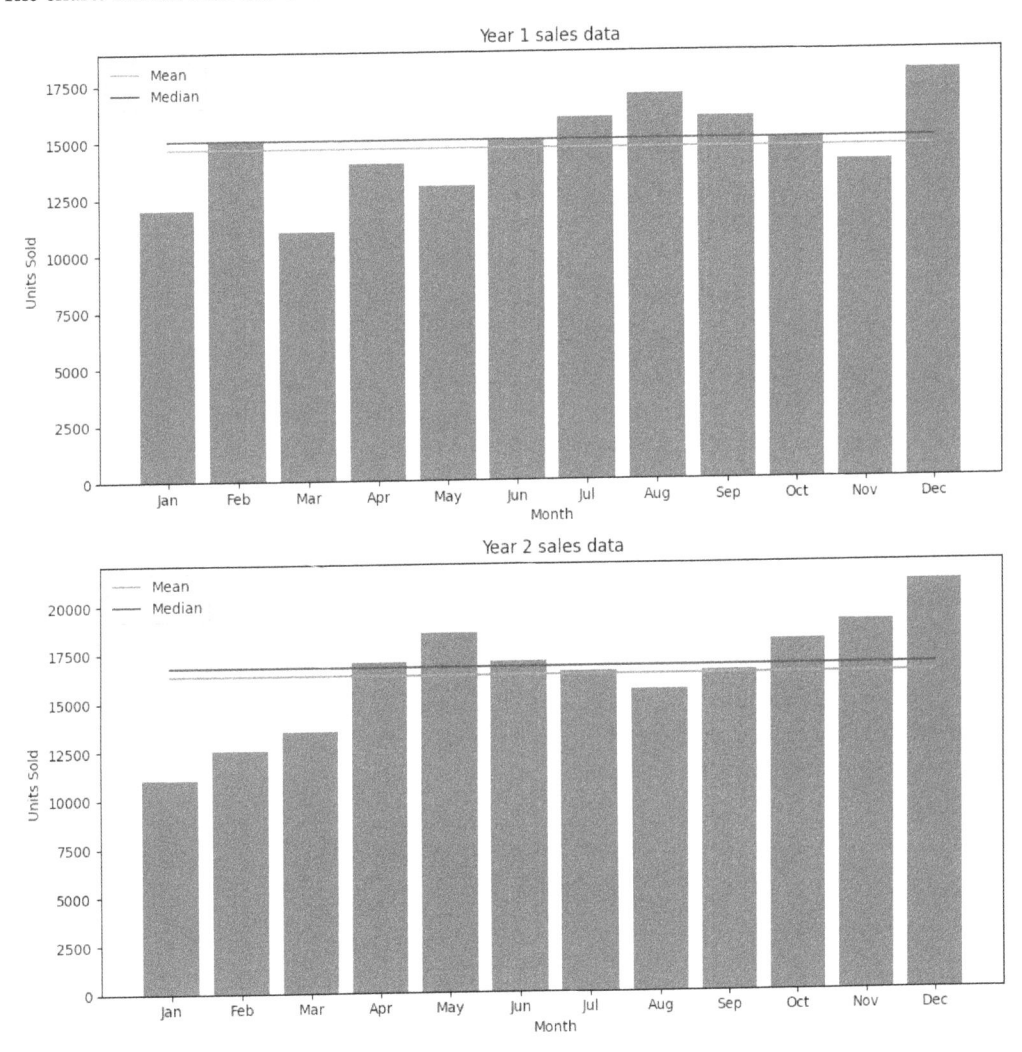

Figure 3.1: Units sold for year 1 and year 2 by month

By looking at the bar plot, we can observe the sales figures for each month. The red line represents the mean, while the blue line represents the median. As you can see, year 2 had higher sales figures, which is consistent with the calculations from the previous section.

With visualizations, it becomes easier to observe trends, fluctuations, and other characteristics of your dataset that may not be apparent from the raw numbers alone. For instance, in year 2, you may have noticed a certain fluctuation in the sales figures, which is causing a higher standard deviation, or you might have observed that the mean and median are more spread apart.

Always remember that visualizing your data is a key step in the data exploration process. It allows you to better understand the data before you apply more complex analyses or modeling techniques.

Histograms

A histogram is a simple and easy-to-understand visual tool that helps us see how data is spread out and organized. Think of it as a bar chart where each bar represents a range or group of data, called a "bin." The height of each bar shows how many data points fall into that specific range. The higher the bar, the more data points are within that range. A histogram can help us quickly grasp the overall shape and distribution of the data, making it easier to identify patterns or trends and spot any unusual values.

For example, let's say we have data on the heights of a group of people, measured in inches. We can create a histogram to visualize this information by dividing the heights into bins or groups, such as 150-159 centimeters, 160-169 centimeters, 170-179 centimeters, and so on. Then, we can count how many people fall into each height range and represent that count as a bar on the chart. So, if we have 12 people with heights between 150-159 centimeters, the bar representing that range would be of a certain height, and if there are 20 people with heights between 160-169 centimeters, the bar for that range would be taller.

By looking at the histogram, we can easily see where most people's heights are concentrated (for example, if many people are between 160-169 centimeters tall, there will be a taller bar in that range) and if there are any outliers (for example, if only one person is over 190 centimeters tall, there would be a very short bar for that range). This visual representation allows even those who are non-technical to quickly grasp the distribution and patterns in the data, making histograms a valuable tool for understanding and communicating data insights:

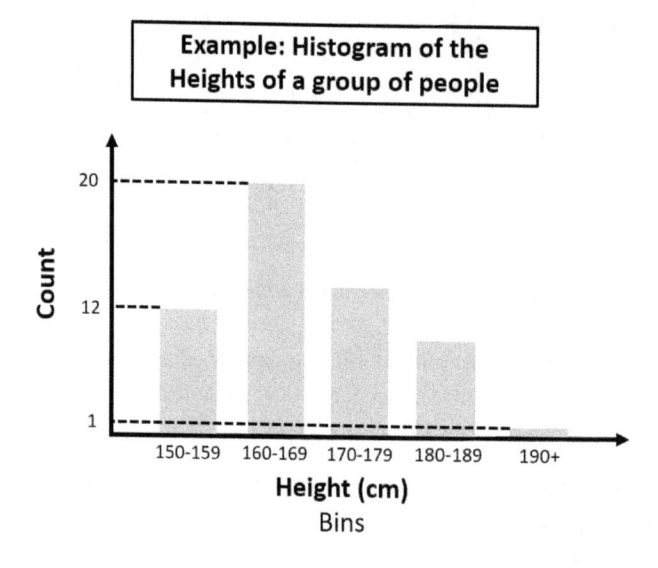

Figure 3.2: A histogram showing the counts from a group of people in different ranges of heights

Density curves

A density curve is a smooth, continuous line that represents the distribution of data in a way that is easy to understand for non-technical readers. It provides a clear picture of how data is spread out and helps us visualize the overall shape and pattern of the data. The curve is drawn in such a way that the total area under it equals one, which means that it shows the relative frequencies or proportions of data points in different ranges, rather than the actual counts. The height of the curve at any point indicates the density of the data at that value, meaning that higher points on the curve represent areas where more data points are concentrated.

For example, imagine that we have data on the test scores of a group of students.

Instead of using a histogram, which consists of bars representing the number of students in each score range, we can use a density curve to show the same information in a smoother, more visually appealing manner. To create the curve, we must estimate the frequency distribution of the test scores and then draw a smooth line that closely follows the shape of the data. The peaks and valleys of the curve will indicate where the scores are more or less dense, respectively.

By looking at the density curve, we can easily see the overall distribution of test scores, such as whether the majority of students scored within a specific range (indicated by a peak on the curve) or if there are any unusual patterns, such as multiple peaks or a wide spread of scores. The curve also helps us identify the central tendency (for example, the mode, where the curve is at its highest point) and the dispersion or spread of the data (for example, a wider curve indicates a larger range of scores). This smooth, visually intuitive representation makes it simple for non-technical readers to grasp and interpret the underlying patterns and characteristics of the data:

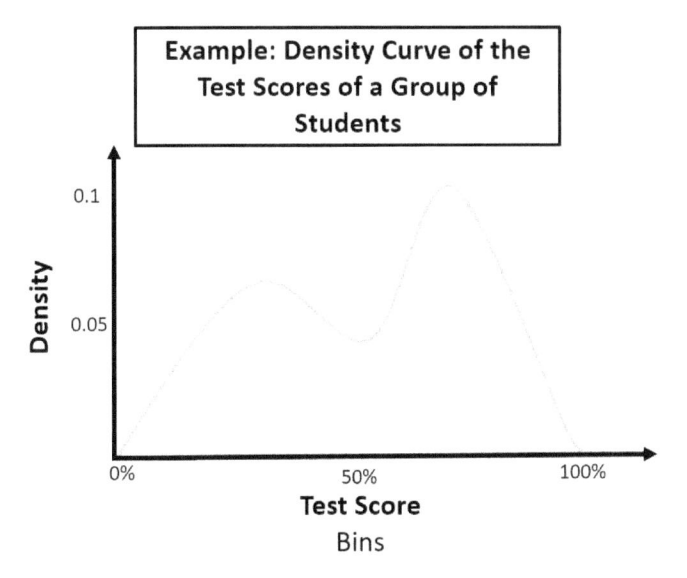

Figure 3.3: A density curve showing the distribution of test scores among a group of students

Boxplots

A boxplot, also known as a box-and-whisker plot, is a straightforward and easy-to-understand visualization that displays key information about the distribution of a dataset. It consists of a rectangular box and two lines (whiskers) extending from the box, representing different aspects of the data. Boxplots are particularly useful for identifying the central tendency, spread, and potential outliers in the data, making them excellent tools for non-technical readers.

To understand a boxplot, let's break down its components using an example. Imagine that we have data on the ages of people attending a community event. We can use a boxplot to visualize the age distribution clearly and concisely. The box in the plot represents the middle 50% of the data, also known as the **interquartile range (IQR)**. The lower edge of the box, called the **first quartile (Q1)**, marks the age at which 25% of the attendees are younger, while the upper edge, the **third quartile (Q3)**, marks the age at which 75% of the attendees are younger. The line inside the box is the median, representing the exact middle age of the dataset, where 50% of the attendees are younger and 50% are older.

The whiskers extending from the box help us understand the spread of the remaining data. Typically, the whiskers extend to the smallest and largest values within 1.5 times the IQR. In other words, they show the range of "typical" ages, excluding any potential outliers. Any data points outside of the whiskers are considered outliers and are often plotted as individual points or circles. These can be seen as the "Xs" in the chart.

By looking at a boxplot, non-technical readers can quickly grasp essential information about the data, such as the median age (the line inside the box), the overall age distribution (the size of the box and whiskers), and any unusual ages that stand out from the rest (outliers). This simple yet powerful visualization provides a clear snapshot of the data's characteristics, making it an invaluable tool for understanding and communicating data insights:

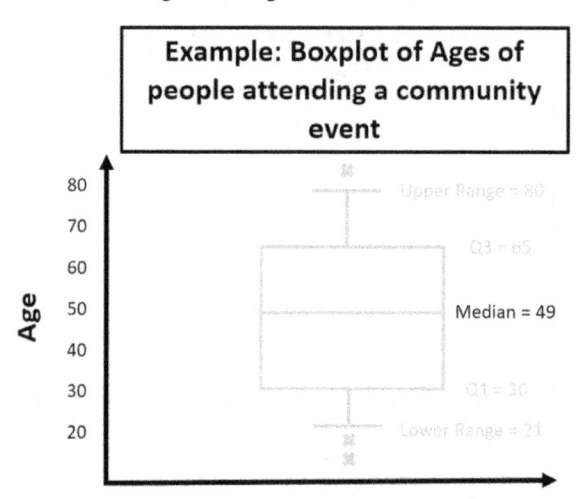

Figure 3.4: A boxplot (box-and-whisker chart), showing the median, Q1, Q3, and lower and upper ranges for the ages of people attending an event

Heatmaps

A heatmap is a visually intuitive and easy-to-understand representation of data that uses colors to display the values or frequencies of variables in a two-dimensional grid. Each cell in the grid corresponds to a specific combination of the two variables, and the color of the cell represents the value or frequency associated with that combination. The color scale typically ranges from one color representing low values to another color representing high values, with a gradient in between. Heatmaps are especially useful for examining patterns, trends, or relationships between variables in large datasets, making them a valuable tool for non-technical readers.

To illustrate how a heatmap works, let's consider an example. Imagine that we have data on the sales of different products in a store across various months. We can create a heatmap to visualize this information clearly and concisely. In the heatmap, one axis (that is, the rows) represents the products, and the other axis (that is, the columns) represents the months. Each cell in the grid corresponds to the sales of a particular product in a specific month. The color of the cell represents the sales amount, with a color scale ranging from light green for low sales to dark green for high sales.

By looking at the heatmap, non-technical readers can quickly identify patterns and trends in the data, such as which products tend to have higher sales in certain months or whether there are seasonal variations in sales. The color-coded cells make it easy to spot high and low values at a glance, allowing users to focus on areas of interest or concern. For instance, a row of dark green cells for a specific product may indicate consistently high sales, while a column of light green cells may suggest that sales are generally low during a particular month.

In summary, heatmaps offer a visually appealing and easily interpretable way to display complex data, allowing non-technical readers to quickly identify patterns, trends, and relationships between variables. This powerful visualization technique simplifies the process of understanding and communicating data insights, making heatmaps an essential tool in any data analysis toolkit:

Example: Heatmap of Product Sales by Month

Product	Jan	Feb	Mar	Apr	May	Jun	Jul	Aug	Sep	Oct	Nov	Dec
T-Shirts	$3.5m	$4.8m	$4.7m	$5.1m	$5.3m	$5.5m	$5.6m	$4.8m	$4.7m	$4.5m	$3m	$3m
Sunglasses	$0.2m	$0.5m	$3m	$4.1m	$5m	$4.6m	$4.8m	$5.2	$2.1m	$0.1m	$0.1m	$0.1m
Winter Jackets	$5.1m	$3.1m	$0.1m	$0.3m	$0.2m	$0.1m	$0.4m	$3.6m	$4.2m	$5.2m	$5.1m	$5.4m
Boots	$4.9m	$3.2m	$1.2m	$1.1m	$0.6m	$0.4m	$0.6m	$3.2m	$4.5m	$5.4m	$5.6m	$5.9m

Figure 3.5: A heatmap showing the monthly sales of different product categories for an example fashion store

Dimensionality reduction

Dimensionality reduction is a technique that's used to simplify complex data by reducing the number of variables or dimensions while still retaining as much of the original information as possible. This process makes it easier for non-technical readers to understand and analyze the data, and it also improves the performance of various machine learning algorithms. The idea behind dimensionality reduction is to find the most important features or patterns within the data and represent them using fewer dimensions, effectively condensing the data while preserving its essential structure.

A popular method for dimensionality reduction is **principal component analysis (PCA)**.

PCA is a mathematical technique that transforms the original data into a new set of variables, called principal components. These principal components are chosen in such a way that they capture the most important patterns and variations in the data. By selecting a few principal components, we can create a simplified representation of the data that still captures most of the essential information.

To illustrate this concept, let's consider an example. Imagine that you have a dataset containing information about various cars, including their price, fuel efficiency, horsepower, and weight. Each of these attributes represents a dimension in the data. However, some of these dimensions may be related or redundant. For instance, a car's weight and horsepower are often correlated – heavier cars tend to have more horsepower.

PCA can help identify these relationships and combine related dimensions into a single principal component. In this case, PCA might create a new component called **performance** that combines information from both horsepower and weight. By focusing on this single component, we can simplify the data while still capturing the essential information about the cars' performance.

PCA is a complex mathematical technique, but as a decision maker, you don't need to understand all the technical details. The key takeaway is that PCA helps simplify data by identifying the most important patterns and representing them using fewer dimensions, making the data easier to understand and analyze.

In summary, dimensionality reduction techniques such as PCA are valuable tools for simplifying complex data and making it more accessible to non-technical readers. By reducing the number of dimensions while preserving the essential structure of the data, PCA facilitates more effective communication of data insights and improves the performance of machine learning algorithms:

Example: Principal Components of Customer Preferences

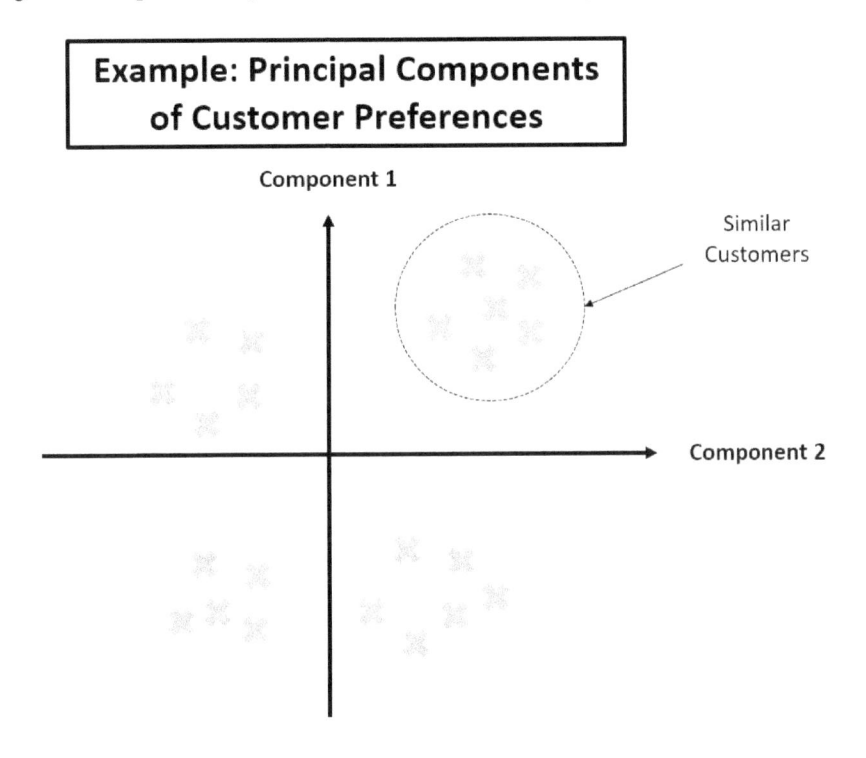

Figure 3.6: An illustration of principle components calculated on customer preference data

Correlation analysis

By calculating the correlation coefficients between variables, decision-makers can identify relationships and dependencies among the data features, which can help inform further analysis and modeling decisions.

Correlation analysis is a statistical technique that's used to evaluate the strength and direction of the relationship between two variables. Simply put, it helps us understand whether changes in one variable are associated with changes in another variable, and if so, how strongly they are related. Correlation analysis is valuable for non-technical readers as it provides a clear and easy-to-understand measure of how variables are connected. This can then be used to identify patterns, make predictions, or inform decision-making.

The result of correlation analysis is typically expressed as a correlation coefficient, a number between -1 and 1. A positive correlation coefficient (between 0 and 1) indicates that as one variable increases, the other variable also tends to increase. A negative correlation coefficient (between -1 and 0) indicates that as one variable increases, the other variable tends to decrease. The closer the correlation coefficient is to 1 or -1, the stronger the relationship between the variables. A correlation coefficient close to 0 indicates that there is little or no relationship between the variables.

For example, let's say we want to understand the relationship between the amount of time students spend studying and their exam scores. We can use correlation analysis to calculate the correlation coefficient between the study time variable and the exam score variable. If we find a positive correlation coefficient of 0.8, this suggests a strong positive relationship between the time spent studying and exam scores, meaning that students who study more tend to have higher scores. Conversely, a negative correlation coefficient, such as -0.3, would suggest a weak negative relationship, indicating that students who study more might have slightly lower scores:

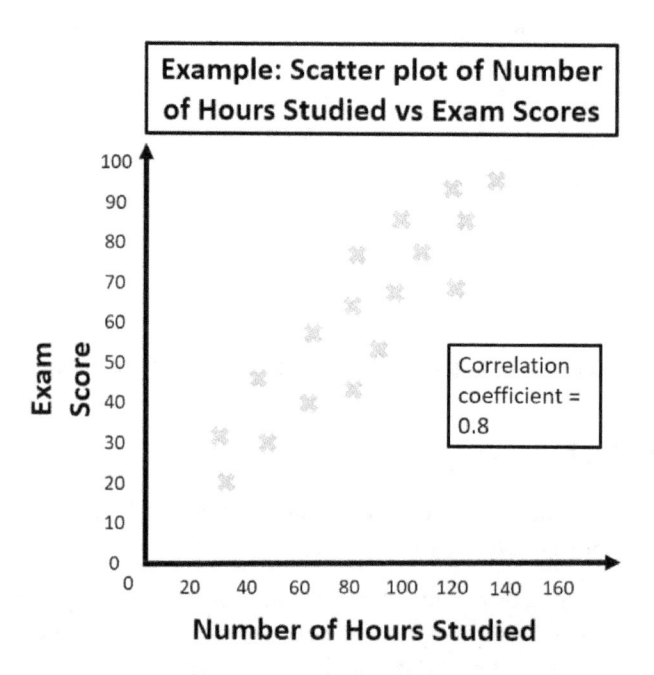

Figure 3.7: A chart illustrating the correlation between exam scores and the number of hours studied for a group of students

It's important to note that correlation does not imply causation. A strong correlation between two variables does not necessarily mean that one variable causes change in the other; it merely indicates that there is a relationship between them. Other factors or variables might be responsible for the observed relationship.

In summary, correlation analysis is a powerful tool for non-technical readers to assess the relationship between variables, providing a straightforward measure of the strength and direction of the association. This information can be used to identify patterns, inform decision-making, and generate hypotheses for further investigation, making correlation analysis a valuable method for understanding and communicating data insights.

Outlier detection

Identifying and addressing outliers in data can help improve the accuracy and reliability of subsequent analyses. Techniques such as the Z-score method or the IQR method can be used to detect and handle outliers.

It is essential to select the most appropriate EDA techniques and tools based on the nature of the data and the specific goals of the analysis.

Outlier detection is the process of identifying data points that are significantly different from the majority of the data in a dataset. These unusual data points, called outliers, can sometimes be the result of errors, anomalies, or exceptional cases that warrant further investigation. Identifying outliers is important because they can have a significant impact on the analysis and interpretation of the data, potentially skewing results or leading to incorrect conclusions. Outlier detection is especially valuable for non-technical readers as it helps ensure the data is accurate and reliable, leading to better insights and decision-making.

There are several methods for detecting outliers, including the Z-score method, the IQR method, and other techniques.

Z-score method

The Z-score measures how far a data point is from the mean (average) of the dataset, expressed in terms of the standard deviation (a measure of the spread of the data). A high Z-score indicates that the data point is far from the mean, potentially making it an outlier. Typically, a Z-score threshold (for example, 2 or 3) is chosen, and data points with Z-scores greater than this threshold are considered outliers. This method is most effective when the data is normally distributed (that is, it follows a bell-shaped curve).

For example, imagine that we have data on the heights of a group of people. If we find one person with a Z-score of 3.5, it means their height is 3.5 standard deviations away from the average height, indicating that this person is unusually tall and could be considered an outlier.

IQR method

The IQR method is another way to detect outliers by looking at the spread of the data. The IQR is the difference between the Q1 and the Q3 values of the data, representing the range in which the middle 50% of the data lies. Outliers are typically defined as data points that fall below Q1 - 1.5IQR or above Q3 + 1.5IQR. This method is more robust than the Z-score method as it is less sensitive to extreme values and works well for data that is not normally distributed.

Continuing with the height example, if we calculate the IQR of the heights and find that a few people's heights fall below Q1 - 1.5IQR or above Q3 + 1.5IQR, we will consider them outliers.

Other techniques

There are numerous other outlier detection methods, including machine learning algorithms such as clustering or classification models, and statistical tests such as Grubbs' test or the Tukey method. The choice of method depends on the nature of the data, the distribution of the data, and the specific goals of the analysis.

In summary, outlier detection is an essential step in the data analysis process, helping non-technical readers ensure the accuracy and reliability of the data. Methods such as the Z-score and IQR can be used to identify unusual data points that may impact the analysis or reveal interesting patterns. By detecting and understanding outliers, data science teams can make more informed decisions and gain deeper insights from their data:

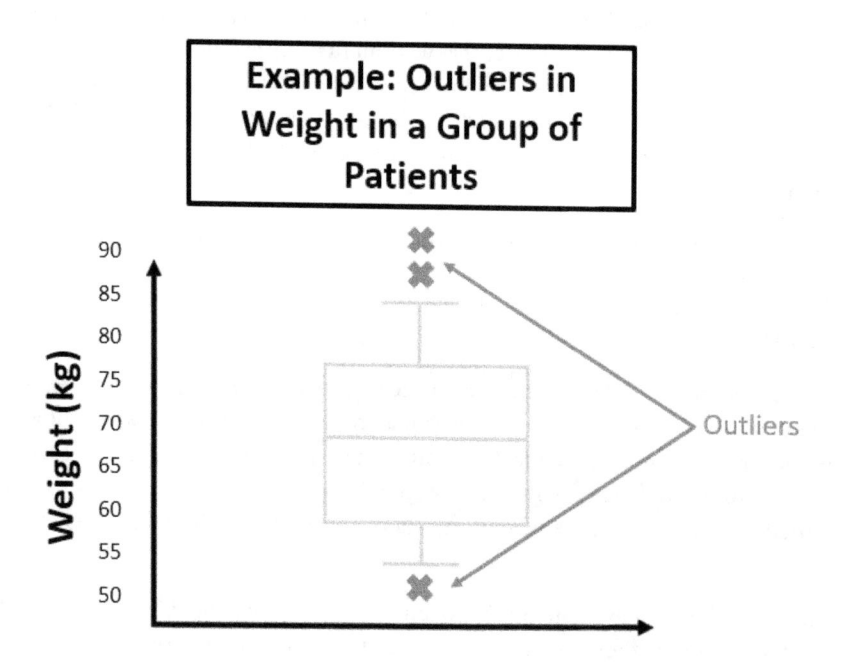

Figure 3.8: A chart illustrating outliers in a dataset containing the weights (in kilograms) of patients

Summary

In this chapter, we learned how EDA is an important stage in the data science project process and provides the means to understand the characteristics and limitations of data, as well as to find insightful patterns within the data before machine learning or statistical models can be developed based on it.

This initial analysis also allows teams to present results and train models with more confidence since they have a deeper understanding of the data they are working with and the issues it may present.

In this chapter, we covered a large range of methods that can be used for EDA. Not all of them are always necessary, but hopefully, these tools will allow you to analyze data for yourself and give you the knowledge to interpret these visualizations and analyses when they are presented to you.

In the next chapter, we'll learn how to test business hypotheses with statistics. This technique, known as significance testing, is critical in validating the findings from your data, ensuring that your decisions are grounded in statistical rigor.

4

The Significance of Significance

We are constantly bombarded with new figures and statistics, whether it's within a business where we may see sales figures or consumer survey results, or in the news where we may see economic statistics or political polls.

How can we make sense of this information and understand what constitutes significant results and what is statistical noise?

This is where the concept of statistical significance becomes important, and we will gain an understanding of statistical hypotheses and how to carry out hypothesis testing (also known as significance testing) in practice in this chapter. By mastering these techniques, you'll be equipped to make data-driven decisions with confidence and avoid costly mistakes based on misleading results.

To illustrate the importance of significance testing, let's consider a common scenario. Suppose your data science team is tasked with reducing customer churn within your company and they observe a 2% increase in the percentage of customers churning (i.e., leaving or unsubscribing) over the past quarter. Is this change a cause for concern or could it be due to random chance?

Significance testing helps you to answer this question and make informed decisions about where to focus your team's efforts.

Another example might be that your team has A/B tested a new machine learning model that has demonstrated an improvement in accuracy of 4% over the previous model.

Significance testing can show us whether this improvement is statistically significant.

In this chapter, we will learn how to formulate business hypotheses and put them to the test with statistics. We will gain an understanding of statistical hypotheses, the concept of statistical significance, and how to carry out hypothesis testing in practice.

These tools will enable you to determine the reliability and relevance of the data and metrics you use so you can make decisions with greater confidence.

This chapter will cover the following topics:

- The idea of testing hypotheses
- Significance tests for a population proportion
- Significance tests for a population average (mean)
- Walking through a case study

The idea of testing hypotheses

Within every organization, there are ideas and concepts we would like to test to make more informed decisions. In many situations, decisions are made based upon intuition or "gut feel," but human intuition is fallible, so we need a framework to test ideas before making critical decisions.

Let's consider a scenario that you might face as a data science leader. Suppose you manage an online brand and are considering running a promotion on an e-commerce marketplace to increase sales of a particular product. Before investing resources in the promotion, you want to determine its potential effectiveness.

This is where hypothesis testing comes in – it provides a framework for making data-driven decisions and avoiding costly mistakes based on assumptions.

In this section, we will briefly introduce hypothesis testing and how it can help you make informed decisions in various scenarios.

What is a hypothesis?

A hypothesis is a statement or claim about a particular situation or phenomenon that we want to test or verify. In our product promotion example, our hypothesis might be, *"The promotion will increase the sales of the product in the marketplace."*

How does hypothesis testing work?

Hypothesis testing is a method used in statistics and data science to test the validity of a claim or hypothesis. The idea is to gather data, analyze it, and then determine whether the evidence supports or contradicts the hypothesis.

To understand the process, let's break it down into four simple steps, we will cover each of these steps in more detail later in this chapter:

1. **Formulate the hypotheses**: First, we need to state our alternative hypothesis, which is the claim we want to test. In addition to this, we also define a null hypothesis, which is the opposite of our original claim. In our brand promotion example, the alternative hypothesis might be, *"The new promotion increased the sales of the product."*

2. **Determine the significance level**: Before we begin testing our hypothesis, we need to decide on a significance level, which is a threshold used to determine whether any observed difference is likely due to chance or an actual effect.

3. **Collect the relevant data**: Now, we collect data relevant to our hypothesis. In our example, we might gather sales data for the product before and after the promotion.

4. **Perform a statistical test**: Next, we perform a statistical test on the data, to determine whether there is a significant difference in the sales before and after the promotion.

5. **Make a decision**: Based on the results of our statistical test, we can either accept or reject our original null hypothesis. If the test shows a significant difference in sales, we might conclude that the promotion was effective and reject the null hypothesis. On the other hand, if the test reveals no significant difference, we might accept the null hypothesis that the new promotion did not increase the sales of the product.

Formulating null and alternative hypotheses

In hypothesis testing, formulating clear and well-defined null and alternative hypotheses is important for making accurate and informed decisions.

In this section, we'll delve deeper into the process of formulating these hypotheses and explain why they are essential for effective hypothesis testing.

The null hypothesis (H_0)

The null hypothesis, denoted as H_0, is a statement that assumes there is no effect or relationship between the variables being studied. In other words, it represents the "status quo" or a baseline scenario. The purpose of the null hypothesis is to provide a starting point for hypothesis testing, allowing us to evaluate the evidence and decide whether it supports or contradicts our original claim.

When formulating the null hypothesis, it's important to ensure that it's testable and specific.

Here are a few examples of null hypotheses:

- "There is no difference in customers' perception of quality between the two products"
- "A new marketing campaign has had no impact on product sales"
- "The awareness of a brand has not changed this quarter compared to the previous quarter"

The alternative hypothesis (H_1)

The alternative hypothesis, denoted as H_1, is a statement that directly contradicts the null hypothesis and represents the effect or relationship we want to prove or investigate. The alternative hypothesis is essentially what we hope to demonstrate through our analysis.

Similar to the null hypothesis, the alternative hypothesis should be testable and specific.

Here are the alternative hypotheses for the examples mentioned previously:

- "There is a significant difference in customers' perception of quality between two products"
- "A new marketing campaign has had a positive impact on product sales"
- "The awareness of a brand has changed this quarter compared to the previous quarter"

Choosing the right hypotheses

Selecting appropriate null and alternative hypotheses is essential for a successful hypothesis test. Here are some guidelines to help you choose the right hypotheses:

- Ensure that the hypotheses are mutually exclusive. This means that if one hypothesis is true, the other must be false.
- Keep the hypotheses clear and specific. Vague or ambiguous hypotheses can lead to confusion and incorrect conclusions.
- Align the hypotheses with the objectives of your study. Your hypotheses should address the key questions you want to answer through your analysis.

Formulating well-defined null and alternative hypotheses is a critical step in the hypothesis testing process. By establishing a clear starting point (the null hypothesis) and a desired outcome (the alternative hypothesis), you can effectively evaluate the evidence and make informed decisions based on your analysis. Remember to keep your hypotheses specific, testable, and mutually exclusive to ensure a successful hypothesis test.

Determining the significance level

The significance level, denoted by the symbol α (alpha), is a crucial concept in hypothesis testing. It represents the probability of making a Type I error, which occurs when we reject the null hypothesis even though it is true. In simpler terms, it's the risk we are willing to take when making a decision based on our data.

Here's an example: let's say you're testing whether a new marketing campaign increases sales. The significance level is the probability of concluding that the campaign is effective when it isn't.

Common significance levels

Significance levels are usually expressed as a percentage or decimal:

- **1% (0.01)**: This strict level is used when we want to be highly confident and minimize Type I errors
- **5% (0.05)**: This is the most widely used level, balancing the risks of Type I and Type II errors

Here's an example: in a market research study investigating customer preferences, using a 1% significance level means there's only a 1% chance of concluding that customers prefer a new product feature when they don't.

Choosing the right significance level

Consider these factors when selecting a significance level:

- **Consequences of errors**: If a Type I error is more serious (e.g., releasing a faulty product), use a lower level. If a Type II error is worse (e.g., failing to detect a disease), use a higher level.
- **Sample size**: With a larger sample, you can use a lower level. With a smaller sample, you may need a higher level due to increased uncertainty.
- **Field conventions**: Follow the established conventions in your field of study.

Let's consider an example.

In a study evaluating the impact of a new employee training program on productivity, the consequences of implementing an ineffective program (false positive) may be less severe than failing to adopt a beneficial one (false negative). In this case, a higher significance level, such as 10%, might be appropriate.

Conversely, consider the following example.

A pharmaceutical company is testing a new drug for treating a serious medical condition. In this case, the consequences of releasing a drug that is not effective (false positive) could be more severe than not releasing a potentially effective drug (false negative). The company would not want to risk patients' health by releasing an ineffective or harmful drug, therefore a lower significance level, such as 1%, might be more appropriate to minimize the risk of a Type I error and ensure that the drug is safe and effective before releasing it to the market.

By carefully considering the context and potential consequences, you can choose a significance level that aligns with your objectives and provides a solid foundation for your analysis.

Understanding errors

In hypothesis testing, there are two types of errors we need to know: Type I and Type II errors. These errors happen when we make the wrong decisions based on our data analysis. Let's explore these errors with simple explanations and examples.

Type I error – false positive

A Type I error happens when we think there is an effect or relationship between the variables, but there isn't. It's like a false alarm.

For example, imagine you're testing whether a new medicine works. If you wrongly conclude that the medicine works when it doesn't, that's a Type I error, also known as a **false positive**.

Type II error – false negative

A Type II error happens when we think there is no effect or relationship between the variables when there is. It's like a missed opportunity.

Using the medicine example, if you wrongly conclude that the medicine doesn't work when it does, that is a Type II error, also known as a **false negative**.

You can see Type I and Type II errors visualized in this chart:

Null hypothesis (H0) is:	True	False
Rejected	Type I error False positive Probability = α	Correct decision True positive Probability = $1 - \beta$
Not rejected	Correct decision True negative Probability = $1 - \alpha$	Type II error False negative Probability = β

Figure 4.1: Type I and Type II errors

In the chart, you can see that if the null hypothesis is rejected, but there is no relationship or effect, this is a Type I error (a.k.a. a **false positive**).

In the chart, you can see that if the null hypothesis is accepted, but there is a real relationship or effect, this is a Type II error (a.k.a. a **false negative**).

The chart also shows the correct decisions, **true positives** and **true negatives**.

Balancing errors

In hypothesis testing, we want to minimize both Type I and Type II errors, which we can achieve using some simple strategies:

- **Choose the right significance level**: This helps manage the risk of making a Type I error. A lower level means a lower chance of making a Type I error, but it might increase the chance of making a Type II error.

- **Use a larger sample size**: More data can help reduce the risk of making a Type II error. However, getting more data isn't always possible due to time or resources.
- **Design your test well**: A good test can help reduce both errors. This might involve picking the right statistical test or accounting for other factors that might affect the results.

Knowing about Type I and Type II errors is important for accurate hypothesis testing. By considering these errors and making smart choices, you can draw better conclusions from your data.

Getting to grips with p-values

P-values are an important concept in hypothesis testing and help us understand the relationship between our data and the hypotheses we're testing. In simple terms, a *p*-value is the probability of getting the observed data (or more extreme results) if the null hypothesis is true.

We will go through a simple explanation of p-values and their relationship to significance tests.

P-value as a measure of evidence

A p-value gives us a way to measure the evidence against the null hypothesis. A small p-value (typically less than 0.05) means the observed data is unlikely to occur if the null hypothesis is true. In other words, a small p-value suggests that there's a real effect or relationship between the variables, and the null hypothesis may be false.

On the other hand, a large p-value means that the observed data is likely to occur if the null hypothesis is true. In this case, the evidence doesn't support the alternative hypothesis, and we cannot reject the null hypothesis.

Significance tests, comparing p-values to significance level

In a significance test, we compare the p-value to our predetermined significance level (α). The significance level represents the maximum probability of making a Type I error (rejecting the null hypothesis when it is true) that we're willing to accept.

If the p-value is less than or equal to the significance level (p ≤ α), we reject the null hypothesis and conclude that the alternative hypothesis is more likely to be true. This means that the observed effect or relationship is statistically significant.

If the *p*-value exceeds the significance level (p > α), we cannot reject the null hypothesis, and the observed effect or relationship is not statistically significant.

Example

Let's say we're testing a new medicine, and our null hypothesis (H_0) is that the medicine has no effect. The alternative hypothesis (H_1) is that the medicine has an effect. We choose a significance level of 5% (0.05).

After conducting the test, we found a p-value of 0.02. Since the p-value (0.02) is less than the significance level (0.05), we reject the null hypothesis and conclude that the medicine has a statistically significant effect.

P-values play an important role in significance testing by helping us measure the evidence against the null hypothesis. By comparing the p-value to the significance level, we can make informed decisions about whether to reject the null hypothesis and accept the alternative hypothesis. Keep in mind that while p-values are a useful tool, they should be interpreted with caution and considered in the context of all your available information and not blindly accepted as absolute proof of a hypothesis.

We've covered the important topic of p-values, explaining how they serve as a measure of evidence against the null hypothesis. Understanding p-values is fundamental to interpreting results in hypothesis testing, whether you're looking to evaluate the impact of a marketing campaign or measure the effectiveness of a machine learning algorithm.

Here are the key takeaways:

- A small p-value indicates that the observed data is unlikely under the null hypothesis, lending support to the alternative hypothesis
- A large p-value suggests that there is not enough evidence to reject the null hypothesis
- In significance tests, we compare the p-value to a predetermined significance level to make informed decisions about the hypotheses

By understanding these principles, executives and decision-makers can make more accurate and reliable conclusions based on their data, reducing the likelihood of costly mistakes.

In the next section, *Significance tests for a population proportion – making informed decisions about proportions*, we'll build on this foundational knowledge. We will explore how to apply *p*-values in practical scenarios, specifically focusing on tests for population proportions. This is particularly relevant where understanding the characteristics of a larger group based on a sample is essential, such as market research.

Significance tests for a population proportion – making informed decisions about proportions

As a decision-maker, you often need to compare proportions to make informed choices. For example, you might want to know if there's a significant difference in the proportion of satisfied customers between two product lines or if a new marketing campaign has a higher success rate than the previous one. This is where significance tests for population proportions are useful because they can allow you to compare proportions between groups and see if they are significantly different.

To provide a simple example, imagine that you wanted to run two email marketing campaigns with different content in each email and compare which was more successful. The more successful campaign could be expanded to more recipients. This is known as an A/B test and can also be a useful approach when deploying an update to a machine learning model, comparing the results between the new model and the existing one.

One metric that could be a useful indicator of the campaign's success would be the **click through rate (CTR)**, the proportion of people who received the email who clicked through on the link.

Look at the following example:

Click Through Rate by Campaign

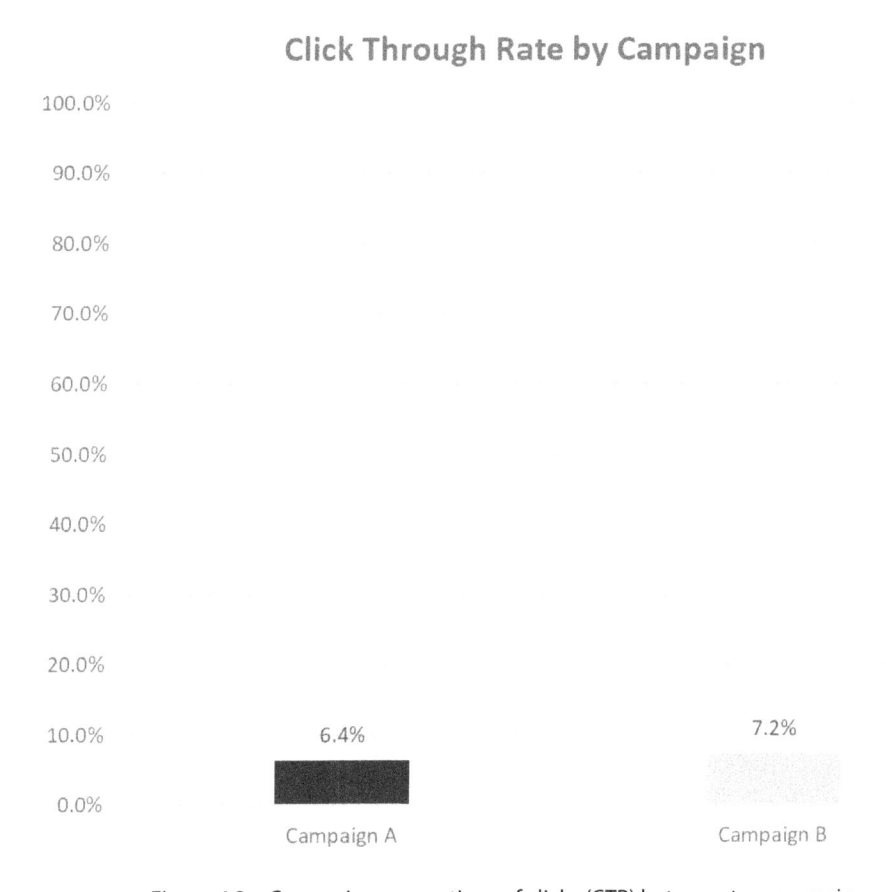

Campaign A: 6.4%
Campaign B: 7.2%

Figure 4.2 – Comparing proportions of clicks (CTR) between two campaigns

You can see that the second campaign had a higher CTR, but how do you know whether this difference is significant or due to random chance?

To test this, you need to know the raw counts of the number of emails sent and the number of emails clicked, and with this data, you can carry out a significance test for proportions.

In this section, we'll explore two commonly used significance tests for population proportions: the **z-test** and the **chi-squared** test. We'll keep the explanations simple and provide plenty of examples to help you grasp the concepts and apply them to your work.

The z-test – comparing a sample proportion to a population proportion

The z-test is a statistical tool that helps you determine whether a sample proportion is significantly different from an expected population proportion. It answers the question, "Is the difference I'm seeing in my sample meaningful, or could it just be due to random chance?"

Understanding the z-test

Before we look into the mechanics of the z-test, it's important to become familiar with the terminology that underpins this statistical method. These key components lay the groundwork for interpreting results effectively:

- **Null hypothesis (H_0)**: The null hypothesis is like our starting assumption. We assume that the population proportion (P) is equal to a specific value we're interested in (P_0).

- **Alternative hypothesis (H_1)**: The alternative hypothesis is the opposite. It suggests that the population proportion (P) isn't equal to, is less than, or is greater than the specific value (P_0).

- **Z-score**: The z-score is a number that shows how far away our sample proportion (P) is from the expected population proportion (P_0), in terms of standard deviations.

- **P-value**: The p-value helps us understand how likely it is to see a sample proportion as extreme as ours (or more extreme) if the null hypothesis were true.

Performing a z-test in simple steps

So, you've grasped the key components of the z-test. What's next? The actual application. Whether you're analyzing the behaviors and preferences of your customers or attempting to compare the accuracy of two machine learning models, being able to perform a z-test is an indispensable skill. Here are the steps to get you there:

1. **Set up the hypotheses**: The first step is formulating your null and alternative hypotheses. Remember, the null hypothesis is your starting point, asserting that there's no effect or difference.

2. **Calculate sample proportion (P)**: Divide the number of successful outcomes by the sample size n. This proportion represents the characteristic or effect you're interested in within your sample.

3. **Determine the standard error (SE)**: Use the formula:

$$SE = \sqrt{\frac{P_0(1-P_0)}{n}}$$

Where P_0 is the expected population proportion (not to be confused with the p-value). The standard error measures how much your sample proportion is expected to vary from the actual population proportion.

4. **Compute the z-score**: The z-score is calculated as:

$$Z = \frac{P - P_0}{SE}$$

It tells you how many standard errors away your sample population is from the null hypothesis proportion.

5. **Find the p-value**: Based on the z-score, determine the p-value. You can determine the p-value based on the z-score from a lookup table or an online calculator (https://www.socscistatistics.com/pvalues/normaldistribution.aspx). This will show you how likely it is to get a z-score as extreme as yours, assuming the null hypothesis is true. The programming language or software of your choice (e.g., Excel, Python, R) will also include functions to calculate the p-value and carry out z-tests.

6. **Compare against a significance level**: Finally, contrast the p-value with your predetermined significance level (α). If $p \leq α$, then you have grounds to reject the null hypothesis.

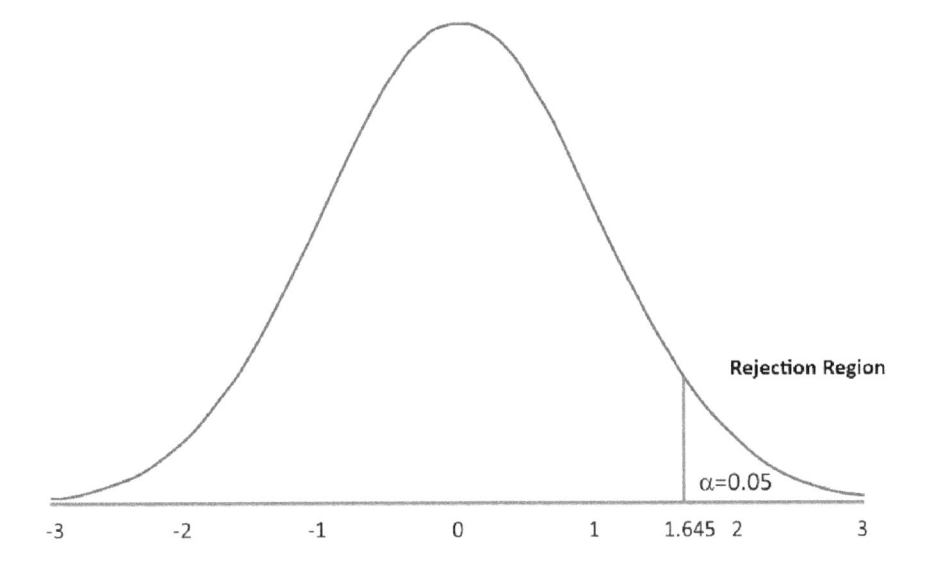

Figure 4.3 – One-tailed z-test

The preceding chart illustrates the standard normal distribution, which is what is being used to carry out a z-test.

The z-score, calculated from the sample proportion and population proportion, determines the position of the sample proportion on this distribution.

The rejection region on the right side represents the area where the z-score would fall if the sample proportion was significantly different from the population proportion.

To conclude that there is a significant difference, the p-value (the area under the curve beyond the z-score) must be less than or equal to the significance level (0.05), which corresponds to the z-score being greater than or equal to the critical value (1.645 in this example. You can say that the difference between your sample proportion and the population proportion is not due to random chance.

We will illustrate a z-test with a more concrete example.

Z-test example made easy

Now that we've gone through the steps to carry out a z-test for a proportion, let's look at a real example.

Imagine we have an assumption that 60% of people ($P_0 = 0.60$) prefer a certain brand of coffee and we want to test this hypothesis with real data. We asked 200 people ($n = 200$) and found out that 130 of them liked the brand ($x = 130$). Our sample proportion would be $p = 130 / 200 = 0.65$.

Our null hypothesis (H_0) is that the population proportion (P) is equal to 0.60. The alternative hypothesis (H_1) is that the population proportion (P) isn't equal to 0.60.

We calculate the SE as $SE = \sqrt{\frac{0.60(1 - 0.6)}{200}} \approx 0.0346$

Next, we find the z-score as $Z = \frac{0.65 - 0.60}{0.0346} \approx 1.445$

Using a z-table or software, we discover that the two-tailed p-value is around 0.148. Since the p-value (0.148) is greater than the significance level (let's say 0.05), we can't reject the null hypothesis. In other words, there's not enough evidence to suggest the proportion of people who prefer that brand of coffee is different from 60%.

Now we have shown how to use z-tests to test hypotheses around proportions, what else can they be used for? That is the topic of the next section, where we will see how z-tests can be used to test hypotheses around the average (mean) of a value for a population.

Significance tests for a population average (mean)

In this section, we'll dive into significance tests about a mean, which are used to determine whether a sample mean is significantly different from a hypothesized population mean. We'll cover various aspects, including writing hypotheses, conditions for a t-test, when to use z or t statistics, examples, and one-tailed and two-tailed tests.

Writing hypotheses for a significance test about a mean

When conducting a significance test about a mean, you'll start by formulating the null and alternative hypotheses:

- **Null hypothesis (H_0)**: The null hypothesis states that the population mean (μ) is equal to a specific value (μ_0).
- **Alternative hypothesis (H_1)**: The alternative hypothesis states that the population mean (μ) is not equal to, less than, or greater than the specific value (μ_0), depending on the research question.

Conditions for a t-test about a mean

A t-test is commonly used for testing hypotheses about a mean when the population standard deviation (σ) is unknown. The following conditions should be met for a *t*-test:

- The sample is randomly selected.
- The sample size is small ($n < 30$), or the population is normally distributed. If the sample size is large ($n \geq 30$), the *t*-test is still robust even if the population is not normally distributed.

When to use z or t statistics in significance tests

- Use a z-statistic when the population standard deviation (σ) is known, and the sample size is large ($n \geq 30$)
- Use a t-statistic when the population standard deviation (σ) is unknown, and you rely on the sample standard deviation (s) as an estimate

Example – calculating the t-statistic for a test about a mean

Suppose we want to test whether the average weight of apples in a sample is different from the hypothesized mean weight of 150 grams. We have a random sample of 25 apples (n = 25) with a sample mean weight of 155 grams ($\bar{x} = 155$) and a sample standard deviation of 20 grams (s = 20).

The null hypothesis (H_0) is that the population mean (μ) is equal to 150 grams. The alternative hypothesis (H_1) is that the population mean (μ) is not equal to 150 grams.

The t-statistic can be calculated using the formula:

$$t = \frac{(\bar{x} - \mu_0)}{\frac{s}{\sqrt{n}}}$$

$$t = \frac{(155 - 150)}{\frac{20}{\sqrt{25}}} = \frac{5}{4} = 1.25$$

Using a table to estimate the p-value from the t-statistic

To find the p-value from the t-statistic, you'll need a t-distribution table or software. In our example, we have a t-statistic of 1.25 and a **degree of freedom (df)** equal to n - 1, which is 24. Using a table or software, we can estimate the two-tailed p-value to be approximately 0.22.

Comparing the p-value from the t-statistic to the significance level

Now, compare the p-value to the significance level (α) to make a decision. If we choose a significance level of 0.05 and the p-value (0.22) is greater than α, we fail to reject the null hypothesis. This means we don't have enough evidence to conclude that the average weight of apples is different from 150 grams.

One-tailed and two-tailed tests

Before diving into conducting significance tests, it's also important to differentiate between two types of hypothesis tests, namely one-tailed and two-tailed tests:

- **One-tailed test**: A one-tailed test is used when you're interested in determining if the population mean is either greater than or less than the hypothesized mean value. In this case, you'll use a one-tailed alternative hypothesis (e.g., $\mu > \mu_0$ or $\mu < \mu_0$). The p-value from a one-tailed test represents the probability of observing a test statistic as extreme or more extreme in the direction specified by the alternative hypothesis.

- **Two-tailed test**: A two-tailed test is used when you want to determine if the population mean is different from the hypothesized mean value, without specifying the direction of the difference. The two-tailed alternative hypothesis is written as $\mu \neq \mu_0$. The p-value from a two-tailed test represents the probability of observing a test statistic as extreme or more extreme in either direction.

So far, we have been considering our significance tests as two-tailed tests. If you want to specify the direction of your hypothesis, you could specify a one-tailed test, and many tools for statistical analysis (Python, R, Excel) will allow you to do this.

In summary, significance tests about a mean are important for determining whether a sample mean is significantly different from a hypothesized population mean. We've covered the necessary steps and conditions for a t-test, when to use z or t statistics, and the differences between one-tailed and two-tailed tests. By understanding these concepts and applying them to real-world scenarios, you'll be well equipped to analyze data and draw meaningful conclusions about population means.

Walking through a case study

To consolidate all that we have learned in this chapter, let's walk through the example we used at the beginning of the chapter about product promotion on an online store.

Walking through a case study 73

Let's say we have data showing the daily sales volume for the 14 days before the promotion and the 14 days after the promotion. Our hypothesis is that the product's daily sales have significantly increased following the promotion.

How could we use significance testing to test this hypothesis?

Let's go through the steps we set out at the beginning of this chapter:

1. **Formulate the hypotheses**: First, we need to state our null and alternative hypotheses.

   Question: Before reading on, can you try to formulate a null and alternative hypothesis?

   A. **Null hypothesis (H_0)**: Our null hypothesis is that there was no significant increase in average daily sales following the promotion.

   B. **Alternative hypothesis (H_1)**: Our alternative hypothesis is that there was a significant increase in average daily sales following the promotion.

2. **Determine the significance level**: Secondly, we decide on a significance level.

   Question: Before reading the following, can you try to decide on a significance level?

   We will use a significance level of 0.05, which is common in business applications of statistics; however, other choices are also acceptable depending on how confident you want to be in rejecting the null hypothesis.

3. **Collect the relevant data**:

   Now, we collect data relevant to our hypothesis. In our example, let's say we have gathered data showing that the average daily sales were $9,000 during the 30 days before the promotion and $9,200 during the 30 days after the promotion with a sample standard deviation of $50.

4. **Perform a statistical test**:

   Next, we perform a statistical test on the data, to determine if there is a significant difference in the sales before and after the promotion.

   Question: Before reading on, try to answer the following questions:

   A. Are we testing for differences in a population proportion, or a population mean?

   B. Which statistical test do you think would be appropriate for this use case?

   C. Should we be using a one-tailed or a two-tailed statistical test?

   In this case, we are testing for differences in a population mean. The sample size is small (n = 14) so a t-test would be appropriate in this case. Since our alternative hypothesis has a direction (that the daily sales are higher after the promotion) we should use a one-tailed t-test.

   Let's now perform this statistical test with our data. We have a random sample of 14 days (n = 14) with a sample mean weight of $9,200 ($\bar{x}$ = 9,200) and a sample standard deviation of $75 grams (s = 75).

The null hypothesis (H$_0$) is that the population mean (μ) is equal to $9,000. The alternative hypothesis (H$_1$) is that the population mean (μ) is greater than $9,000. Using these numbers to find the *t*-statistic we find:

$$t = \frac{(\bar{x} - \mu_0)}{\frac{s}{\sqrt{n}}} = \frac{(9200 - 9000)}{\frac{75}{\sqrt{14}}} = \frac{200}{20.04} = 9.98$$

5. **Make a decision**: Based on the results of our statistical test, we can either accept or reject our original hypothesis.

    Entering these values into a calculator for a one-tailed t-test table, for example, via the following link:

    `https://www.socscistatistics.com/tests/studentttest/`

    We find that $p < 0.001$, which indicates there is a significant increase in the sales of the product following the promotion.

Based on this test showing a significant increase in sales, we might conclude that the promotion was effective and accept our original hypothesis. This may help inform future decisions on running similar promotions in the same e-commerce store or across other stores. Statistics provides us with a mechanism to make decisions with more confidence and evidence, rather than based upon gut feel or intuition, thereby increasing our chances of making correct decisions.

Summary

Congratulations, you have managed to apply statistical thinking and test a hypothesis resembling a real-world business use case, there may be situations in your own business or life where testing hypotheses can be applied.

In this chapter, we have learned about using statistical tests to test different hypotheses. We have learned about the different types of error, about choosing significance levels, and understood how p-values relate to significance levels. Then we learned about significance tests for population proportions and significance tests for population means. Finally, we have worked through an example based on our case study of a product promotion on an online store.

In the upcoming chapter, we'll switch gears and dive into regression analysis. This powerful statistical technique goes beyond identifying whether variables are related, allowing you to predict future outcomes based on these relationships. If you've ever wondered how to forecast sales, gauge the impact of social media marketing, or learn a foundational technique for machine learning, you won't want to miss what comes next.

5

Understanding Regression

In this chapter, we will learn about *regression*, a powerful statistical tool that can enable decision-makers to identify and understand relationships between variables, uncover trends, and forecast future trends.

You might be asking yourself the following question:

How can I benefit from understanding regression?

Regression, in simple terms, is a statistical method that helps uncover patterns and relationships within data.

Within businesses, regression can allow decision-makers to better understand how different factors or variables impact their key performance indicators, such as sales, revenue, or customer satisfaction. By identifying these relationships, businesses can make more informed decisions, optimize their strategies, and improve their overall performance.

Here are some use cases for regression in a business context:

- **Forecasting**: Regression techniques help businesses forecast future trends, sales, and demands by analyzing historical data. Accurate forecasting is crucial for strategic planning, resource allocation, and budgeting.
- **Identifying relationships**: Regression analysis can help businesses uncover relationships between variables, such as the impact of advertising spending on sales or the influence of pricing on customer demand. Understanding these relationships can help businesses optimize their strategies.
- **Efficient resource allocation**: By understanding how different factors impact business performance, companies can allocate resources more effectively and make better investment decisions.
- **Risk management**: Regression analysis can help businesses identify potential risks and vulnerabilities in their operations by understanding the factors that contribute to variability in outcomes.

- **Evaluating performance**: Businesses can use regression analysis to evaluate the performance of different departments, teams, or employees by examining the relationship between inputs (for example, resources and time) and outputs (for example, sales and productivity).
- **Price optimization**: By understanding how price changes affect demand, businesses can use regression analysis to determine optimal pricing strategies to maximize revenue and profit.
- **Policy evaluation**: Regression analysis can help businesses assess the effectiveness of various policies and initiatives by comparing their outcomes with expected results.

Before we dive into the complexities of regression analysis, it's essential to start with a foundational concept that you've likely come across, albeit perhaps not in a statistical context – trend lines. While trend lines might seem straightforward, understanding their nuances can offer a wealth of insights.

Introduction to trend lines

By the end of this section, you'll have a firm grasp of trend lines, the foundation of regression analysis.

Let's begin with a practical example. Suppose you own an e-commerce store and have been recording your daily sales for the past few months. With a list of numbers at hand, you're curious about any patterns in the data that could inform your business decisions. This is where trend lines come into play.

A trend line is a line that represents the general direction or pattern in a dataset. It allows us to visualize the relationship between data points and helps us make predictions about future values. In simple terms, it connects the dots in a way that best illustrates the overall trend.

Returning to our e-commerce store scenario, imagine plotting your daily sales on a graph, with days on the horizontal axis and sales on the vertical axis. Each day's sales become a data point on the graph. Your goal is to draw a line that best fits these data points, which represent the general trend in your sales data. A positive slope indicates increasing sales over time, while a negative slope suggests decreasing sales.

How would you fit a line that best fits this data? Would it have a positive or negative slope?

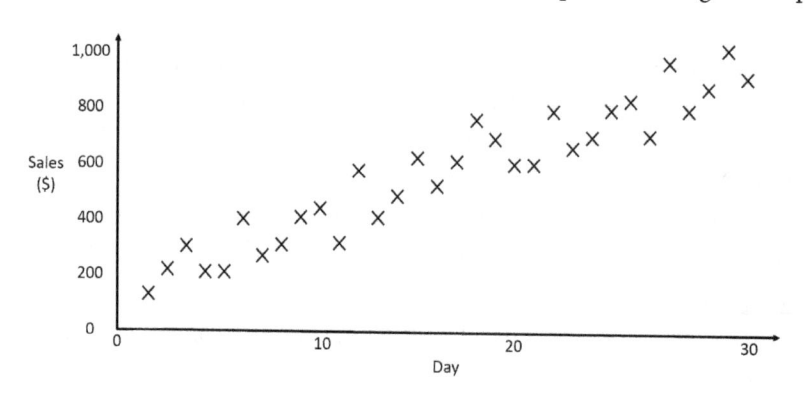

Figure 5.1: An e-commerce store's daily sales

Real-world data, however, is rarely so straightforward. Fluctuations in the data may occur due to various factors, such as holidays, promotions, or even the weather. This is where regression shines. Regression helps us fit a trend line to the data while accounting for these fluctuations, resulting in a more accurate representation of the overall pattern.

Consider another example to further understand trend lines. As a marketing manager, you might be interested in the relationship between your advertising budget and product sales. You could plot your monthly advertising budget on the horizontal axis and monthly product sales on the vertical axis, with each data point representing a specific advertising budget and its corresponding sales. Fitting a trend line to this data allows you to see if there's a general trend suggesting that higher advertising budgets lead to higher sales:

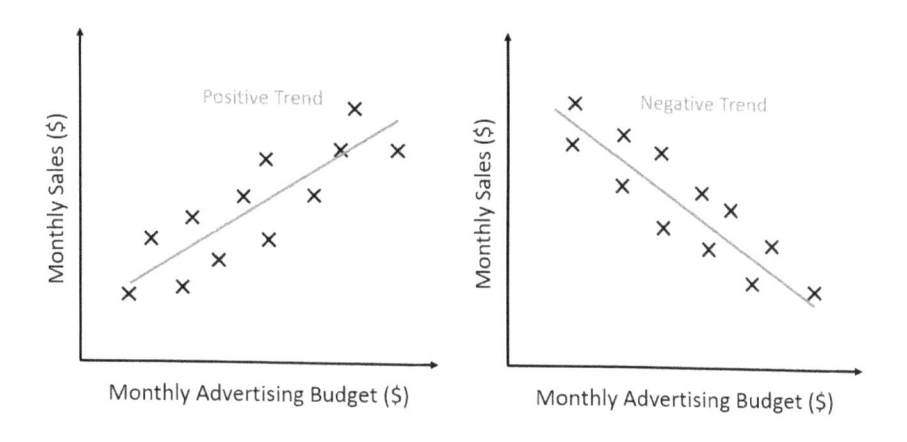

Figure 5.2: Positive and negative trend lines when comparing Monthly Advertising Budget to Monthly Sales

Now that we understand what a trend is, how do we go about estimating it based on our data? This is the topic of the next section.

Fitting a trend line to data

In this section, we'll explore the process of fitting a trend line to a dataset and the techniques that can be used to minimize error and maximize accuracy.

The art of fitting a line to data is all about finding the line that best represents the underlying pattern or trend. But how do we define "best?" The answer lies in minimizing the *error* between the predicted values generated by our trend line and the actual data points. The most commonly used method for achieving this is known as the **least squares** technique.

Imagine you've drawn a line through your data points, and for each point, you measure the vertical distance between the actual data point and the corresponding point on the line. This distance is known as the "residual" or the "error." The goal of the least squares technique is to find the line that minimizes the sum of the squared residuals. Squaring the residuals is crucial because it eliminates any negative values and emphasizes larger deviations, ensuring the line fits the data as closely as possible.

Looking at the following diagram, each data point is represented by black dots, and the line we are trying to fit is represented by a long red line. The "residuals" or "errors" are represented by the red lines perpendicular to the line we are trying to fit. It is the sum of the squares of all these distances that we minimize in the least squares method:

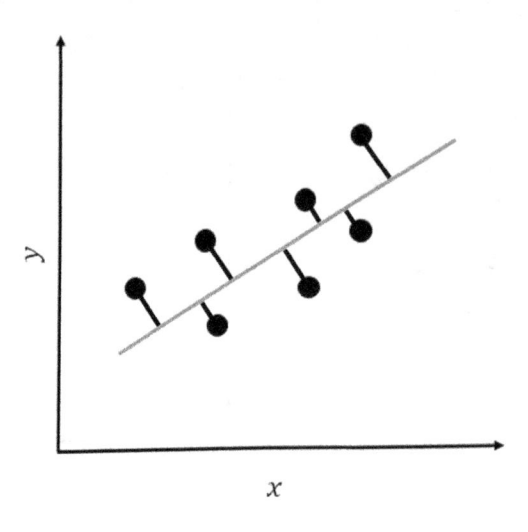

Figure 5.3: Line of best fit through a set of data points and the residuals/errors between the line of best fit and the data points

To illustrate this process, let's return to our marketing manager example. Once you've plotted your advertising budget and corresponding product sales data points, you'll need to find the line that best fits the data. By applying the least squares technique, you'll minimize the overall error between the predicted sales values generated by the line and the actual sales data points. This line will then give you valuable insights into the relationship between your advertising budget and product sales, helping you make more informed decisions.

While fitting a line to data might seem intimidating at first, modern software tools and programming languages make this process easier than ever. Many tools, such as Excel, Python libraries, Tableau, and PowerBI, offer built-in functions to fit trend lines and perform regression analysis with just a few clicks or lines of code. As a decision-maker, you don't need to be an expert in the mathematical details, but understanding the concept and its applications is crucial for effectively leading data-driven projects.

Fitting a trend line to a dataset is a powerful technique that helps us uncover the hidden patterns within our data, allowing for better decision-making. By minimizing the error between the actual data points and the predictions generated by the line, we can extract valuable insights to drive business decisions and achieve desired outcomes. In the next section, we'll explore how to estimate the line of best fit.

Estimating the line of best fit

In this section, we'll dive deeper into the least squares method, the gold standard for estimating the line of best fit. We'll explore the intuition behind this technique and walk through various examples to illustrate its power in uncovering patterns in data.

To better understand the least squares method, let's walk through a couple of examples:

- **Example 1**: A school principal wants to understand the relationship between students' study hours and their test scores. The principal plots the data on a graph, with study hours on the horizontal axis and test scores on the vertical axis. Each data point represents a student's study hours and the corresponding test score.

    Applying the least squares method, the principal aims to find the line that minimizes the sum of the squared residuals – the squared vertical distances between the actual test scores and the predicted scores generated by the line. Once the line of best fit is determined, the principal can identify patterns in the data, such as whether longer study hours generally lead to higher test scores, and use this information to inform school policies and study programs.

- **Example 2**: A fitness coach wants to evaluate the correlation between a person's daily calorie intake and weight loss. The coach plots the data, with daily calorie intake on the horizontal axis and weight loss on the vertical axis. Each data point represents an individual's daily calorie intake and the corresponding weight loss.

With the line of best fit in place, the coach can analyze the relationship between calorie intake and weight loss, providing tailored recommendations to clients based on their goals and dietary preferences.

As a decision-maker, it's essential to understand the core concepts of the least squares method and its applications in various scenarios. In the following sections, we'll expand upon this foundation, exploring more advanced regression techniques and tools.

Calculating the equations of the lines of best fit

In this section, we'll dive into the process of calculating the equation of the line of best fit for both simple and multiple linear regression. While equations may seem daunting, we'll break them down step by step to ensure a clear understanding. By mastering the equations behind the lines of best fit, you'll gain a deeper appreciation for the underlying mechanics of linear regression.

For simple linear regression, the equation of the line of best fit can be represented as follows:

$$y = a + bx$$

Here, y is the dependent variable, x is the independent variable, a is the y-intercept (the point where the line intersects the Y-axis), and b is the slope (which determines the steepness of the line):

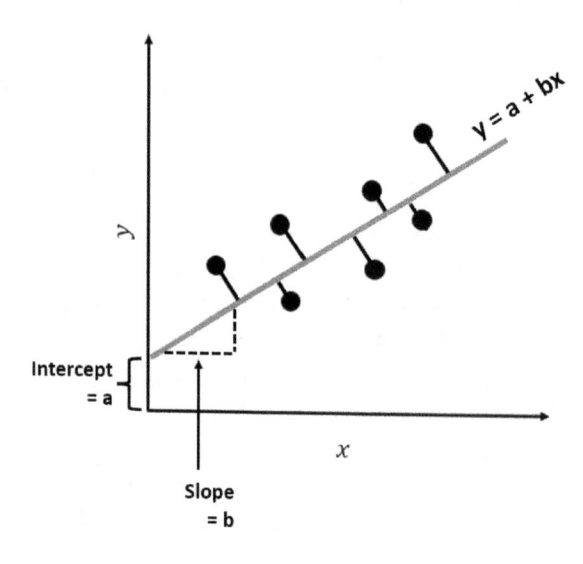

Figure 5.4: Line of best fit and the equation of the line

To calculate a and b, we can use the following formulas:

$$b = \sum_{i=1}^{n} \frac{(x_i - \bar{x})(y_i - \bar{y})}{(x_i - \bar{x})^2}$$

$$a = \bar{y} - b\bar{x}$$

In these formulas, x_i specifies the individual data points, $\bar{x}$ and $\bar{y}$ represent the mean (average) of the x and y values, and Σ denotes summation.

Let's illustrate this process with an example.

Example: A small business owner wants to predict their monthly revenue based on the number of items sold. The owner has the following data for the past 4 months:

- **Month 1:** Items sold = 10, Revenue = $1,060
- **Month 2:** Items sold = 15, Revenue = $1,400
- **Month 3:** Items sold = 18, Revenue = $1,580

- **Month 4**: Items sold = 26, Revenue = $2,150
- **Month 5**: Items sold = 31, Revenue = $2,320

To find the equation of the line of best fit, follow these steps:

1. Calculate the mean of the *x* values (items sold) and the *y* values (revenue):

$$\bar{x} = \frac{(10 + 15 + 18 + 26 + 31)}{5} = 20$$

$$\bar{y} = \frac{(1{,}060 + 1{,}400 + 1{,}600 + 2{,}150 + 2{,}320)}{5} = \$1{,}702$$

2. Apply the formulas to find the slope, *b*, and the y-intercept, *a*, shown previously. After making the calculations in the equations for *a* and *b*, we obtain the line of best fit equation:

$$y = \$467.03 + \$61.75x$$

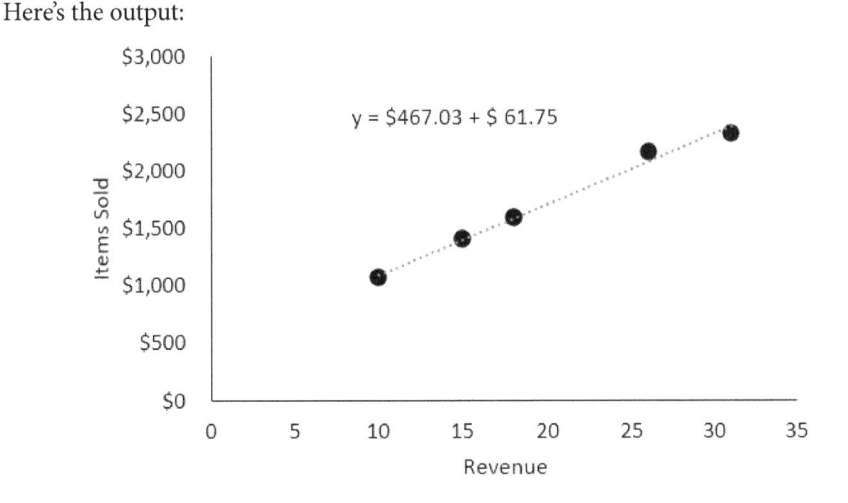

Here's the output:

Figure 5.5: Line of best fit equation, estimated for a scatter plot of Items Sold against Revenue

Armed with the line of best fit equation, y = $467.03 + $61.75, the small business owner can confidently make predictions about their monthly revenue. For example, if they plan to sell 22 items in the upcoming month, they can estimate the revenue by plugging the value of *x* (number of items sold) into the equation:

$$y = \$467.03 + \$61.75(22) = \$467.03 + \$1{,}358.50 = \$1{,}825.53$$

According to the model, the business owner can expect a monthly revenue of approximately $1,825.53 when they sell 22 items. This estimate can be useful for budgeting, resource allocation, and setting sales targets. By continually updating the model with new data, the business owner can refine the predictions and make well-informed decisions that contribute to the growth and success of their small business.

For multiple linear regression, the process is more complex as it involves multiple independent variables. The general equation is represented as follows:

$$y = a + b_1 x_1 + b_2 x_2 + \ldots + b_n x_n$$

Here, a is the constant, and b_1, b_2, ..., b_n are the coefficients for each independent variable, x_1, x_2, ..., x_n. Calculating the coefficients in multiple linear regression typically requires specialized software or programming languages such as Python or R.

Understanding the equations behind the lines of best fit is essential for comprehending the mechanics of linear regression. By calculating these equations, you'll be better equipped to interpret and apply the results of linear regression models in real-world scenarios.

Now that we know how to estimate the equation for a line of best fit (regression line), let's learn how to interpret the parameters of the equation.

There are two important parameters to interpret: the **slope** of the regression line and the **intercept**.

First, we'll interpret the slope; then, we'll interpret the intercept.

Interpreting the slope of a regression line

In this section, we'll focus on the significance of the slope of a regression line and how it informs our understanding of the relationship between variables. By studying the slope, we can derive meaningful insights from our regression models and make well-informed decisions. We'll illustrate this concept through various examples, highlighting the practical implications of interpreting the slope.

Recall that the equation for a simple linear regression line is as follows:

$$y = a + bx$$

The slope, b, represents the average change in the dependent variable, y, for each one-unit increase in the independent variable, x. In other words, it tells us how y is expected to change as x changes.

Let's explore some examples to better understand the interpretation of the slope.

Example 1: A fitness coach has developed a simple linear regression model to predict weight loss based on the number of calories burned during exercise. The equation of the line of best fit is as follows:

$$y = 5 - 0.01x$$

Here, *y* is the weight loss in pounds and *x* is the number of calories burned. The slope, -0.01, indicates that for every additional calorie burned, the expected weight loss increases by 0.01 pounds, on average. In this case, a negative slope is expected since burning more calories should lead to weight loss.

Example 2: An e-commerce company has built a model to predict revenue as a function of marketing spend. The equation of the line of best fit is as follows:

$$y = \$10{,}000 + 2x$$

In this scenario, *y* represents the monthly revenue and *x* denotes the number of website visitors. The intercept suggests that there is a baseline revenue of $10,000 even without marketing spend. The slope, 2, suggests that for every additional dollar of marketing spend, the expected monthly revenue increases by $2, on average. Here, the positive slope indicates a positive relationship between marketing spend and revenue.

Understanding the slope of the regression line is essential because it quantifies the relationship between the dependent and independent variables. A positive slope implies that as the independent variable increases, so does the dependent variable, while a negative slope suggests that as the independent variable increases, the dependent variable decreases.

Now that we've learned how the slope of the regression line can be interpreted, let's move on to the intercept.

Interpreting the intercept of a regression line

In this section, we'll explore the importance of interpreting the intercept of a regression line, which provides crucial context for understanding the baseline level of the dependent variable when the independent variable is equal to zero. We'll investigate various examples to demonstrate the practical relevance of interpreting the intercept in linear regression models.

In our equation for a simple linear regression line, we have the following:

$$y = a + bx$$

The intercept, *a*, represents the expected value of the dependent variable, *y*, when the independent variable, *x*, is equal to zero.

Let's examine some examples to better understand the interpretation of the intercept.

Example 1: An energy provider has developed a simple linear regression model to predict monthly electricity bills based on the number of **kilowatt-hours** (**kWh**) consumed by a household. The equation of the line of best fit is as follows:

$$y = \$20 + \$0.12x$$

In this case, *y* represents the monthly electricity bill and *x* denotes the number of kWh consumed. The intercept, *20*, suggests that when a household consumes zero kWh (that is, $x = 0$), the expected monthly electricity bill is $20. This value can be interpreted as the base charge or fixed cost that households need to pay regardless of their electricity consumption.

Example 2: A marketing analyst has built a model to predict the number of sales leads generated based on the advertising budget. The equation of the line of best fit is as follows:

$$y = 30 + 5x$$

Here, *y* represents the number of sales leads and *x* is the advertising budget in thousands of dollars. The intercept, *30*, indicates that when the advertising budget is zero (that is, $x = 0$), the expected number of sales leads generated is 30. This value could be understood as the baseline number of leads generated through organic, non-advertising methods, such as referrals or search engine traffic.

It's essential to note that interpreting the intercept may not always be meaningful, especially if the value of the independent variable, *x*, cannot be zero or if the regression model is not valid in that range. For example, when making a prediction based on the age of a customer, such as predicting the number of insurance claims based on the customer's age, the age cannot be zero, so the intercept doesn't relate to a specific meaning. In such cases, the intercept serves mainly to fine-tune the position of the regression line, rather than providing direct insights.

As a decision-maker, interpreting the intercept of the regression line helps you understand the baseline level of the dependent variable when the independent variable is zero, offering valuable context for your data. This understanding enables you to make more informed decisions and capitalize on the relationships between variables.

At this point, we understand a lot about our line of best fit, but what about how well the real data matches our line of best fit? This will be the topic of the next section, where we'll measure the difference between our line of best fit and the actual data via **residuals**.

Understanding residuals

In this section, we'll explore the concept of residuals in depth, focusing on their role in linear regression and their importance in assessing the accuracy and quality of our models. We'll illustrate the significance of residuals through various examples, ensuring you have a comprehensive understanding of this critical aspect of regression analysis.

Residuals are the differences between the actual observed values (data points) and the values predicted by the regression model (the line of best fit). In simple terms, residuals represent the errors in our model – how far off our predictions are from reality. By analyzing the residuals, we can evaluate the performance of our regression model and identify potential areas for improvement.

The formula to calculate the residual for a specific data point is as follows:

residual = observed value − predicted value

Let's explore the concept of residuals through an example.

Example: A sales manager has built a simple linear regression model to predict monthly revenue based on the number of sales calls made. The equation of the line of best fit is as follows:

$$y = \$1{,}000 + \$50x$$

Here, y is the predicted monthly revenue and x is the number of sales calls.

For a specific month, the team made 30 sales calls and generated $2,300 in revenue. To calculate the residual for this month, we must find the predicted revenue using the following equation:

*Predicted revenue = $1,000 + $50 * 30 = $2,500*

Now, we can calculate the residual:

Residual = observed value − predicted value

Residual = $2,300 − $2,500 = −$200

In this case, the residual is -$200, indicating that the actual revenue was $200 lower than the predicted revenue based on the model.

When analyzing residuals, it's essential to look for patterns or trends that may suggest issues with our regression model. Ideally, the residuals should be randomly distributed around zero, with no discernible patterns. If the residuals exhibit trends or systematic patterns, it may indicate that the model isn't adequately capturing the underlying relationship between the variables, and adjustments may be necessary.

Some common residual patterns and their potential causes are provided here:

- **A U-shaped or inverted U-shaped pattern**: This may suggest that a quadratic term (a variable squared) needs to be added to the model to better capture the relationship between the variables
- **A pattern showing residuals increasing or decreasing as the predicted value increases**: This could indicate that the relationship between the variables is not strictly linear, and a transformation (for example, logarithmic) might be required

By understanding and analyzing residuals, decision-makers can evaluate the accuracy and reliability of their regression models, leading to better predictions and more effective data-driven decisions.

How can we use residuals to evaluate how well our model fits our data? This is what we'll explore in the next section.

Evaluating the goodness of fit in least-squares regression

In this section, we'll discuss how to evaluate the goodness of fit in least-squares regression, a critical step in determining the accuracy and effectiveness of our models.

By understanding how well our model fits the data, we can make more informed decisions and improve our predictions. We'll investigate various examples and introduce key metrics for evaluating the goodness of fit in regression analysis.

The goodness of fit is a measure of how well the regression line represents the relationship between the dependent and independent variables. A model with a high goodness of fit accurately describes the underlying data, while a model with a low goodness of fit may not capture the true relationship between the variables. To evaluate the goodness of fit, we commonly use two key metrics: the coefficient of determination (R-squared) and the **root mean square error (RMSE)**:

- **Coefficient of determination (R-squared)**: R-squared is a measure that ranges from 0 to 1 and represents the proportion of the total variation in the dependent variable, y, that is explained by the independent variable, x. An R-squared value close to 1 indicates that the model explains a high percentage of variation in the data, while a value close to 0 suggests that the model has little explanatory power. However, it's important to note that a high R-squared value does not necessarily imply a good model as it could be the result of overfitting or the presence of irrelevant variables.

    Example: A car rental company has built a regression model to predict daily revenue based on the number of vehicles rented. The R-squared value for this model is 0.85. This indicates that 85% of the variation in daily revenue can be explained by the number of vehicles rented, suggesting a strong relationship between the two variables.

- **RMSE**: RMSE is a measure of the average difference between the actual observed values and the values predicted by the regression model. Lower RMSE values indicate that the model's predictions are closer to the true values, while higher RMSE values suggest larger discrepancies between the predictions and the actual data.

    Example: A clothing retailer has developed a regression model to predict monthly sales based on the amount spent on advertising. The RMSE for this model is $500. This means that, on average, the model's predicted sales differ from the actual sales by $500. The retailer can use this information to assess the accuracy of the model and determine whether adjustments are necessary.

Evaluating the goodness of fit is crucial in determining the effectiveness of our regression models. By understanding key metrics such as R-squared and RMSE, decision-makers can assess the reliability of their models.

Summary

In this chapter, we introduced the concept of trend lines and their significance in visualizing patterns in datasets. We explored the least squares method for estimating the line of best fit, discussed the importance of understanding residuals, and explained how to interpret the slope and intercept of the regression line. Finally, we covered how to evaluate a model's goodness of fit using R-squared and RMSE. This knowledge has equipped you to carry out (or interpret from your team) regression analysis and apply it to various business scenarios. These scenarios could include forecasting sales, optimizing advertising budgets, and assessing the impact of different factors on key performance indicators, leading to informed data-driven decisions and business growth.

As we transition into *Part 2* of this guide, we're about to open a new dimension of analytical capabilities: machine learning. You'll learn how to move from understanding relationships between variables to predicting future outcomes and even making automated decisions.

Machine learning algorithms have a plethora of applications across many industries, from optimizing supply chains to helping in customer segmentation and targeted marketing, and even automating the process of gathering insights from textual data. As the capabilities of machine learning models grow, the number of applications is ever-expanding, with too many to list here. However, by understanding the core concepts and some of the well-understood applications, you will be able to better identify which business problems can be properly framed as machine learning problems, and the pitfalls to avoid.

The next chapter kicks off with an introduction to machine learning, where we'll lay the groundwork for more advanced techniques and applications. The focus will be on how machine learning can bring scalability and automation to your data analysis and business decisions.

Part 2: Machine Learning – Concepts, Applications, and Pitfalls

This part focuses on machine learning, covering its importance, types of machine learning techniques, supervised and unsupervised learning, model evaluation and interpretation, and common pitfalls to avoid. This part has the following chapters:

- *Chapter 6, Introducing Machine Learning*
- *Chapter 7, Supervised Machine Learning*
- *Chapter 8, Unsupervised Machine Learning*
- *Chapter 9, Interpreting and Evaluating Machine Learning Models*
- *Chapter 10, Common Pitfalls in Machine Learning*

6
Introducing Machine Learning

In the rapidly evolving world of data-driven decision-making, machine learning has emerged as a game-changer. As a decision-maker, understanding the fundamentals of this powerful tool is essential to leverage its potential and stay ahead in today's competitive landscape.

In this chapter, we will demystify machine learning, exploring its roots in statistics and its pivotal role within **artificial intelligence** (**AI**). We'll break down the different types of machine learning techniques and walk through the process of training, validating, and testing models. Moreover, we'll dive into the exciting world of deep learning and its transformative impact on various industries.

By the end of this chapter, you'll have a solid grasp of the following topics:

- The evolution from traditional statistics to machine learning
- The significance of machine learning in data-driven decision-making
- The diverse applications of machine learning across different fields
- The key steps in the machine learning process
- Harnessing machine learning for unstructured data
- The relationship between deep learning and artificial intelligence

Machine learning is not just a buzzword; it's a field of study that can help you uncover hidden insights, make accurate predictions, and automate complex decision-making processes.

From statistics to machine learning

In this section, we step beyond the known confines of statistics. We're about to investigate a field that's become the beating heart of business intelligence and innovation – machine learning.

What is machine learning?

Machine learning is a subfield of AI that employs statistical techniques to enable computer systems to learn from data. It centers on developing algorithms that can learn patterns from data to make predictions or decisions. The keyword here is *learn*, as unlike rule-based algorithms within computer science, machine learning systems operate by training a model based on input data, then using that model to make predictions or understand patterns in the data, rather than following static program instructions.

To put it simply, think of a child first learning to speak. After hearing many people speak around them – parents, relatives, and friends – the child learns language and grammar without being taught the specific grammatical rules that the language follows.

Incredibly, children can learn all the grammatical complexities – the different tenses, cases, and conjugations – of their native language. In contrast, adults struggle to learn a foreign language even when they have learned formal explanations of the grammatical rules.

Machine learning algorithms operate similarly, learning from examples in data rather than by following hardcoded rules.

Another example is to think of a child learning to identify animals. After seeing several examples of dogs and being told each time that the animal is a dog, the child begins to understand what characteristics define a dog. Later, when they encounter a new animal that resembles the previous examples, they can identify it as a dog.

It's crucial to note that machine learning systems are not programmed explicitly for specific tasks. Instead, they rely on patterns and inferences derived from data to accomplish those tasks. Hence, a machine learning system's effectiveness heavily depends on its training data's quantity, quality, and relevancy.

Ultimately, machine learning's fundamental aim is to create systems that can independently learn, adapt, and improve, thereby reducing human intervention and error while increasing efficiency and accuracy across different tasks where it is applied.

How does machine learning relate to statistics?

Concerning statistics, you can consider machine learning as a form of applied statistics focusing on prediction and decision-making. While statistics emphasize inference and understanding relationships between variables, machine learning emphasizes accuracy in prediction.

Let's consider an example: predicting housing prices. A statistician might create a model using variables such as square footage, number of rooms, and location to infer how these factors relate to and impact the price. On the other hand, a machine learning model would utilize the same data, but its primary goal is to predict the prices as accurately as possible. It might find complex relationships, perhaps even ones that humans fail to spot, to improve the prediction's accuracy.

Understanding the subtle differences and the overarching connections between statistics and machine learning will serve as a valuable compass as we continue our journey in this exciting domain. It is essential to remember that both are tools in your decision-making arsenal, each powerful in its own right and even more so when used together.

Why is machine learning important?

In today's rapidly changing digital landscape, machine learning is a pivotal technology transforming how businesses operate, compete, and grow. Its importance extends beyond merely automating routine tasks. Machine learning is reshaping industries by enabling businesses to extract valuable insights from data, leading to more intelligent decision-making, improved productivity, and competitive advantage. Here are some current applications of machine learning that underline its significance.

Customer personalization and segmentation

Today's consumers expect personalized experiences. Machine learning is instrumental in making this a reality. By analyzing a wealth of customer data, machine learning algorithms can identify unique customer segments based on various factors, including purchasing behavior, preferences, or demographics. Such granular segmentation enables businesses to provide contextualized offers, recommendations, and services, enhancing customer satisfaction and loyalty. For instance, streaming services such as Netflix and Spotify use machine learning to offer personalized content recommendations, tailoring their services to each user's unique tastes.

Fraud detection and security

Machine learning is playing an increasingly crucial role in fraud detection and security. Traditional rule-based systems can be inflexible and unable to keep up with sophisticated, evolving threats. On the other hand, machine learning algorithms can learn from fraud incidents to detect patterns and anomalies that may indicate fraudulent activity. For example, credit card companies utilize machine learning to identify unusual transactions that could indicate credit card fraud, thereby improving security while minimizing false positives.

Supply chain and inventory optimization

Efficient supply chain management and inventory control are vital for businesses, particularly in sectors such as retail and manufacturing. Machine learning can provide accurate demand forecasts by analyzing historical sales data, market trends, and other relevant factors. These forecasts aid in maintaining optimal inventory levels, reducing holding costs, and preventing stockouts or overstock scenarios. Machine learning can also optimize routing in the supply chain, reducing delivery times and costs.

Predictive maintenance

Predictive maintenance powered by machine learning can be a game-changer in industries where equipment uptime is crucial, such as manufacturing, aviation, or energy. Machine learning algorithms can analyze data from sensors on equipment to detect patterns that precede failures, enabling maintenance scheduling before a breakdown occurs. This pre-emptive maintenance reduces downtime and prevents unnecessary issues and fixes, saving time and resources.

Healthcare diagnostics and treatment

Machine learning is making waves in healthcare, particularly in diagnostics. Deep learning models can analyze medical images to detect diseases, sometimes with accuracy surpassing human experts. For example, algorithms have been developed to detect certain types of cancer in medical images. Machine learning is also used to predict patient risk, helping doctors make better-informed treatment decisions.

In an era of data-driven decision-making, machine learning is a critical tool for businesses. It unlocks the potential to glean actionable insights from vast amounts of data, leading to more informed decisions, improved operational efficiency, and a significant competitive edge. By understanding and leveraging machine learning, business leaders can drive innovation and growth in their organizations.

> **Question**
> Can you think about where in your industry or business machine learning could be applied or where you have heard it being applied? When thinking about use cases for machine learning in your organization, it can often help to start by looking at typical applications within your industry rather than trying to find novel applications, as not every business problem is easily framed as a machine learning problem.

Now that we have understood how machine learning is defined and explored some of the common applications of machine learning, in the next section, we will go a little deeper and introduce the different domains *within* machine learning.

The different types of machine learning

Akin to an artisan's toolbox filled with various tools, each designed for a specific task, machine learning is not a one-size-fits-all solution. It's a spectrum of methodologies, each tailored to different types of problems and data. This section will examine four major types:

- Supervised learning
- Unsupervised learning
- Semi-supervised learning
- Reinforcement learning

Supervised learning

Imagine trying to learn a new language with a tutor who corrects your mistakes and guides you as you practice. Supervised learning operates on a similar principle. You provide the machine with input data (the features) and the correct output (the target). The machine learns a model mapping inputs to outputs and then uses this model to make predictions on new, unseen data. This type of learning is called "supervised" because you are supervising the model's learning process with correct answers.

A common example might be the fraud detection your bank account uses. The data may be information about your transaction, the transaction amount, the transaction time, the recipient, and so on. A supervised machine learning model trained on historical transactions, both normal transactions and fraudulent ones, would be able to discriminate whether your transaction is more likely to be a usual transaction or a fraudulent one, and the bank may block the account until the matter is investigated.

Unsupervised learning

Imagine trying to learn a language without a tutor, using only books or media in the target language. This situation is akin to unsupervised learning, where the machine receives input data without corresponding output labels. The goal is to identify underlying patterns or structures within the data.

An example would be customer segmentation in marketing. An unsupervised learning algorithm can identify groups or "clusters" of customers with similar behaviors, preferences, or characteristics without being explicitly told what these groups might be.

Semi-supervised learning

In a perfect world, we'd have a label for every piece of data. But in reality, labeled data can be expensive or time-consuming to obtain. This is where semi-supervised learning comes in. It uses a small amount of labeled data and the rest unlabeled data for training.

Consider a social media company trying to identify harmful content. They might have a small set of posts labeled as "harmful" or "safe," but millions of unlabeled posts. Semi-supervised learning can use unlabeled data to improve its understanding of what constitutes harmful content.

Reinforcement learning

Finally, consider a scenario where you have reinforcement learning. An agent learns to make decisions by performing actions in an environment to maximize cumulative reward.

A classic example is using machine learning to play a game of chess. The machine, or agent, learns by playing numerous games, receiving a reward when it wins and a penalty when it loses. Over time, the agent learns which moves will likely maximize its chances of winning the game.

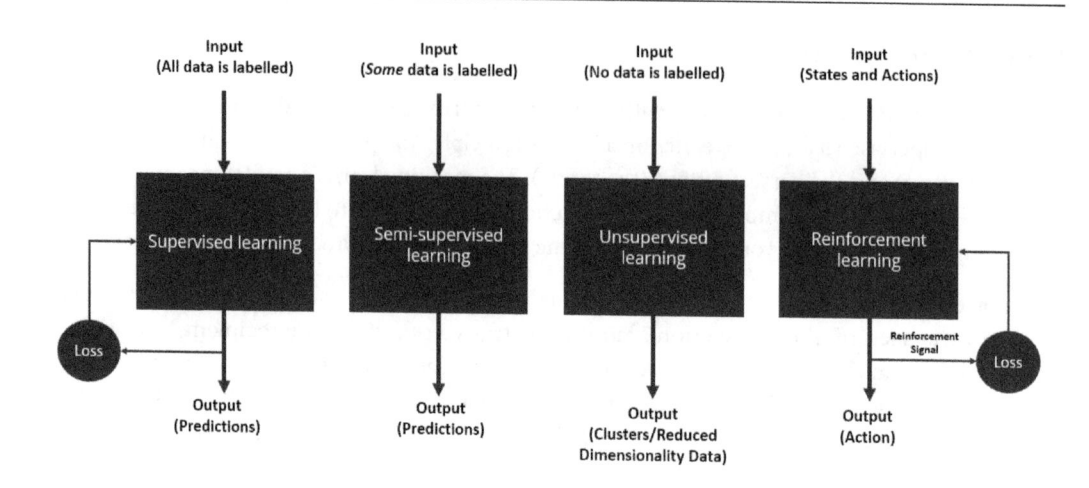

Figure 6.1: Different types of machine learning

Transfer learning

Finally, there's another intriguing approach within machine learning: transfer learning. This concept is grounded in the idea that knowledge learned in one domain can be transferred and applied to a different but related domain.

Picture this: you're a skilled tennis player aiming to learn squash. Many skills and techniques you've honed while playing tennis, such as racket handling, agility, and strategic court movement, can be transferred and adapted to squash. You're not starting from scratch – you're transferring your learning from one domain (tennis) to another (squash).

Similarly, transfer learning in machine learning leverages a pre-trained model's knowledge from a large dataset (such as identifying objects or animals in millions of images). It applies this understanding to a different but related problem (such as diagnosing diseases from medical images).

Transfer learning offers a significant advantage when you have limited data for your specific task or when training a complex model from scratch is computationally expensive or impractical. In deep learning, where models with millions of parameters are not uncommon, transfer learning has become the de facto standard for many applications, from image recognition to natural language processing tasks.

By applying transfer learning, models can achieve better performance, require less training data, and save valuable computational resources, thus offering practical solutions in various real-world scenarios.

Each of these types of machine learning has its strengths and uses, and understanding when to apply each is a fundamental aspect of leveraging machine learning effectively for decision-making.

As we continue, we'll explore how these tools can be applied to generate actionable insights for your business.

Popular machine learning algorithms

Machine learning employs many algorithms to model and understand complex data. When learning from data, these algorithms can be viewed as the machine's "recipe." While it's not necessary to understand the intricate workings of each algorithm, it is helpful to have an overview of some commonly used ones and their general applications.

Linear regression

In *Chapter 5*, we explored linear regression, a technique traditionally rooted in statistics. However, linear regression can also be considered one of the simplest examples of a supervised machine learning technique.

Linear regression, in a machine learning context, involves training a model to predict a dependent variable (such as sales) based on one or more independent variables (such as advertising spend and market conditions). The algorithm learns from historical data, identifying patterns and relationships. For instance, in a business setting, a company might use linear regression to forecast sales based on past sales data and other relevant factors, such as marketing budget, seasonal trends, or economic indicators. This predictive insight can inform decision-making, such as budget allocation or strategic planning, demonstrating how a classical statistical method adapts effectively to the dynamic needs of modern business analytics.

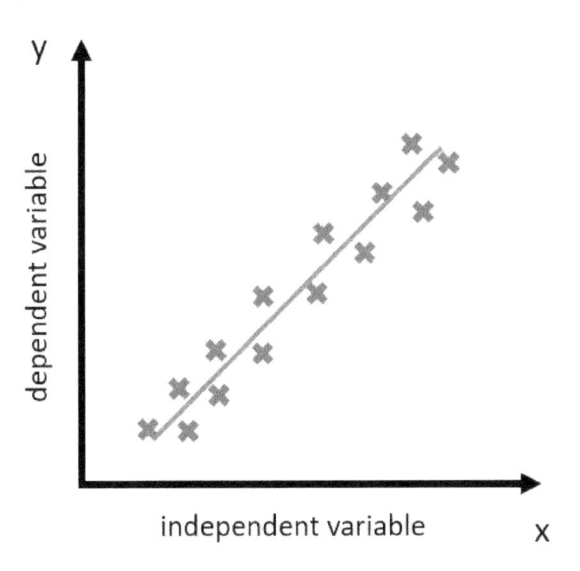

Figure 6.2: Linear regression

Logistic regression

Logistic regression is a tool used for making decisions when there are two possible outcomes, much like choosing between "yes" and "no." Unlike linear regression, which predicts values (such as how much a house might sell for), logistic regression predicts the likelihood of something happening, such as whether a loan will be defaulted or an email is spam.

In this model, we use data (such as by how many days a payment is late) to calculate a probability between 0 and 1. This tells us how likely it is that the event we're concerned about (such as a late payment) will occur. The process involves a special S-shaped curve, known as the sigmoid function, which you can see in your chart. This curve shows that at first, the probability of a default is low, but as the payment becomes more overdue, the likelihood of a default increases significantly.

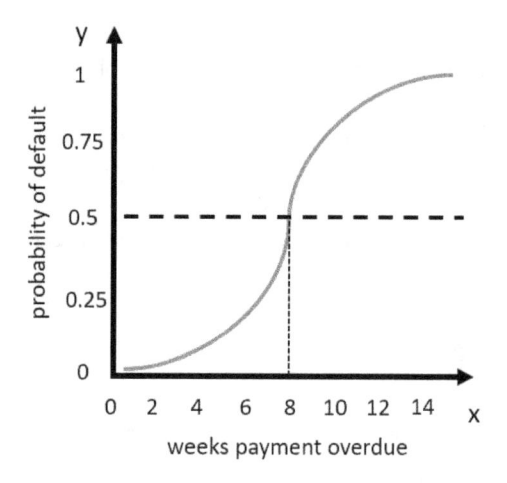

Figure 6.3: Logistic regression

For instance, in the preceding business scenario, logistic regression could help predict the chance of a company failing to pay an invoice on time, based on how overdue the payment is.

The curve in your chart illustrates the S-shaped logistic function, known as the sigmoid function. At the lower end of the weeks overdue, the probability of default is low. At around 8 weeks, the probability of default is 0.5 (50%). We can think of this as the threshold where it is more likely that the company is to default than pay their invoice.

As the weeks increase, the probability of default rises until it reaches a point where further delay doesn't significantly change the probability. This is because the model recognizes a pattern: once a payment is significantly overdue, the likelihood of default is already high and stabilizes.

Logistic regression can be a practical way to gauge risks and make decisions, offering a balance between complex mathematical predictions and accessible, actionable insights.

Decision trees

Decision trees are intuitive and easy-to-understand algorithms used for both regression and classification tasks. They learn a series of explicit if-then rules on the features to predict the target variable. They're like playing a "20 questions" game with your data, helping you deduce the answer by asking the right questions.

For example, in customer service management, a decision tree could help classify customer complaints based on their severity.

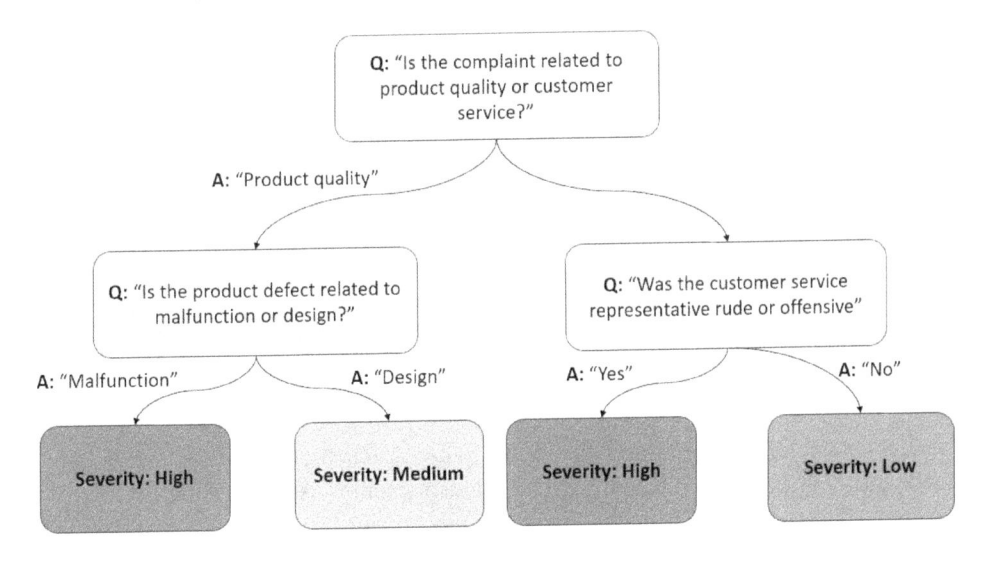

Figure 6.4: Decision tree for complaint severity

It could start by asking simple questions such as, "Is the complaint related to product quality or service?" Based on the answer, it delves deeper with more specific questions, such as "Is the product defect related to design or malfunction?" This step-by-step approach efficiently categorizes complaints, allowing for tailored responses and quicker resolution.

By breaking down complex decision-making processes into a series of simple questions, decision trees provide clear and actionable insights, making them invaluable in business operations.

Random forests

Random forests are an "ensemble" method for decision trees that combines the insights of multiple decision trees to improve prediction accuracy. You can think of them as a team of experts (the individual trees) where each contributes their opinion, and the final decision is made based on the majority vote. This method enhances the strengths and balances the weaknesses of single decision trees, leading to more reliable results.

In practice, random forests work by having each tree in the forest give its prediction, with the most common outcome becoming the final prediction.

Ensemble techniques, such as Random Forests, often outshine even deep learning models, particularly when working with structured, table-like data. Their effectiveness is proven across various fields, from detecting fraudulent activities to predicting customer churn, showcasing their versatility and robustness in tackling complex problems.

Support vector machines

Support vector machines (**SVMs**) are a supervised machine learning technique that is particularly useful when you need to categorize or predict certain outcomes.

Imagine you have a bunch of data points that belong to two different categories. SVMs help by finding the maximum margin hyperplane – a line (or a more complex boundary in the case of more complicated data) that best separates these categories with the widest possible gap, known as the maximum margin, on either side.

The maximum margin is important because it helps the SVM find the most robust separation between the classes. By maximizing the margin, the SVM ensures that the decision boundary is as far away from the data points as possible, which makes the classification less sensitive to noise and more likely to generalize well to new, unseen data.

For a business example, consider a bank that wants to decide whether to approve loans. They have information such as credit scores, income levels, and loan amounts. An SVM can help by analyzing this data and finding the maximum margin hyperplane that divides applicants into two groups: those likely to repay the loan and those who are high-risk. The maximum margin ensures that the bank's decision boundary is robust and less likely to misclassify applicants. This separation helps the bank make more informed and safer lending decisions, reducing the risk of default.

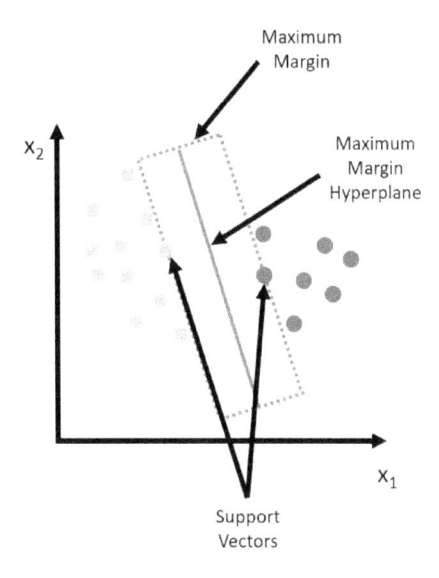

Figure 6.5: Support vector machines

k-nearest neighbors

k-nearest neighbors (**k-NN**) is a machine learning approach used in making predictions or categorizing things based on data. Think of it like finding the closest match. In k-NN, the idea is that similar items are usually found close to each other.

For instance, in a business setting such as customer service, k-NN can help categorize customer inquiries. If a new inquiry comes in, the algorithm looks at past inquiries that are most similar (or "nearest") to it. It then categorizes the new inquiry based on what it's closest to. This is like saying, "This new customer problem is most similar to these previous ones, so it probably needs a similar kind of response." This method helps quickly sort and respond to customer needs by using patterns from past data.

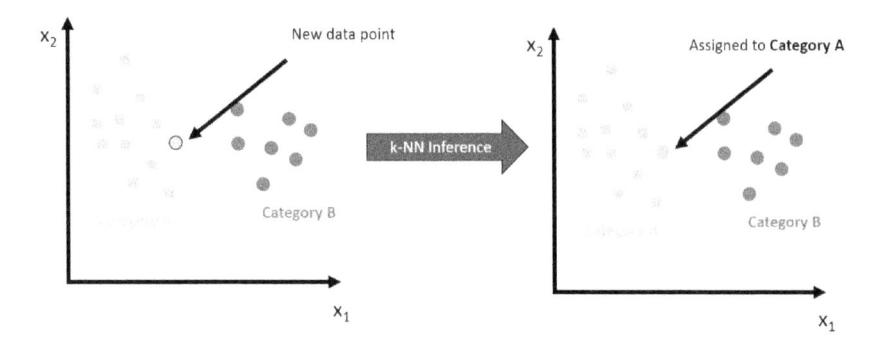

Figure 6.6: k-nearest neighbors

Neural networks

Neural networks, especially deep neural networks, are at the heart of today's AI boom. They're the backbone of most modern machine learning, from speech recognition to image classification. They work by simulating a network of interconnected neurons inspired by the human brain to learn patterns in data.

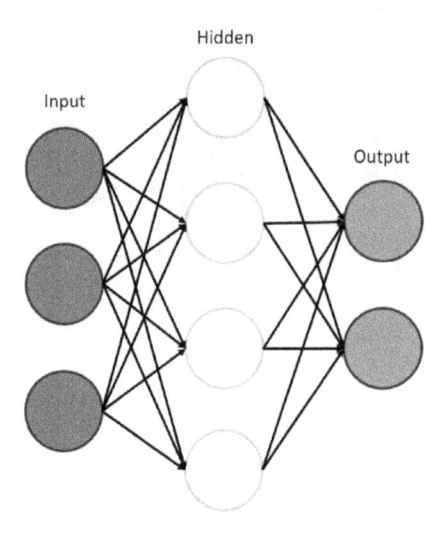

Figure 6.7: A simple artificial neural network

Consider a factory that produces electronic components. A neural network could be trained to inspect these components as they come off the assembly line, using images captured by high-resolution cameras.

The network learns to identify what a perfect component should look like and then compares each produced item against this standard. It can detect even the smallest deviations or defects, such as misalignments, incorrect sizes, or surface blemishes, which might be challenging for human inspectors to catch consistently.

Alongside computer vision tasks such as this, neural networks are at the heart of many state-of-the-art machine learning models, such as speech recognition models and large language models including OpenAI's GPT family of models.

These are just a few examples of the plethora of algorithms used in machine learning, each with its strengths, weaknesses, and application areas. The beauty of Machine Learning lies in its flexibility: the appropriate algorithm can be chosen or custom-designed based on the problem at hand. This variety makes machine learning applicable and valuable across many industries and domains.

In the next section, we will walk through the process involved in training, testing, and deploying machine learning models.

The machine learning process

Machine learning is a broad field that encompasses various approaches to training models. Each machine learning approach has its own process for developing and optimizing models.

In unsupervised learning, the model learns from unlabeled data to discover hidden patterns or structures. The process typically involves data preprocessing, model training, model evaluation, and model tuning.

Reinforcement learning is a type of machine learning where an agent learns to make decisions by interacting with an environment. The process involves environment setup, agent training, policy evaluation, and policy improvement.

For supervised learning and transfer learning, establishing a reliable machine learning model involves carefully progressing through three essential stages: training, validation, and testing. These stages represent a structured approach to bringing a model to life, optimizing its performance, and ensuring its readiness for real-world application.

We will focus on the training process for a supervised machine learning model.

Training a supervised machine learning model

Training is the initial phase where the supervised machine learning model learns from the data. We feed the model a "training dataset" that includes both input data and the correct output. The model works to identify patterns and relationships between the input and output.

For example, let's consider that we are building a machine learning model to predict the weather. In the training phase, we expose the model to historical weather data such as temperature, humidity, wind speed, and weather conditions such as "sunny," "rainy," or "snowy." The model will attempt to discern patterns between these weather variables and the resulting weather conditions.

Validation of a supervised machine learning model

Once the model has been trained, we need to fine-tune it. Here, the validation stage plays a crucial role. We use a separate "validation set" to adjust the model's parameters for better performance.

Let's return to our weather prediction model. We might use another subset of historical weather data during validation to see how well our model predicts the weather based on the patterns learned during the training phase. If it does not meet expectations, we will adjust the model's parameters or complexity. This process is repeated until the model's performance on the validation set is satisfactory.

Testing a supervised machine learning model

After training and validation, we reach the final stage – testing. This stage is a litmus test for our model's performance. We expose the model to a "test set," a separate dataset the model hasn't seen before. The purpose here is to ensure that the model performs well on the training and validation data and generalizes well to new, unseen data.

Our weather prediction scenario might have a set of recent weather data that our model has never seen before. We would use this data to test how accurately our model predicts weather conditions. If the model performs well, we can confidently use it for real-time weather prediction.

These three stages—training, validation, and testing—form the bedrock of developing and deploying a machine learning model. They help us ensure that our model learns effectively, generalizes well, and is ready to make reliable predictions when deployed in a live environment. This is often a long, iterative process, where experiments will be carried out to train, validate, and test a model, before it reaches a level of accuracy ready to be deployed into production.

Evaluating machine learning models

Once a machine learning model is trained, evaluating its performance is crucial to determine its effectiveness and reliability. Understanding model evaluation techniques helps you gauge whether your model is performing well or requires tweaking and tuning. This section overviews some key concepts and metrics used in model evaluation.

Training, validation, and test sets

Building a machine learning model involves splitting the available data into three sets: training, validation, and test sets. The model learns from the training set, which is the most significant portion of the data. The validation set is used to adjust parameters for improved performance during model tuning. The test set, which the model has not seen during the training phase, is used to assess the model's final performance, providing a measure of how well the model generalizes to unseen data.

Classification metrics

For classification problems where the aim is to predict a discrete label, several metrics are used:

- **Accuracy** measures the proportion of correct predictions out of all predictions. It is a good measure when the classes are balanced but can be misleading when the classes are imbalanced.
- **Precision** is the proportion of true positive predictions (correctly predicted positives) out of all positive predictions. It is a measure of the model's exactness.
- **Recall (sensitivity)** is the proportion of true positive predictions out of all actual positives. It measures the model's completeness.

To illustrate why accuracy can be misleading with imbalanced classes, consider a hypothetical problem of predicting a rare disease that only affects 1% of the population.

A model that simply predicts "no disease" for everyone would achieve 99% accuracy but would fail to identify any actual cases of the disease. In this scenario, precision and recall provide a more informative assessment of the model's performance.

Accuracy, precision, and recall can be calculated based on the Type I (false positives) and Type II (false negatives) errors we discussed in an earlier chapter. The following chart provides a visual representation of how these metrics relate to the different types of predictions:

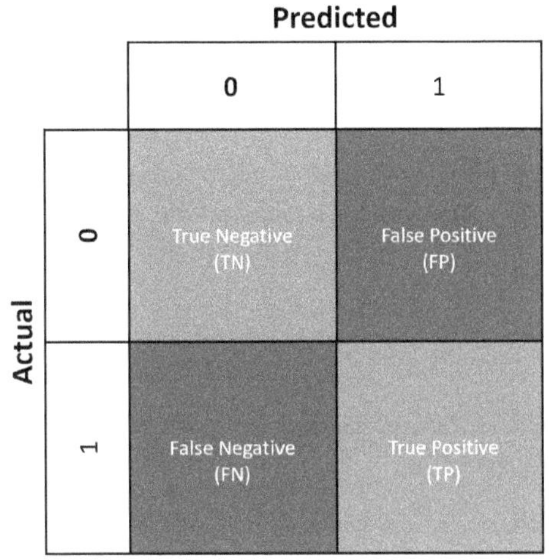

$$Accuracy = \frac{TP + TN}{TP + FP + FN + TN}$$

$$Precision = \frac{TP}{TP + FP} \quad Recall = \frac{TP}{TP + FN}$$

Figure 6.8: Accuracy, precision, and recall

The columns represent the predicted classes (0 or 1), while the rows represent the actual classes (0 or 1).

The green quadrants represent **correct** predictions:

- **True Negative (TN)**: Actual, 0; predicted, 0
- **True Positive (TP)**: Actual, 1; predicted, 1

The red quadrants represent **incorrect** predictions:

- **False Negative (FN)**: Actual, 1; predicted, 0
- **False Positive (FP)**: Actual, 0; predicted, 1

The formulas at the bottom show how accuracy, precision, and recall are calculated based on the counts in each of these four quadrants.

In addition to accuracy, precision, and recall, the following metrics are incredibly useful in understanding the performance of a supervised machine learning model, and less prone to the issues with class imbalance causing accuracy to be a misleading metric:

- **F1-score** is the harmonic mean of precision and recall, providing a balanced measure when the class distribution is uneven.
- **Area under the ROC (AUC-ROC)** is a comprehensive performance measurement for classification problems. It tells how much the model is capable of distinguishing between classes.

Regression metrics

For regression problems, where the aim is to predict a continuous value, we have the following:

- **Mean absolute error (MAE)** measures the average magnitude of the errors in a set of predictions without considering their direction.
- **Mean squared error (MSE)** is similar to MAE but squares the errors before averaging. It gives more weight to larger errors.
- **R-squared (coefficient of determination)** represents the proportion of variance in the dependent variable that is predictable from the independent variables. It indicates the goodness of fit of the model.

Understanding these metrics is fundamental to assessing the quality and reliability of machine learning models. It's important to note that no single metric tells the complete story. The choice of evaluation metrics should align with the business objective and the nature of the problem.

In the next section, we will consider something very important to understand when working with machine learning models, namely, the risks and limitations of machine learning.

Risks and limitations of machine learning

As much as machine learning has revolutionized various aspects of business and society, it's essential to recognize that it comes with risks and limitations. Understanding these can guide decision-makers to take better, more informed actions and mitigate potential negative consequences.

Overfitting and underfitting

Overfitting occurs when a model learns the training data too well. It becomes so engrossed in the specific details and noise in the training set that it performs poorly on unseen data. An overfitted model has a low bias but a high variance.

On the other hand, underfitting happens when a model is too simple to capture all the relevant relationships in the data. It may perform poorly on both the training data and unseen data. An underfitted model has a high bias but low variance.

Balancing the trade-off between overfitting and underfitting is critical in creating a model that generalizes well to unseen data.

Bias and variance

Bias in a machine learning model is its tendency to consistently learn the wrong thing by not considering all the information in the data. Variance, on the other hand, refers to the model's sensitivity to small fluctuations in the training set. High variance can cause overfitting, leading the model to capture random noise in the training data.

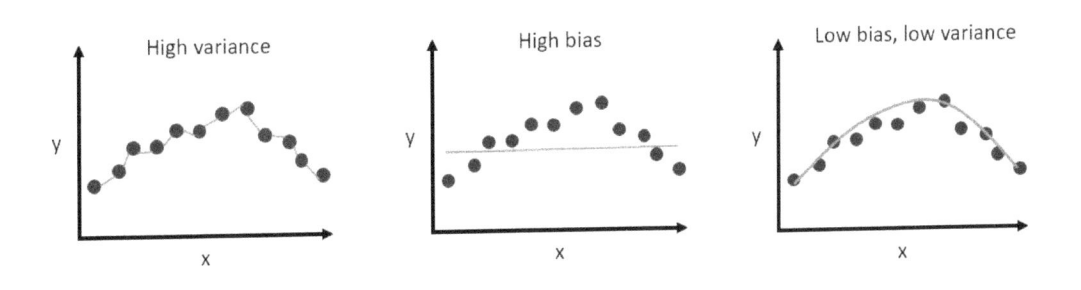

Figure 6.9: Charts showing the bias-variance trade-off for models that are overfitting, underfitting, and correctly fitting, respectively

Balanced dataset

The quality and composition of the training data can significantly impact machine learning models. Suppose the dataset is imbalanced, meaning that one class of outputs is overly represented compared to others. In that case, the model may be biased toward the majority class and perform poorly on the minority class. Techniques such as oversampling the minority class, undersampling the majority class, or using synthetic data augmentation methods can help address this issue.

Models are approximations of reality

It's crucial to remember that machine learning models are, at their core, approximations of reality. They are constructed based on the data they were trained on and the assumptions they make. Consequently, they are inherently imperfect and come with a degree of uncertainty. They should not be seen as absolute oracles of truth but tools to assist decision-making, always subject to scrutiny, revision, and validation.

Understanding these risks and limitations encourages a mindful and responsible approach to machine learning. This understanding serves as a reminder that while machine learning can be a powerful tool, human oversight, continuous monitoring, and ethical considerations remain paramount to ensure its positive and fair application.

Machine learning on unstructured data

Traditionally, machine learning has been applied to structured data – neat, tabulated data that fits nicely into a spreadsheet. However, most data being created and stored is unstructured – it doesn't come pre-packaged in a friendly, orderly format. Examples of unstructured data are text documents, images, audio files, and videos. Luckily, machine learning is well equipped to handle this type of data, leading to the development of specialized fields such as **natural language processing** (**NLP**) and computer vision.

Natural language processing (NLP)

NLP is a field at the intersection of computer science, AI, and linguistics. It focuses on how computers can understand, interpret, and generate human language in a valuable way.

The following are applications of NLP:

- **Sentiment analysis**: Companies often use sentiment analysis to understand customer opinions about their products or services. For instance, NLP can analyze social media posts, customer reviews, and comments to determine whether the sentiment expressed about a product is positive, negative, or neutral.
- **Chatbots**: Chatbots are becoming increasingly popular for customer service. They use NLP to understand customer queries and respond to them effectively.
- **Automated summarization**: Summarizing long documents can be extremely valuable, saving time and effort. For example, a business might use this to quickly understand the main points of a lengthy market research report.

Computer vision

Computer vision aims to give machines the ability to understand and interpret visual data, akin to how humans use their eyesight.

The following are applications of computer vision:

- **Image recognition**: One of the most common applications of computer vision is recognizing what's in an image, ranging from identifying items in a photograph to detecting faces in a crowd.
- **Medical imaging**: Computer vision is used extensively in healthcare, particularly in interpreting medical images. Algorithms can help detect anomalies in X-rays, MRIs, or CT scans that could indicate conditions such as cancer or brain injury.
- **Autonomous vehicles**: Self-driving cars rely heavily on computer vision to navigate the world. They use it to recognize traffic signs, pedestrians, and other vehicles and to understand road conditions.

Working with unstructured data opens up a vast world of possibilities. It allows us to tackle more complex problems and generate insights from broader data sources. Understanding how to apply NLP and computer vision techniques can significantly enhance your ability to make data-driven decisions.

Deep learning and artificial intelligence

AI has experienced monumental strides in recent years, primarily driven by advancements in an area known as deep learning. As we continue our exploration of machine learning, it's critical to understand these concepts, their relationship, and their profound impact on our modern technological landscape.

Artificial intelligence

AI, at its core, is the pursuit of creating machines that can perform tasks requiring human intelligence. These tasks include understanding natural language, recognizing patterns, making decisions, and perceiving environments.

AI can be broadly classified into two categories:

- **Narrow AI**: These are systems designed to perform specific tasks, such as recommending songs on a music streaming app or providing driving directions on a navigation app. Most of the AI that we interact with today falls under this category.
- **General AI**: These systems can understand, learn, adapt, and implement knowledge across various tasks, much like humans. While the notion is exciting and often dramatized in science fiction, we're still far from achieving this level of AI.

Deep learning

Deep learning is a subset of machine learning that's been making waves in the AI space. It employs artificial neural networks with many layers (hence the "deep" in deep learning) to model and understand complex patterns in datasets. Deep learning models excel with large, high-dimensional datasets such as images, audio, or text.

Notable applications of deep learning include the following:

- **Speech recognition**: Deep learning models are at the core of voice assistants such as Siri, Alexa, or Google Assistant, helping them understand and respond to various voice commands
- **Image recognition**: Advanced image recognition, such as the facial recognition used in biometric security systems or identifying diseases in medical images, is primarily powered by deep learning
- **Natural language processing**: While we discussed NLP earlier, it's worth noting that many of the recent advances in this field, including machine translation and sentiment analysis, have been driven by deep learning

Deep learning's impact on AI has been transformative. By enabling machines to learn from vast amounts of data, it has significantly expanded the possibilities of what AI can achieve. It's the driving force behind many AI applications that seemed like science fiction not too long ago.

However, it's essential to understand that AI is more than just deep learning. AI encompasses many techniques and methodologies, with deep learning being one of the most prominent examples. The AI landscape continues to evolve rapidly, and keeping abreast of these developments will be crucial for decision-makers looking to leverage AI's power effectively.

Summary

In this chapter, we have introduced machine learning, understood the different types of machine learning, introduced some of the common machine learning algorithms, gone through the machine learning process, and discussed some of the risks and limitations of machine learning. That's quite a lot to have covered!

Now that you have a good high-level view of machine learning, in the next chapter, we will dive further into supervised machine learning and better understand what it is and its use cases and techniques.

7

Supervised Machine Learning

Within machine learning, supervised learning is one of the most used and most useful subfields. It is often the first area students learn within machine learning and what people think of when first hearing about machine learning, as it involves learning on annotated or labeled data, similar to how we learn from correct examples.

The applications of supervised machine learning are wide and varied. From the spam detection on your email inbox, through to recommendation systems used when recommending TV shows and movies on your favorite streaming service, through to the call you get from your bank when its systems believe they may have detected fraudulent transactions, these are all applications of supervised machine learning.

In this chapter, we will discuss in more detail the steps involved in training and deploying supervised machine learning models, some of the core supervised machine learning models, factors to consider when training and evaluating supervised machine learning models, and applications of supervised machine learning.

This chapter covers the following topics:

- Defining supervised learning
- Steps within supervised learning
- Characteristics of regression and classification algorithms
- Applications of supervised learning

Defining supervised learning

Building upon the foundations covered in the previous chapter, let's dive deeper into supervised learning. As discussed earlier, supervised learning involves training a model using labeled data, where the correct answers are already known. This process is analogous to a student learning under the guidance of a knowledgeable teacher.

In the context of business, imagine you're trying to predict future sales based on historical data. The historical sales data, along with the factors that influence sales (such as marketing spend, seasonality and more), are your labeled data. Your machine learning model learns from this data to predict future sales.

Before getting into the detail of the process of supervised machine learning and different supervised learning algorithms, let's look at some common applications.

Applications of supervised learning

Supervised learning has a broad range of applications across various industries, such as the following:

- **Consumer goods and retail**:

    - **Demand forecasting**: Retailers can use supervised learning to forecast product demand. By training a model on historical sales data, including product features, store locations, promotions, and external factors such as weather and holidays, along with corresponding sales figures, the model can learn patterns that influence demand. This allows retailers to optimize inventory management, reduce stockouts, and improve supply chain efficiency.

- **Financial services**:

    - **Credit risk assessment**: Financial institutions can use supervised learning to assess the creditworthiness of loan applicants. By training a model on historical data of loan repayments, along with relevant features such as credit score, income, and employment status, the model can learn to predict the likelihood of an applicant defaulting on a loan. This helps institutions make informed lending decisions and manage risk.

- **Utilities**:

    - **Customer churn prediction**: Utilities companies, such as electricity, gas, and water companies, as well as telecoms and broadband companies, can use supervised learning to predict which customers are likely to churn (i.e., switch to a competitor). By training a model on historical customer data, including usage patterns, customer service interactions, and demographic information, along with churn labels, the model can identify customers at high risk of churning. This allows companies to proactively offer personalized incentives, such as discounts or loyalty rewards, or improve targeted aspects of their services based on the identified churn drivers, ultimately reducing customer attrition.

The two types of supervised learning

Supervised learning can be further divided into two main categories: **regression** and **classification**. The key difference between them lies in the type of output they predict.

Regression

Regression is used when the output variable is a continuous value. The goal is to predict a numerical value based on input features. Here are some examples:

- **Sales forecasting**: A company can use regression to predict sales figures for the next quarter based on historical sales data, marketing expenditure, and economic indicators. The model learns the relationship between these input features and the continuous output variable (sales figures).
- **House price prediction**: A real estate company can use regression to predict the price of a house based on features such as square footage, number of bedrooms, location, and age of the property. The model learns from past housing data to estimate the continuous output variable (house price).

Classification

Classification is used when the output variable is a categorical value. The goal is to predict the class or category to which an input belongs. Here are some examples:

- **Talent acquisition**: HR departments can use classification to screen and shortlist job applicants. The model is trained on a dataset of past applicants, including their resumes, qualifications, and interview performance, along with hiring decision labels. Given a new applicant's information, the model predicts whether they are likely to be accepted for the role, streamlining the recruitment process.
- **Survey fraud detection**: Within market research surveys, particularly those provided online, there is often a high proliferation of fraudulent responses, as fake respondents aim to get the reward for taking the survey without providing accurate answers. To prevent this, supervised machine learning can be used to classify and filter out fraudulent responses, looking at aspects such as the length of time taken to answer the survey, the answers selected, and even the location of the IP address.

Key factors in supervised learning

As we touched upon in the previous chapter, there are several factors and risks to consider when training a machine learning model. Factors such as the bias-variance trade-off, the amount of training data, the dimensionality of the input space, and noise in the target values play a crucial role in supervised learning. Let's investigate how these factors specifically impact supervised learning algorithms.

The bias-variance trade-off – balancing simplicity and complexity

In supervised learning, it's important to strike the right balance between a model that is too simple (high bias) and a model that is too complex (high variance):

- A model that is too simple may miss important patterns in the data, while a model that is too complex may memorize noise and irrelevant details
- The goal is to find a model that captures the underlying patterns without being overly influenced by random fluctuations

Quantity of training data

- The amount of data used to train the model is **pivotal** to its performance.
- Generally, having more training data allows the model to learn better and make more accurate predictions.
- However, it's also important to consider the relationship between the number of data points and the number of input variables (features). If there are too many features compared to the number of data points, the model may become overly complex and perform poorly on new, unseen data.

Number of input variables

- The number of input variables, also known as features or attributes, can impact the model's performance
- When dealing with a large number of input variables (high-dimensional data), the model becomes more complex and may require more data to learn effectively
- In such cases, techniques such as variable selection or dimensionality reduction can be used to identify the most important variables and simplify the model

Quality of the target data

- The quality of the labeled data used for training is crucial to the model's performance
- If the target data contains errors or inconsistencies (noise), it can mislead the model during the learning process, leading to inaccurate predictions
- Techniques such as data cleaning and outlier detection can help improve the quality of the target data and enhance the model's performance

To summarize, when implementing supervised learning, it's important to consider the trade-off between model simplicity and complexity, the quantity and quality of training data, the number of input variables, and the presence of noise in the target data. By carefully managing these factors, businesses can develop effective supervised learning models that make accurate predictions and support decision-making.

Steps within supervised learning

In this section, we will explore in more detail all the steps involved in supervised learning. From data preparation to model deployment, we'll walk through each stage, providing insights and examples along the way.

Data preparation – laying the foundation

The success of any supervised learning project hinges on the quality of the data. Data preparation is an important first step that involves the following:

- **Data cleaning**: Identifying and correcting erroneous, incomplete, or inconsistent data points to ensure the integrity of your dataset.

- **Feature selection**: Choosing the most informative and relevant attributes that contribute to the predictive power of your model, while discarding irrelevant or redundant features.

- **Data transformation**: Converting raw data into a format that can be effectively processed by machine learning algorithms. This may involve scaling numerical features, encoding categorical variables, or handling missing values.

Example: A retail company preparing customer purchase data might clean up inconsistencies, select key features such as purchase history and demographics, and transform them into numerical representations.

Algorithm selection – choosing the right tool

With a wide array of supervised learning algorithms available, selecting the most appropriate one is essential. The choice depends on the nature of your problem:

- **Regression algorithms**: Used for predicting continuous target variables. Popular choices include linear regression, polynomial regression, ridge regression, and lasso regression.

- **Classification algorithms**: Used for predicting categorical target variables. Common options include logistic regression, **Support vector machines (SVMs)**, **k-nearest neighbors (k-NN)**, decision trees, and random forests.

Example: A real estate company might use regression algorithms to predict house prices based on features such as location, size, and property age, while a marketing firm could employ classification algorithms to predict customer behavior based on demographic and interaction data.

Model training – learning from data

Once you've selected an algorithm, it's time to train your model using the prepared training data. This step involves feeding the algorithm with input features and corresponding target values, allowing it to learn the underlying patterns and relationships.

During training, the algorithm iteratively adjusts its internal parameters to minimize the difference between predicted and actual target values. This process enables the model to capture the complex mappings between inputs and outputs.

Model evaluation – assessing performance

Before deploying your trained model, it's crucial to assess its performance using evaluation metrics. This step helps you understand how well the model generalizes to unseen data and identifies potential areas for improvement.

- **Regression metrics: mean absolute error (MAE), mean squared error (MSE), and root mean squared error (RMSE)** are commonly used to measure the average difference between predicted and actual values
- **Classification metrics:** Accuracy, precision, recall, and F1 score provide insights into the model's ability to correctly classify instances across different categories

By evaluating your model on a separate validation set, you can gauge its performance and make informed decisions about further refinements or parameter tuning.

Prediction and deployment – putting the model to work

Once you're confident in your model's performance, it's time to deploy it for real-world predictions. This step involves integrating the trained model into your application or system, allowing it to generate predictions based on new, unseen input data.

Example: A consumer goods company can use a trained sales forecasting model to predict future demand based on factors such as marketing spend, seasonality, and competitor activity, enabling proactive inventory management and resource allocation.

By carefully following the key steps of data preparation, algorithm selection, model training, evaluation, and deployment, you can realize the full potential of supervised learning.

In the next section, we'll dive deeper into specific algorithms for supervised learning, for both regression and classification. We'll explore their characteristics and how they can be used to predict continuous and categorical data respectively.

Characteristics of regression and classification algorithms

In this section, we'll explore the characteristics of a range of different regression and classification algorithms. We will explore their practical applications and how they can be used to drive decision-making in various industries.

Regression algorithms

We have already covered regression, which is a form of supervised machine learning. Regression algorithms are used when the output or target variable is continuous or numerical. They are primarily used for forecasting, predicting trends, and determining relationships between variables. Beyond the ordinary least squares regression we have already covered, there are other, more advanced variations of regression. These variations can be used to account for different interactions between variables, or to mitigate overfitting by applying what is known as **regularization**.

Polynomial regression

Polynomial regression extends linear regression by adding extra predictors, obtained by raising each of the original predictors to a power – for example, x^2 or x^3. This provides a broader range of functions to fit the data.

In market research, polynomial regression can capture non-linear relationships between input variables and sales. For example, it might reveal that sales increase with advertising spend up to a certain point, but then level off or decline past that threshold, helping inform optimal budget allocation.

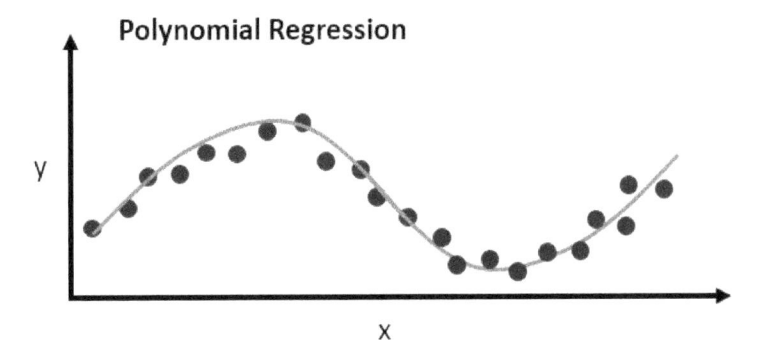

Figure 7.1: Polynomial regression

Take, for example, this chart of polynomial regression, which has been fit to a set of data points. Remember that with ordinary least squares regression, we could only fit a linear, straight-line relationship between the points. However, polynomial regression allows us to model a more complex relationship between the variables, which may not be a straightforward, linear relationship, as in the previous example.

Ridge regression

Often within regression, we have many input variables to consider, which can lead to problems such as overfitting or what is known as **multicollinearity**, where the input variables are correlated with one another. This can lead to less reliable inferences from our model.

To deal with this, there are different forms of "regularized" regression that add terms to our regression equation to help mitigate the aforementioned issues.

Ridge regression is a regularization method used to analyze multiple regression data that suffer from multicollinearity – when predictor variables are highly correlated. By adding a degree of bias to the regression estimates, ridge regression reduces the standard errors. This could be useful in retail, where one might want to understand the relationship between advertising spend and sales while considering multicollinearity between different advertising channels.

Lasso regression

Lasso (least absolute shrinkage and selection operator) regression is another regularization technique for linear regression that allows for the selection of variables in a regression model, such that not all the input variables have an effect on the outcome variable. This can reduce the likelihood of overfitting and is particularly useful when dealing with high-dimensional data. In the consumer goods industry, lasso regression can be used to predict demand based on various factors while avoiding overfitting.

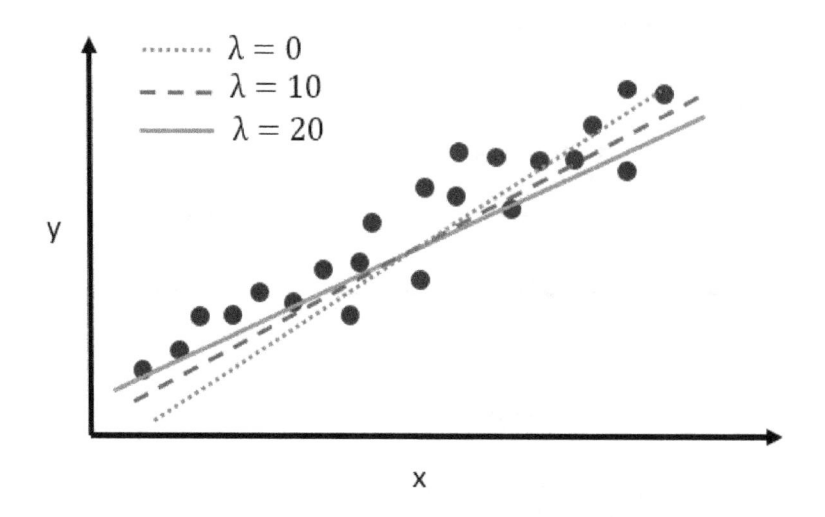

Figure 7.2: Regularized regression (e.g., ridge regression/lasso regression)

Classification algorithms

Classification algorithms are used when the output or target variable is categorical or discrete. They are mainly used for categorizing data into specific groups.

SVM

An SVM is a powerful classification algorithm that seeks the best hyperplane separating different classes. It's particularly effective in high-dimensional spaces and situations where the number of dimensions exceeds the number of samples. In marketing, SVM can be used to segment customers into different groups for targeted advertising.

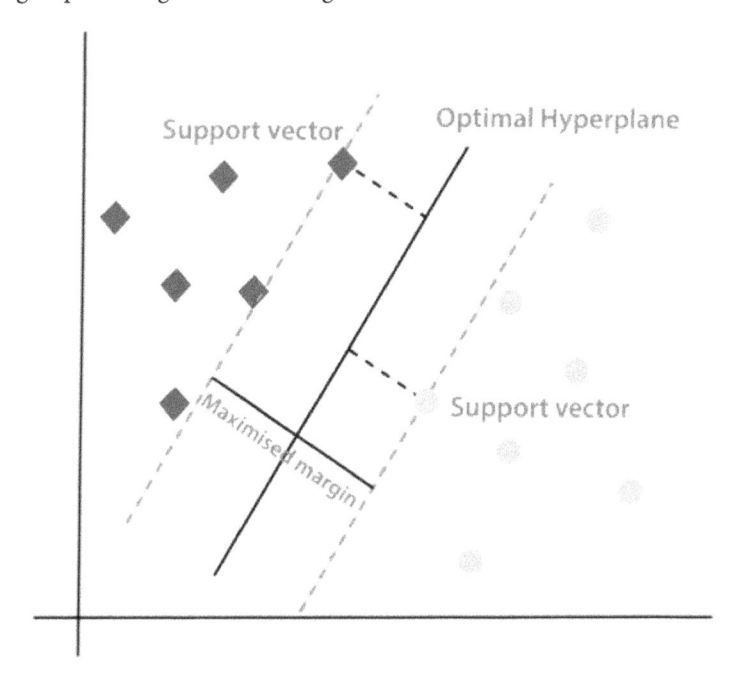

Figure 7.3: SVM

k-NN

k-NN is a simple, easy-to-understand algorithm that classifies a data point based on how its neighbors are classified. It's widely used in preliminary studies to gain insights from the data. For example, in retail, k-NN can be used to predict whether a customer will make a purchase based on the behavior of similar customers.

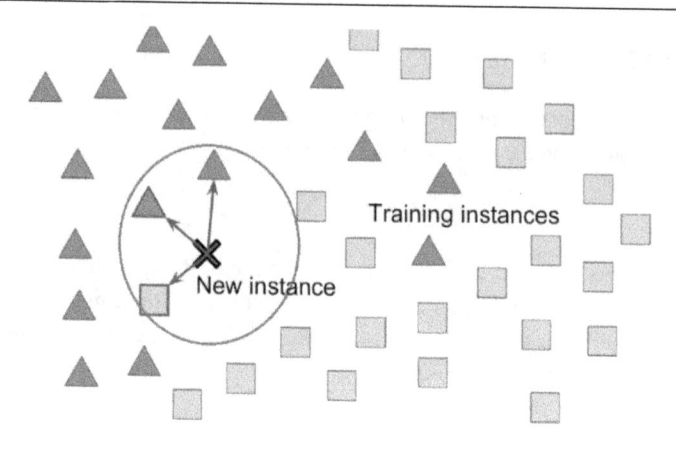

Figure 7.4: k-NN

Decision trees and random forests

Decision trees split the data into multiple sets based on certain conditional control statements. They are easy to understand and interpret, making them useful for exploratory research. Random forests, an ensemble of decision trees, can improve prediction accuracy. In the consumer goods industry, these algorithms can be used to predict whether a new product will be successful based on features such as price, marketing spend, and competition.

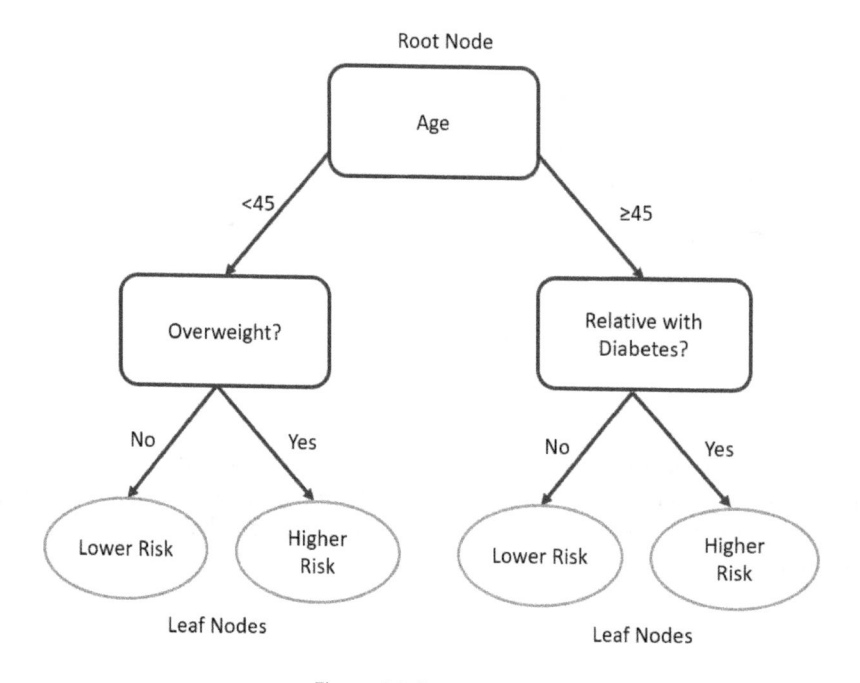

Figure 7.5: Decision tree

Take, for example, a decision tree that has been fitted to data to predict whether a patient is at higher risk or lower risk of type 2 diabetes. We can see that a decision tree can split the population on the variables it has been trained on, including variables such as age (are they older or younger than 45?), as well as whether they are overweight or have a relative with type 2 diabetes. This is a simple example but illustrates how you can go down a decision tree to predict an outcome.

Key considerations in supervised learning

While applying these algorithms, it's important to consider factors such as the bias-variance trade-off, the amount of training data, the dimensionality of the input space, and noise in the target values. Striking a balance between bias and variance ensures that your model is neither too simple (underfitting) nor too complex (overfitting). Having sufficient training data, managing high-dimensional input spaces, and dealing with noise in target values are also crucial to building robust models.

Evaluation metrics

Evaluation metrics play a vital role in assessing the performance of supervised learning models. While the previous chapter introduced some common metrics, let's now explore their specific applications in supervised learning:

- **Regression metrics**:

  - **MAE**: MAE measures the average absolute difference between the predicted and actual values. It provides a clear interpretation of the model's average prediction error in the same units as the target variable.

  - **MSE**: MSE calculates the average squared difference between the predicted and actual values. It emphasizes larger errors and is sensitive to outliers. Taking the square root of MSE gives the RMSE, which is in the same units as the target variable.

  - **R-squared**: R-squared represents the proportion of variance in the target variable that is predictable from the input features. It ranges from 0 to 1, with higher values indicating a better fit of the model to the data.

- **Classification metrics**:

  - **Accuracy**: Accuracy measures the proportion of correct predictions out of the total predictions made. It is a simple and intuitive metric but can be misleading when dealing with imbalanced classes.

  - **Precision**: Precision represents the proportion of true positive predictions out of all positive predictions made by the model. It focuses on the model's ability to avoid false positives.

  - **Recall (sensitivity)**: Recall measures the proportion of true positive predictions out of all actual positive instances. It emphasizes the model's ability to identify positive instances correctly.

- **F1 score**: The F1 score is the harmonic mean of precision and recall. It provides a balanced measure of the model's performance, especially when dealing with imbalanced classes.
- **Area under the ROC (AUC-ROC)**: AUC-ROC evaluates the model's ability to discriminate between classes across different probability thresholds. It is particularly useful when the decision threshold needs to be adjusted based on the specific problem requirements.

By understanding and applying these evaluation metrics, businesses can gain valuable insights into the performance of their supervised learning models, identify areas for improvement, and make informed decisions based on the models' predictions.

Applications of supervised learning

Supervised learning has found its place in numerous industries. It enables many businesses to predict future outcomes based on historical data. Let's explore some more practical examples of how supervised learning algorithms are applied in different industries.

Consumer goods

In the consumer goods industry, supervised learning is being leveraged for various applications:

- **Consumer trend identification**: By analyzing data from eCommerce platforms, social media, search engines, sales, and surveys, companies can identify emerging consumer trends – for example, trending product categories, ingredients, flavors, and claims that are predicted to see future growth. This helps in developing new products or making changes to existing ones that align with consumer preferences, potentially leading to increased revenue.
- **Price optimization**: By considering factors such as historical sales data, competitor pricing, and marketing initiatives, companies can determine the optimal price for their products to maximize profitability.

Retail

In the retail industry, supervised learning is transforming various aspects of the business:

- **Product recommendations**: By analyzing customers' purchase histories and product similarities, retailers can recommend products that are likely to interest specific customers, potentially increasing sales and customer loyalty.
- **Customer feedback classification**: By categorizing customer feedback from various sources such as call centers, social media, and website forms, retailers can identify common issues and concerns. This information can be used to prioritize customer service efforts and address areas that need improvement.

- **Demand forecasting**: By analyzing historical sales data, retailers can predict future demand for products. This helps in optimizing inventory management, reducing stockouts or overstocking, and improving overall operational efficiency.
- **Workforce optimization**: By forecasting customer traffic and sales patterns, retailers can optimize staff scheduling to ensure adequate coverage during peak hours while minimizing labor costs during slower periods.

Manufacturing

Supervised learning is transforming the manufacturing industry in several ways:

- **Predictive maintenance**: By analyzing sensor data from equipment, supervised learning algorithms can predict when a machine is likely to fail, allowing for proactive maintenance and minimizing downtime
- **Quality control**: By analyzing product data and identifying patterns, supervised learning can help detect defects or anomalies in the manufacturing process, ensuring higher product quality and reducing waste

These are just a few examples of how supervised learning is being applied across a few major industries to drive business value.

Think about potential use cases for supervised machine learning within the industries you are interested in. Are there existing, common use cases for supervised machine learning that other companies in your industry have successfully applied?

When evaluating potential use cases within your organization, it's important to have a clear understanding of the expected benefits and costs associated with implementation. With a well-defined value proposition, supervised learning can help transform various aspects of these industries and contribute to successful outcomes.

Source: `https://www.qualifai.co.uk/post/ai-use-cases-in-consumer-goods-retail`

Summary

In this chapter, we've explored the applications of supervised learning in various industries, walked through the steps involved in supervised learning, discussed important considerations, and touched on different algorithms and evaluation metrics.

With this knowledge, you're now equipped to harness the power of supervised learning in your business.

But remember, the journey doesn't end here. In the next chapter, we'll delve into unsupervised learning – another exciting domain of machine learning.

8

Unsupervised Machine Learning

Unlike the more familiar terrain of **supervised learning** (**SL**), where data comes neatly labeled and the learning path is predefined, **unsupervised learning** (**UL**) ventures into the territory of unlabeled data, offering an opportunity to uncover hidden patterns and insights.

This chapter delves into the field of UL, where we will learn about some practical examples of UL, the key steps involved in UL, and techniques around clustering, anomaly detection, dimensionality reduction, and association rule learning.

This chapter covers the following topics:

- Defining UL
- Steps in UL
- Clustering – unveiling hidden patterns in your data
- Association rule learning
- Applications of UL

Defining UL

UL is a type of **machine learning** (**ML**) that finds patterns in data without any prior training. Distinct from its counterpart, SL, where the model is trained using labeled data, UL algorithms work with unlabeled data. The aim is to model the underlying structure or distribution in the data to learn more about it.

Think of it as a detective who walks into a crime scene with no initial clues or suspects. The detective's job is to uncover patterns, find hidden groups, or establish relationships between different elements at the scene.

Practical examples of UL

To make this concept more tangible, let's look at some practical examples:

- **Market research**: A company wants to understand its customer base better and tailor their marketing to different consumer segments. They have a wealth of data (for example, customer data or consumer survey data) but no specific categories or labels. UL can help identify distinct groups or segments within their customers. The company can then better understand the demographics, behaviors, and opinions of these different segments, leading to more targeted marketing strategies.

- **Consumer goods and retail**: An e-commerce store wants to understand the buying behavior of its customers. Using UL, they can discover associations between different products. For instance, they might find that customers who buy a certain brand of remote control also buy a certain battery type and pack size, enabling the e-commerce store to automatically recommend items the consumer is likely to add to their order.

- **Supplier performance analysis**: By clustering suppliers based on performance metrics such as delivery time, quality of goods, cost, customer support, and reliability, companies can gain insights into their supply chain's strengths and weaknesses. This aids in making informed decisions about which suppliers to prioritize or re-evaluate.

UL is a powerful tool that can uncover hidden patterns and associations in your data. It's like having a detective on your team who can make sense of seemingly unrelated information. Whether you're looking to understand your customers better, optimize your marketing strategies, or discover new opportunities, UL can provide valuable insights.

Now that we've established a solid understanding of what UL is, let's dive deeper into the process. In the next section, we'll explore the steps involved in UL, from data collection to interpretation.

Steps in UL

UL is a type of ML that allows us to draw inferences from datasets consisting of input data without labeled responses. Unlike SL, where we have a clear target or outcome to predict, UL is more about discovering hidden patterns and structures within data. But how does this process work? Let's break it down into digestible steps:

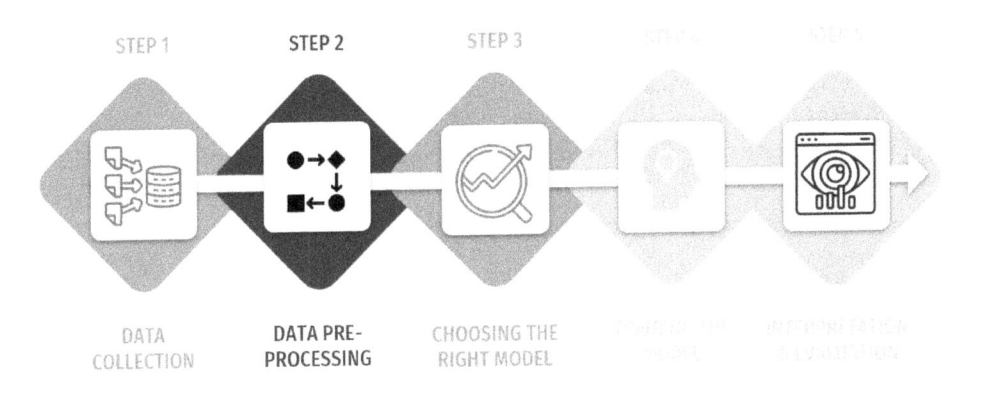

Figure 8.1: Steps involved in unsupervised ML (UML)

> **Note**
> While the diagram presents a linear flow, in practice, these steps may not always follow a strict linear sequence. Throughout the process, insights gained about the data, such as during evaluation, may inform iterations and refinements in data processing or model selection.

Step 1 – Data collection

Just as with any other ML project, UL begins with data collection. This could be customer data for a retail company, patient data for a healthcare organization, or user behavior data for a tech firm. The key here is to gather as much relevant data as possible to help the model learn and make accurate predictions.

Step 2 – Data preprocessing

Once the data is collected, it needs to be cleaned and preprocessed. This step involves handling missing values, removing outliers, and normalizing the data. This step is important as the quality of data impacts the ability of the model to learn effectively.

Step 3 – Choosing the right model

After preprocessing, the next step is to choose the right model for your data. There are various UL algorithms, such as k-means clustering, hierarchical clustering, and **Density-Based Spatial Clustering of Applications with Noise** (**DBSCAN**). The choice of model depends on the problem at hand and the nature of your data.

Step 4 – Training the model

Now comes the exciting part – training the model. Here, the model learns to identify patterns and structures within the data without any supervision. For instance, in a market research context, a UL model could identify distinct segments within your customer base based on purchasing behavior.

Step 5 – Interpretation and evaluation

The final step involves interpreting the results and evaluating the model's performance. As with SL, the unsupervised model performance can be evaluated with evaluation metrics. In UL, evaluation metrics can be a bit tricky as we don't have a clear target to compare our predictions with. However, metrics such as Silhouette Score or the **Davies-Bouldin Index (DBI)** can be used to evaluate the quality of clustering.

In a business context, interpretation is equally important. For example, in a retail setting, understanding the characteristics of different customer segments can help tailor marketing strategies to each segment, ultimately leading to increased sales and customer satisfaction.

In summary

By now, you should have an understanding of the steps involved in UL and how it can be applied in a business context. But we're just scratching the surface here. Next, we'll dive deeper into one of the most common techniques in UL – clustering. Stay tuned!

In the next section, we will delve into the world of clustering algorithms, exploring how they work, their applications, and how they can be used to drive decision-making in business.

Clustering – unveiling hidden patterns in your data

Clustering is a powerful tool in the UL toolkit. But what is it, and how can it help decision-makers in business? Let's dive in.

What is clustering?

Clustering is a method of UL that involves grouping data points together based on their similarity. Unlike SL, where we have a clear target or outcome variable, UL (and, by extension, clustering) is all about finding hidden structures and patterns in data without any predefined labels.

Think of clustering as a way to discover and explore unknown territories in your data. It's like an explorer setting out on a journey without a map, using only their observations to make sense of the landscape.

How does clustering work?

The process of clustering involves several steps:

1. **Feature selection**

    In this step, you choose the characteristics or attributes of your data that you believe can help differentiate between different groups. For example, if you're clustering customers, you might select features such as age, income, and purchase history.

2. **Distance measurement**

    - To group similar data points together, you need to define what "similar" means. This is done by measuring the "distance" or "dissimilarity" between data points.

    - One common distance measure is Euclidean distance, which is the straight-line distance between two points. You can imagine this as the distance "as the crow flies," whereas other distance measures, such as Manhattan distance or cosine similarity, consider different aspects of the data. The cosine distance is the cosine of the angle between two points.

3. **Clustering algorithm**

    - Once you have your features and distance measures, you apply a clustering algorithm to group similar data points together.

    - Different algorithms make different assumptions about the structure of the clusters. Here are some examples:

        * k-means tries to partition n observations into k clusters where each observation belongs to the cluster with the nearest mean.

        * Hierarchical clustering builds a hierarchy of clusters, either from individual elements by merging clusters (agglomerative approach) or from the entire dataset by dividing the dataset into smaller clusters (divisive approach).

        * DBSCAN groups together points that are closely packed together and marks points that are in low-density regions as outliers.

4. **Evaluation**

    - After clustering, you need to evaluate the quality of your clusters. This helps determine if your clustering makes sense and is useful for your problem.

    - Metrics such as Silhouette Score measure how similar an object is to its own cluster compared to other clusters. A high silhouette score indicates that the object is well matched to its own cluster and poorly matched to neighboring clusters.

    - The **Dunn Index** (**DI**) is another metric that measures the ratio between the minimal inter-cluster distance and the maximal intra-cluster distance. A higher DI indicates better clustering.

Remember – clustering is an exploratory technique. It can help uncover patterns and structures in your data that you might not have known about beforehand. Experiment with different features, distance measures, and algorithms to see what insights you can uncover in your data.

k-means clustering

Here is an example of one clustering algorithm called k-means:

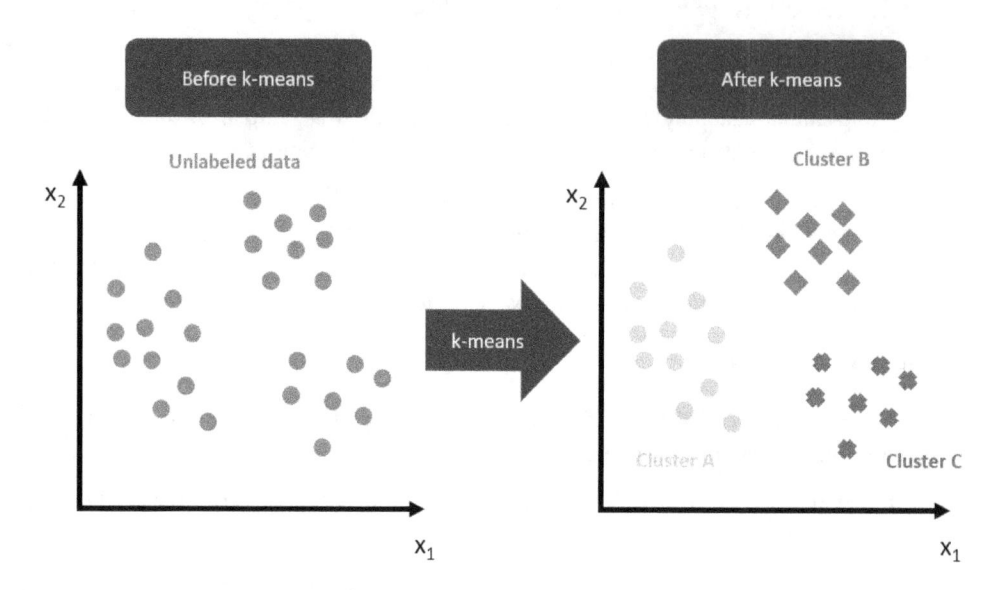

Figure 8.2: k-means clustering

In the preceding diagram, let's look at each side before and after the k-means process.

Before k-means (left side):

On this side, before we carry out k-means, the data points are scattered across the two-dimensional space defined by axes x_1 and x_2. These could be variables such as, say, the total spend (x_1) and the number of visits (x_2) of customers at a store.

At this stage, the data is unlabeled, meaning we don't yet know which cluster each data point belongs to.

After k-means (right side):

After k-means, the data points have been grouped into clusters based on their proximity to one another. These clusters can be informative about underlying patterns within the data.

The k-means clustering process

To carry out k-means, we need to choose the number of clusters we want to identify in our data. Let's say we have visualized the data and decided that *k*=3, meaning we want to find three clusters.

The k-means algorithm follows these steps:

1. **Initialization**: Randomly select *k* points from the data as the initial centroids (the center of each cluster).
2. **Assignment step**: Assign each data point to the nearest centroid based on the distance between the point and the centroid.
3. **Update step**: Recalculate the centroid of each cluster by taking the mean of all points assigned to that cluster.
4. Repeat *steps 2* and *3* until the centroids no longer move significantly or a maximum number of iterations is reached. This indicates that the clusters have stabilized.

After applying the k-means algorithm, the data points are colored differently based on the cluster they belong to. In this case, three clusters have been identified: Cluster A, Cluster B, and Cluster C.

The k-means algorithm is widely used because it's relatively simple and efficient. However, it assumes that clusters are spherical and evenly sized, which might not always be the case in real-world data. Additionally, the number of clusters k needs to be specified beforehand, which can be a drawback if the optimal number of clusters is not known. Despite these limitations, k-means remains a powerful tool for **exploratory data analysis** (**EDA**) and pattern recognition in various fields, which we will explore in this next section.

Practical applications of clustering

Clustering has a wide range of applications across various industries:

- **Risk assessment in insurance**: In the insurance industry, clustering algorithms can be used to group policyholders based on various risk factors. For instance, clustering can identify groups of individuals with similar driving habits in auto insurance or health profiles in life insurance. This segmentation allows insurance companies to tailor their policies and pricing more accurately according to the risk levels, leading to more efficient risk management and pricing strategies.
- **Energy consumption analysis in utilities**: Utility companies can use clustering to analyze energy usage patterns of their customers. By grouping customers into clusters based on their consumption patterns, peak usage times, and seasonal variations, utilities can better understand demand, plan energy distribution, and even design customized energy-saving programs. This can also help in identifying areas where infrastructure improvements are needed or where energy conservation measures can be most effective.

- **Content personalization in digital media**: In the digital media and entertainment industry, clustering is used to analyze user preferences and viewing habits. By clustering users based on their interactions with different content types (such as genres of movies, music, or articles), media companies can provide personalized content recommendations. This not only enhances user experience but also increases engagement and, potentially, subscription retention.

Evaluation metrics for clustering

As decision-makers, it's important to understand how well your clustering model is performing. Here are a few metrics to consider:

- **Silhouette Score:** The Silhouette Score metric is a way to quantify how well data is grouped into clusters. It ranges from -1 to 1. A score close to 1 means that the data points are very similar to others in the same cluster but dissimilar to those in other clusters, which is ideal. Essentially, it's a measure of how appropriately each data point belongs to its cluster: the higher the score, the better each data point fits within its own cluster as opposed to others. This score helps to validate consistency within clusters of data and can be used to determine the optimal number of clusters by comparing scores across different numbers of clusters.

- **DI**: DI is a more nuanced gauge of clustering quality that considers both the compactness of clusters and the separation between them. It does this by examining the smallest distance between points in different clusters and the largest distance between points within the same cluster. A higher DI indicates that the clusters are compact (with data points closely bunched together) and well separated (with each cluster being a good distance away from the others). This index is especially useful when you want to ensure that clusters are distinct from each other while also being internally coherent.

Remember – the choice of metric should align with your business objectives. For instance, if your goal is to create highly distinct customer segments for targeted marketing, a high silhouette score would be desirable.

In summary

Clustering is a powerful UL technique that can reveal hidden patterns and structures in your data. By understanding its process and applications, you can harness its power to make more informed business decisions.

In the next section, we'll explore another key UL technique: association rule learning. This method can help you discover interesting relations between variables in large datasets – an important skill for any data-savvy decision-maker.

Association rule learning

Imagine you're at a supermarket, and you notice that people who buy diapers often also buy beer. This is not a random observation but a result of a powerful UL technique called association rule learning. It uncovers hidden patterns in large datasets, enabling businesses to make data-driven decisions.

What is association rule learning?

Association rule learning is an ML method that identifies frequent if-then associations called "rules" among a set of items. It's like finding relationships between products often grouped together. These rules can be leveraged to predict future behavior, enabling businesses to strategize their marketing efforts effectively.

The Apriori algorithm – a practical example

One of the most popular algorithms used in association rule learning is the Apriori algorithm. Let's break down how it works with a practical example.

Suppose you're a decision-maker at a retail store. You want to understand the buying patterns of your customers to optimize product placement and boost sales. Here's how you can use the Apriori algorithm:

1. **Set a minimum support and confidence**

   These are two key metrics in the Apriori algorithm. **Support** measures the frequency of an item set in all transactions, while **confidence** measures the likelihood that item Y is purchased when item X is purchased.

2. **Generate item sets**

   The algorithm will start by creating a list of all individual items (item sets) that meet the minimum support threshold.

3. **Create rules**

   For each item set, the algorithm will generate rules that meet the minimum confidence threshold.

4. **Rank rules**

   The rules are then ranked by their lift, another metric that measures how much more likely item Y is purchased when item X is purchased, compared to purchasing item Y alone.

By following these steps, you might discover rules such as {Diapers} -> {Beer}, indicating that customers who buy diapers are likely to buy beer as well. This insight can be used to strategically place products in your store to increase sales.

Evaluation metrics

In association rule learning, the key evaluation metrics are support, confidence, and lift. These metrics help in identifying the most relevant rules. However, it's important to strike a balance. High support may lead to obvious rules, while high confidence may lead to overly specific rules. Lift, on the other hand, provides a balance by measuring the strength of a rule over the random occurrence of item sets.

In summary

Association rule learning is a powerful tool in the UL toolkit. It uncovers hidden patterns in large datasets, enabling businesses to make strategic decisions. Whether you're in retail, marketing, or any industry dealing with large datasets, association rule learning can provide valuable insights.

In the next section, *Applications of UL*, we'll explore more applications of UL, diving deeper into how these techniques can be leveraged across various business scenarios.

Applications of UL

UL, as we've discussed, is a type of ML that identifies patterns in data without the need for explicit supervision. It's like a detective who arrives at a crime scene with no witnesses but must still piece together the story from the available evidence. But where does this kind of "detective work" find its application in the business world? Let's explore.

Market segmentation

One of the most common applications of UL is in market segmentation. Businesses with a diverse customer base use clustering algorithms to group customers based on their behavior, demographics, and purchase history. This allows them to tailor their marketing strategies to each group, maximizing engagement and conversion rates.

Consider a global retail brand with millions of customers. They could use UL to segment their customers into groups, such as "young professionals," "parents," or "retirees," each with distinct shopping habits and preferences. The company could then create personalized marketing campaigns for each segment, increasing customer satisfaction and loyalty.

Anomaly detection

UL is also excellent at detecting anomalies or outliers in data. This is particularly useful in industries such as finance and cybersecurity, where identifying unusual patterns can prevent fraud or security breaches.

For instance, a bank could use UL to monitor transactions and flag any that deviate significantly from a customer's usual behavior, as shown in the following simple diagram. UL algorithms can identify anomalies by measuring the distance of a data point from the centroid of its assigned cluster. Data points that are far away from their cluster centroid are considered anomalies. This could indicate fraudulent activity, prompting the bank to take preventive measures:

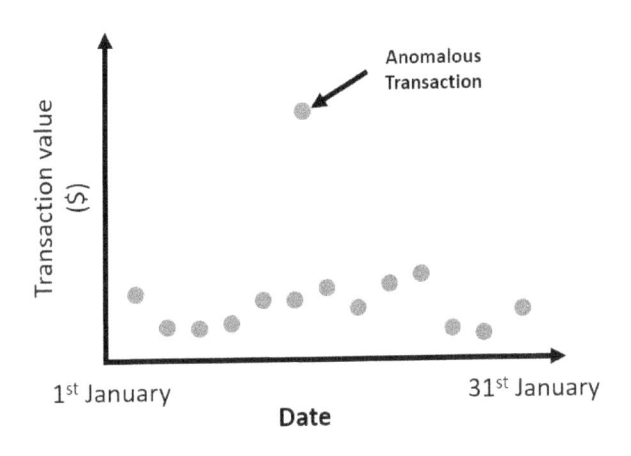

Figure 8.3: Anomaly detection for financial transactions

Feature extraction

UL can also be used for feature extraction, which simplifies complex datasets by reducing their dimensionality. This can make other ML tasks more efficient and accurate.

For example, a car manufacturer might have data on hundreds of features for each vehicle. UL could identify the most important features that affect a car's performance or popularity, allowing the manufacturer to focus on these in their design and marketing efforts.

Summary

We have learned that UL is a versatile tool that can uncover hidden insights from data and applies to many business use cases, such as market segmentation, anomaly detection, and feature extraction.

By grasping the capabilities of UL, decision-makers can harness it to uncover valuable insights, streamline processes, and make data-driven decisions that impact the bottom line.

Throughout this chapter, we've covered the fundamental concepts of UL, outlined its key steps, and explored some of its most prevalent real-world applications. We've also discussed methods for evaluating the performance of UL models in a business setting.

Building on this foundational knowledge of ML, the next chapter will take a closer look at strategies for interpreting and assessing ML models, equipping you with the tools needed to effectively communicate insights and justify decisions based on your ML projects.

9
Interpreting and Evaluating Machine Learning Models

The promise and potential of machine learning systems to create systems that can make decisions without the need for hardcoded rules or heuristics is huge. However, this promise is often far from straightforward to fulfil, and in developing machine learning models or leading teams who develop machine learning models, great care needs to be taken to ensure their accuracy and reliability.

In this chapter, we will explore how to interpret and evaluate different machine learning models.

This is one of, if not the most important skill you can have in your toolkit as a decision-maker working on data science projects.

While it can be convenient to allow data scientists to evaluate their own models and "mark their own homework," this is a risky decision to make and will, invariably, eventually lead to problems.

This chapter covers the following topics:

- How do I know whether this model will be accurate?
- Understanding evaluation metrics
- Evaluating classification models
- Methods for explaining machine learning models

How do I know whether this model will be accurate?

As decision-makers, you need to be confident that the machine learning models you're using provide you with reliable, accurate predictions or insights. However, how can you be sure? What metrics should you use to evaluate your models? And what do these metrics really mean?

Let's attempt to understand how metrics are used to evaluate machine learning models and look at some common examples.

Evaluating on test (holdout) data

Before we get into the specifics around the different types of evaluation metrics, first, you need to understand the importance of evaluating on test (a.k.a. holdout) data.

One very important aspect of model evaluation is the use of holdout (or test) data. This is a subset of your data that the model hasn't seen during training or validation. Evaluating your model on holdout data gives you a more realistic estimate of its performance in the real world.

This test data should follow the same distribution of data that the model would see in the real world once it is in production. It should not be used in the training process or even for tuning different model hyperparameters, and care should be taken such that data do not leak between the training and test sets or between the independent variables and dependent (outcome) variables.

It is only with a good set of test data that you can accurately evaluate a model and gain some confidence in its performance once it goes live in the real world.

Understanding evaluation metrics

In machine learning, an evaluation metric is a measure used to quantify the quality of a model's predictions.

If understood and interpreted correctly, they can provide you with a measure with which to evaluate the quality of a model and, therefore, make more informed decisions about its use or whether more work is needed to train a more accurate model.

There is a wide range of evaluation metrics within machine learning, and different types of machine learning models require different evaluation metrics.

When considering supervised machine learning, which we covered in *Chapter 7*, there are two groups of models: regression models and classification models, each with its own set of evaluation metrics.

First, let's look at some of the more common metrics used for evaluating regression models.

Evaluating regression models

Imagine you're a retail executive trying to forecast the next quarter's sales. You've built a regression model for this purpose. However, how can you assess its accuracy so that you can have some confidence in the next quarter's sales projections?

Three common metrics for evaluating regression models are R-squared, **root mean squared error (RMSE)**, and **mean absolute error (MAE)**. Let's discuss each in turn.

R-squared

The R-squared metric, also known as the coefficient of determination, is a statistical measure in regression analysis that represents the proportion of the variance in the dependent variable that is **explained** by the model. In simpler terms, it's a measure of how well the regression predictions approximate the real data points.

R-squared formula

The formula for R-squared can be seen in the following:

$$R^2 = 1 - \frac{SS_{res}}{SS_{tot}}$$

where we see the following denotations:

- SS_{res} is the sum of the squares of the residuals, also known as the residual sum of squares. It measures the variability of the model's errors.
- SS_{tot} is the total sum of the squares. It measures the total variability of the dependent variable.

The sums of the squares are calculated as follows:

- $SS_{res} = \Sigma(y_i - \hat{y}_i)^2$
- $SS_{tot} = \Sigma(y_i - \bar{y})^2$

In these formulas, we denote the following:

- y_i is the actual observed value
- $\hat{y}_i$ is the predicted value by the regression model
- $\bar{y}$ is the mean of the observed data

Understanding R-squared

An R-squared of 1 indicates that the regression predictions perfectly fit the data.

An R-squared of 0 means that the model does not explain any of the variability of the response data around its mean.

Example of an R-squared calculation

Imagine you work for a retailer and that you have a dataset of monthly sales volumes for one of your top products, as well as the predictions of those sales volumes from a regression model covering the past 6-months:

Observed Data (y): [725, 693, 654, 712, 722, 695]

Predicted Data ($\hat{y}$) : [720, 695, 660, 715, 724, 698]

First, calculate the mean of the observed data ($\bar{y}$):

$$\bar{y} = \frac{725 + 693 + 654 + 712 + 722 + 695}{6} = 700.17$$

Next, calculate SS_{res} and SS_{tot}:

$SS_{res} = (725 - 720)^2 + (693 - 695)^2 + (654 - 660)^2 + (712 - 715)^2 + (722 - 724)^2 + (695 - 698)^2 = 87$

$SS_{tot} = (725 - \bar{y})^2 + (693 - \bar{y})^2 + (654 - \bar{y})^2 + (712 - \bar{y})^2 + (722 - \bar{y})^2 + (695 - \bar{y})^2 = 3442.8$

$R^2 = 1 - \frac{87}{3442.8} = 0.97$

So, in this case, our R-squared value is approximately 0.97, indicating that the regression model can explain 97% of the observed data. This is a high value, suggesting that the model provides a very good fit for the data (this could be due to overfitting, which we will cover in a later chapter).

When interpreting R-squared values, there is no universal benchmark for a "good" R-square value, but understanding that the closer the value is to 1, the better the model is at explaining the data can help when comparing different models.

Two evaluation metrics that can be clearer to interpret are **RMSE** and **RAE**, which we will look into now.

Root mean squared error

RMSE is a widely used metric in regression analysis that measures the average magnitude of the errors between the values predicted by a model and the values observed. It gives an estimate of the standard deviation of the prediction errors.

Unlike R-squared, which is a relative measure of fit, RMSE provides an absolute scale of measurement, giving a direct interpretation of the model's prediction accuracy in the units of the variable of interest. It's particularly useful in evaluating the precision of prediction models and is sensitive to large errors, making it a useful tool for assessing model performance.

RMSE formula

The formula for calculating the RMSE is this:

$$\sqrt{\frac{1}{n} \sum_{i=1}^{n} (y_i - \hat{y}_i)^2}$$

where we see the following denotations:

- n is the number of observations
- y_i is the actual observed value
- $\hat{y}_i$ is the predicted value by the model

Understanding evaluation metrics 141

This formula effectively measures the square root of the average squared differences between the actual and predicted values, providing a clear measure of model accuracy.

Example of an RMSE calculation

By continuing with the retailer's dataset from the R-squared example, where the observed monthly sales volumes (y) are [725, 693, 654, 712, 722, 695] and the predicted sales volumes ($\hat{y}$) are [720, 695, 660, 715, 724, 698], we can calculate the RMSE as follows:

1. Calculate the squared differences between the actual and predicted values.
2. Compute the average of these squared differences.
3. Take the square root of this average to find the RMSE.

Let's calculate the RMSE for this dataset. We know from the R-squared calculation that the sum of squared differences between the actual and predicted values is this:

$$SS_{res} = \Sigma(y_i - \hat{y}_i)^2 = 87$$

In addition, we know the number of observations is $n = 6$ (i.e., 6 months).

By plugging these numbers into our RMSE equation, we find the following:

$$RMSE = \sqrt{\frac{1}{n}\sum_{i=1}^{n}(y_i - \hat{y}_i)^2} = \sqrt{\frac{1}{6}*87} = 3.8$$

Understanding RMSE values

The RMSE value gives insight into the average error in the same units as the response variable, making it intuitively easier to understand. A lower RMSE value indicates a better fit of the model to the data.

However, like R-squared, there's no absolute "good" or "bad" threshold for RMSE, as it depends on the context of the data and the specific domain of its application. It's best used comparatively to assess improvements in model accuracy or to compare performance across different models or datasets.

In our example, the RMSE for the given dataset is approximately 3.8. This indicates that, on average, the model's predictions are within 3.8 units of the actual sales figures. This appears to be a very accurate set of predictions, but the context of the business needs and how this may compare to other models helps us understand the evaluation accuracy in context.

Practical tips for interpreting RMSE

The following are some practical tips for interpreting RMSE:

- **Comparative analysis**: Use RMSE to compare model performance, especially when tweaking models or choosing between different types of models.

- **Unit sensitivity**: Remember that RMSE is sensitive to the scale of the data, so interpret it in the context of the magnitude of your dependent variable.
- **Complement with other metrics**: Combine RMSE with other metrics, such as R-squared, to get a more holistic view of model performance. While RMSE provides a measure of accuracy in the response variable's units, R-squared offers insight into the variance explained by the model.

Now, let's consider one other evaluation metric for regression models: MAE.

Mean absolute error

MAE is a measure used in regression analysis to quantify the average magnitude of the errors between predicted values and observed actual outcomes without considering their direction. It calculates the average of the absolute differences between the predicted values and actual values, making it a simple yet clear metric for assessing model accuracy.

MAE formula

The formula for calculating MAE is the following:

$$MAE = \frac{1}{n}\sum_{i=1}^{n}|y_i - \hat{y}_i|$$

where, as we have seen before, the following applies:

- n is the number of observations
- y_i is the actual observed value
- $\hat{y}_i$ is the predicted value from the model

This formula emphasizes the absolute value of the errors, thereby treating all errors with equal weight, regardless of their direction.

Example of an MAE calculation

Continuing with the retailer example used for the R-squared and RMSE calculations, as an exercise, you can calculate the MAE using the observed sales volume data (y) and predicted data ($\hat{y}$) to understand (using a practical illustration) how MAE is determined.

A reminder that the absolute value of a difference is the positive magnitude of the difference. For example, the absolute value of $|5 - 10| = |-5| = 5$ and the absolute value of, for example, $|7 - 4| = |3| = 3$.

The MAE for the example sales volume data and predictions should be this:

$MAE = 3.5$

See if you can calculate this answer using the sales volume values and predictions provided previously.

Understanding MAE values

MAE provides an intuitive understanding of the average error magnitude. A lower MAE value indicates a model with better predictive accuracy. Unlike RMSE, MAE is not as sensitive to outliers, as it does not square the errors before averaging. This characteristic makes MAE particularly useful in scenarios where you want to avoid the disproportionate effect of large errors.

Practical tips for interpreting MAE

The following are some practical tips for interpreting MAE:

- **Error interpretation**: Use MAE to get a direct understanding of the average error in the same units as the data. This makes it particularly accessible for non-technical stakeholders.
- **Outlier sensitivity**: Consider the nature of your data and whether emphasizing or de-emphasizing outliers is important. MAE treats all errors equally, making it a robust measure against large individual errors.
- **Complementary metrics**: Just as with RMSE, it's advisable to use MAE alongside other metrics to get a fuller picture of model performance. MAE can be particularly informative when used in conjunction with RMSE, as the two metrics together can provide insights into the error distribution and the presence of outliers.

When and how to use each metric

Now that we have seen each of these regression metrics, it is worthwhile discussing when to use each and how they complement each other:

R-squared:

When to use it:

- It is ideal for assessing the explanatory power of the model
- It is useful for comparing the model's performance against a baseline model or other models on the same dataset

How to use it:

Higher values (closer to 1) indicate a better fit.

- Consider using it in conjunction with other metrics for a comprehensive model evaluation

RMSE:

When to use it:

- It is best for models where large errors are particularly undesirable
- It is suitable for comparing across models or model versions to gauge improvement in predictive accuracy

How to use it:

- Lower values indicate a more accurate model
- Use it as a primary metric for precision, but analyze a model alongside R-squared to understand both fit and accuracy

MAE:

When to use it:

- Use it when you require a straightforward metric that is easy to explain and understand
- Use it in scenarios where outliers are present but should not disproportionately impact the model's error metric

How to use it:

- Lower values are better, indicating tighter conformity of predictions to actual values
- Consider using MAE to complement RMSE for a nuanced view of error distribution and to assess the impact of outliers

Practical evaluation strategies

Here are some of the most popular strategies:

- **Balanced approach**: Utilize a combination of these metrics to get a holistic view of model performance. R-squared offers insights into how well the model explains the data. RMSE helps identify how large, on average, the errors are, with a penalty for larger errors. MAE provides a simple average error magnitude, which is useful for understanding the typical error size.
- **Contextual interpretation**: Always contextualize the metrics within your specific business or research objectives. A good metric value in one context might not be acceptable in another, depending on the precision required or the cost of errors.
- **Comparative analysis**: Use these metrics not just in isolation but also comparatively across different models or iterations of the same model. This can help with selecting the best model or refining a model to better meet objectives.

- **Error sensitivity**: Consider the nature of your prediction task and the consequences of errors. If large errors are more problematic, RMSE will be particularly informative. If consistent errors are of concern, regardless of their size, MAE will provide valuable insights.

Summarizing the evaluation of regression models

By leveraging R-squared, RMSE, and MAE thoughtfully, as a decision-maker, you can critically assess model performance beyond just a single dimension of accuracy or fit. This multi-metric approach enables a more nuanced understanding and evaluation of regression models, guiding the selection, development, and refinement of models to align with specific business goals.

Now that we have looked at evaluation metrics for regression models, let's now turn to classification models and how they can be evaluated.

Evaluating classification models

Imagine you are running a business with a large portfolio of customers, and you are trying to predict which customers are likely to stop using your service within the next year. This is a common binary classification model known as a customer churn model; many companies, whether banks, telecoms providers, insurance companies, or streaming services, can benefit from knowing which of their customers are most likely to churn so that they can take action to retain these customers.

You may have evaluated your customer churn model's predictions on a test (holdout) set, for example, for the previous year, where you know whether a customer did, indeed, leave or stay with the company.

> **Important note**
>
> For this example, let's refer to a customer who has churned as a "positive" outcome, as this is the outcome we are trying to predict (in this context, "positive" or "negative" does not have anything to do with the sentiment or favorability of the outcome).

There are four different types of outcomes you would observe when evaluating your model's predictions:

- **True positive**: A true positive would be when our model predicts that the customer churned, and the customer did, indeed, churn (i.e., a correct prediction).
- **False positive**: A false positive, also known as a Type I error, is when our model predicts that a customer churned; however, the actual outcome was that a customer did **not** churn.
- **True negative**: A true negative is when the model predicted that the customer did not churn, and the actual outcome is that the customer did not churn (i.e., another correct prediction).
- **False negative**: A false negative, also known as a Type II error, is when our model predicts that the customer did **not** churn; however, the actual outcome was that the customer did churn.

Each of these four types of results can help inform us how accurate the model (on the test set) is at predicting the different outcomes.

There are different evaluation metrics that we can use to calculate the counts of each of these outcomes, which we will see. A useful way to visualize classification results is with a confusion matrix:

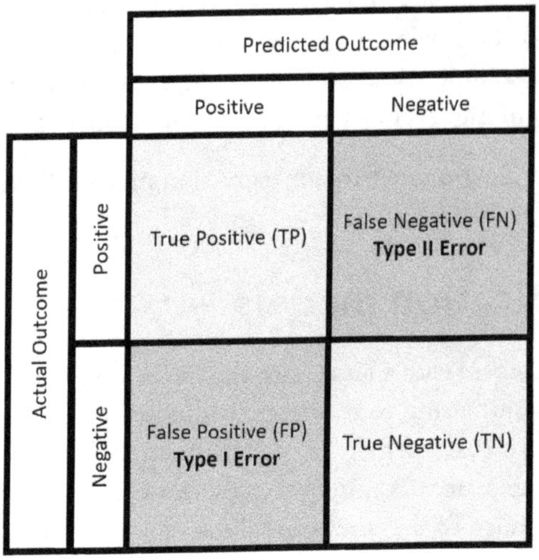

		Predicted Outcome	Predicted Outcome
		Positive	Negative
Actual Outcome	Positive	True Positive (TP)	False Negative (FN) **Type II Error**
Actual Outcome	Negative	False Positive (FP) **Type I Error**	True Negative (TN)

Figure 9.1: Confusion matrix for binary classification

To solidify our understanding of a confusion matrix, let's map the outcomes from our example onto a confusion matrix:

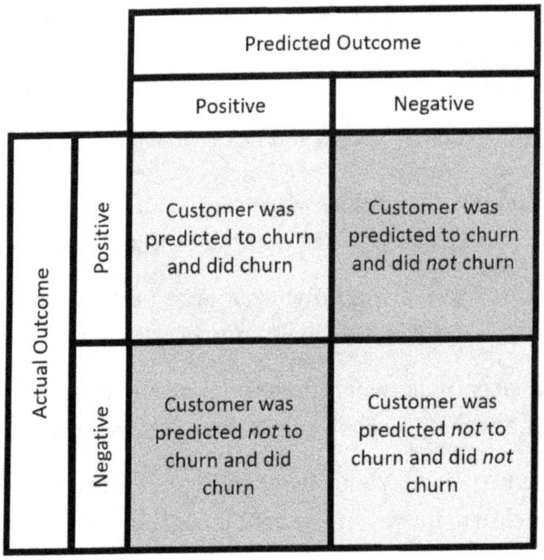

		Predicted Outcome	Predicted Outcome
		Positive	Negative
Actual Outcome	Positive	Customer was predicted to churn and did churn	Customer was predicted to churn and did *not* churn
Actual Outcome	Negative	Customer was predicted *not* to churn and did churn	Customer was predicted *not* to churn and did *not* churn

Figure 9.2: Confusion matrix for the binary classification of the customer churn example

From the counts of these different outcomes on a test (holdout) dataset, we can calculate useful evaluation metrics for a machine learning classification model.

Let's look into some of these metrics and how they can be interpreted to help us understand the predictive power of our models.

Classification model evaluation metrics

First, let's consider our example of the customer churn model. Let's say that on our test data, we predicted the outcome for 1,000 customers. Of these, 150 were predicted to churn, and they did, in fact, churn (true positives), and the 50 who we predicted to churn did not churn and stayed as customers (false positives). We also predicted that 600 customers would not churn, and they did not churn (true negatives). However, 200 customers who we predicted would not churn did churn (false negatives):

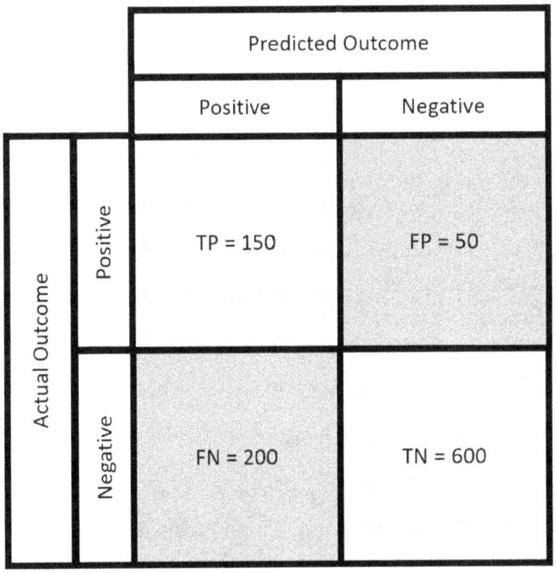

		Predicted Outcome	
		Positive	Negative
Actual Outcome	Positive	TP = 150	FP = 50
	Negative	FN = 200	TN = 600

Figure 9.3: Confusion matrix results for the binary classification of the customer churn example

From these values, we can calculate several useful metrics to help evaluate our model. Let's take a look at some of these evaluation metrics.

Precision, recall, and F1-Score

The first metric we will look at is precision.

Precision allows us to evaluate how **precisely** our model makes positive predictions.

More formally, precision is the ratio of true positive predictions to the **total** number of positive predictions made by the classification model.

It answers the question, Of all the instances labeled as positive by my model, how many are actually positive?

Precision calculation

The formula for calculating precision is given here:

$$Precision = \frac{True\ Positives\ (TP)}{True\ Positives\ (TP) + False\ Positives\ (FP)}$$

In our example, the precision would be calculated as follows:

$$Precision = \frac{150}{150 + 50} = 0.75$$

Precision can vary from 0 to 1, where precision of 1 implies that the model is perfectly precise at predicting the positive outcome (that the customer churns). Here, the precision suggests that when the model predicts that a customer will churn, then three out of four times, they will, in fact, churn.

Understanding precision

Precision focuses solely on the model's performance in accurately predicting the positive class. A high precision score indicates that the model is reliable in its positive classifications, meaning that when it predicts a positive result, you can be quite confident in its accuracy. However, precision does not take into account the false negatives (instances that are positive but predicted as negative) that are covered by another metric, such as recall, which we will discuss.

When to use precision

Here are some examples of when best to use precision:

- **High cost of false positives**: Precision is particularly useful when the cost of a false positive is high. For example, in email spam detection, a high precision is required because classifying an important email as spam (a false positive) could mean missing critical information.

- **Imbalanced datasets**: In datasets where the positive class is rare (imbalanced datasets), precision becomes a crucial measure to ensure that the positive predictions made by the model are, indeed, correct.

Precision is a key metric in classification that helps assess the reliability of the positive predictions made by a model, making it very useful in contexts where false positives have significant consequences.

Recall

Recall, also known as sensitivity or the true positive rate, is a critical performance metric used in classification tasks to evaluate the ability of a model to correctly identify all relevant instances of a particular class. It is especially important in situations where the cost of missing a positive instance (false negative) is high.

Here's a detailed explanation:

Recall measures the proportion of actual positive cases that were correctly identified by the model. It addresses the question, Of all the actual positives in the dataset, how many were correctly identified as positive by the model?

Formula for recall

The formula for calculating recall is given here:

$$Recall = \frac{True\ Positives\ (TP)}{True\ Positives\ (TP) + False\ Negatives\ (FN)}$$

In our example, recall would be calculated according to the following:

$$Recall = \frac{150}{150 + 200} \approx 0.43$$

This suggests that our model correctly identifies less than half of the customers who churned.

Understanding recall

Recall focuses on the model's capability to find all the relevant cases within a dataset. A high recall score indicates that the model is effective at capturing the majority of positive instances, minimizing the number of false negatives. However, it does not account for the correctness of negative predictions, which is covered by specificity.

In the case of our example, it may be the case that recall is more important than precision, as we may want to correctly identify all of the customers who will churn so that we can take some remedial actions to try and retain them, even at the cost of some potential false positives.

In this situation, it is sometimes possible to change the **threshold** that the model uses to predict true or false outcomes to favor increasing recall at the cost of precision or vice versa.

It is important to understand which is more important for your business case: having fewer false positives (i.e., higher precision) or fewer false negatives (i.e., higher recall).

When to use recall

Here are some examples of when best to use recall:

- **High cost of false negatives**: Recall is crucial in contexts where missing a positive instance is more critical than falsely identifying a negative instance as positive. For instance, in medical screening tests for diseases, a high recall is necessary to ensure that as many positive cases as possible are identified for further testing.
- **Imbalanced datasets**: In datasets where the positive class is rare, maximizing recall ensures that the model does not overlook the few positive instances present.
- **Comprehensive coverage**: It is useful when the goal is to ensure no positive instance is missed, even at the expense of higher false positives.

Practical implications

While recall is an essential metric for evaluating the comprehensiveness of a model in identifying positive cases, focusing solely on recall can lead to models that classify too many instances as positive (high false positives), reducing precision. This is why recall is often used alongside precision to understand the trade-offs between capturing all positives and the accuracy of positive predictions.

The balance between recall and precision is quantified by F1-score, which provides a single metric to assess model performance when both recall and precision are considered important, which we will look at now.

F1-score

F1-score is a helpful metric used in the evaluation of binary classification models, especially in situations where the balance between precision and recall is important. It is particularly useful when dealing with datasets that have an uneven class distribution or when the cost of false positives and false negatives varies significantly.

Definition of F1-score

F1-score is the harmonic mean of precision and recall, providing a single metric that balances both the model's ability to correctly identify positive instances (recall) and the accuracy of these positive identifications (precision). Unlike the arithmetic mean, the harmonic mean gives a higher weight to lower numbers, meaning that F1-score will be more influenced by lower precision or recall. This makes F1-score a stringent measure of a model's accuracy, which is especially useful when you seek a balance between precision and recall.

Formula for F1-score

The formula for calculating F1-score is given here:

$$F1\ Score = 2 \times \frac{Precision \times Recall}{Precision + Recall}$$

Understanding F1-score

F1-score ranges from 0 to 1, where a score of 1 indicates perfect precision and recall, and a score of 0 indicates the worst. A high F1-score suggests that the model has a robust balance between precision and recall, managing to accurately identify a high proportion of actual positives while minimizing the number of false positives and false negatives.

When to use F1-score

Here are some examples of when best to use F1-score:

- **Imbalanced classes**: It is particularly useful in scenarios where there are significantly more instances of one class than another, and the cost of false positives and false negatives are both critical.
- **Trade-off analysis**: It is ideal when you need to evaluate models based on their balance between precision (the quality of the positive predictions) and recall (the completeness of the positive predictions).
- **Comparative model evaluation**: When comparing models and a balance between precision and recall is desired, F1-score provides a single metric to assess performance, simplifying decision-making.

Practical implications

F1-score is an essential tool in the model evaluation process, allowing for a more nuanced assessment than evaluating precision or recall independently. However, it's important to consider the specific context of your application.

In some cases, precision might be more important than recall or vice versa. Adjusting the emphasis on one over the other might be necessary.

F1-score assumes the equal importance of precision and recall, which might not always align with business objectives or cost considerations.

F1-score is a powerful metric for assessing the accuracy of binary classification models, particularly in complex scenarios where both the ability to correctly identify positive instances and the precision of these identifications are important.

Alongside evaluating the accuracy of machine learning models, it is also important to understand how they make decisions. This can often be a difficult process, as many machine learning models can seem like a "black box" to the user. However, some machine learning models are more explainable than others, and even for those less explainable models, there exist a number of techniques in the field of "Explainable AI" that aims to shine a light on the decision-making process of what can be opaque models.

Methods for explaining machine learning models

Incorporating methods for interpreting and explaining machine learning models into your analytical toolkit can enhance transparency and provide insight into the decision-making process used by a machine learning model.

In some industries, explainability is an important aspect to consider; for example, in sensitive sectors, such as medicine and law, opaque "black-box" models are insufficient in scenarios where the reasoning behind how a machine learning model made a prediction is needed.

Let's first look at a simple example, using coefficients to understand regression models.

Making sense of regression models – the power of coefficients

Imagine you're using a regression model to predict future sales based on various factors such as marketing spend, seasonality, and product price. In this context, interpreting coefficients becomes akin to decoding the direct influence each factor has on your sales.

A positive coefficient for marketing spend would suggest that increasing your marketing budget is likely to boost sales, whereas a negative coefficient for product price might indicate that higher prices could deter customers. Understanding these coefficients empowers you to prioritize investments and strategic initiatives effectively.

Decoding classification models – unveiling feature importance

When deploying classification models—say, to identify which customers are most likely to churn or to flag potentially fraudulent transactions—understanding feature importance is key. This method ranks the attributes (e.g., customer behavior patterns and transaction sizes) according to their impact on the model's predictions. By focusing on the most influential factors, you can tailor interventions more precisely, whether that's through personalized retention strategies or targeted fraud prevention measures.

Methods for explaining machine learning models | 153

Imagine you had a machine learning model that predicted the predicted the expected spending of a customer in the next year. This machine learning model has been trained on a range of different features to predict the value of a customer. Generating a feature importance plot (by following the training of a model) can explain which of the features are more important to the model in making predictions:

Feature Importance

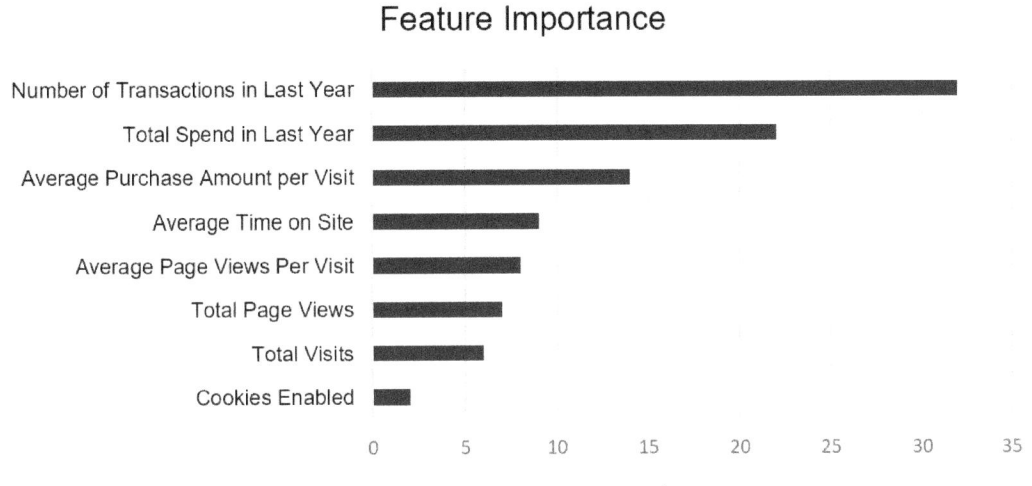

- Number of Transactions in Last Year
- Total Spend in Last Year
- Average Purchase Amount per Visit
- Average Time on Site
- Average Page Views Per Visit
- Total Page Views
- Total Visits
- Cookies Enabled

Figure 9.4: Feature importance plot

In the preceding example, you can see that the features related to the previous number of transactions and spend from the customer are more important to the model in predicting their next year spend, which is contrast to more superfluous information such as page views and whether their cookies are enabled.

Beyond specific models – universal insights using SHAP values

Regardless of whether you're working with regression, classification, or any other predictive model, **SHAP (SHapley Additive exPlanations)** offers a powerful, model-agnostic approach to explanation. SHAP values dissect any prediction to reveal the contribution of each feature.

For instance, if a loan application is predicted to be high risk, SHAP can show you exactly how factors such as the applicant's credit score, income, and loan amount contributed to this assessment. This level of insight is invaluable for refining risk models, addressing customer inquiries about decision outcomes, and ensuring compliance with regulatory requirements for explainability.

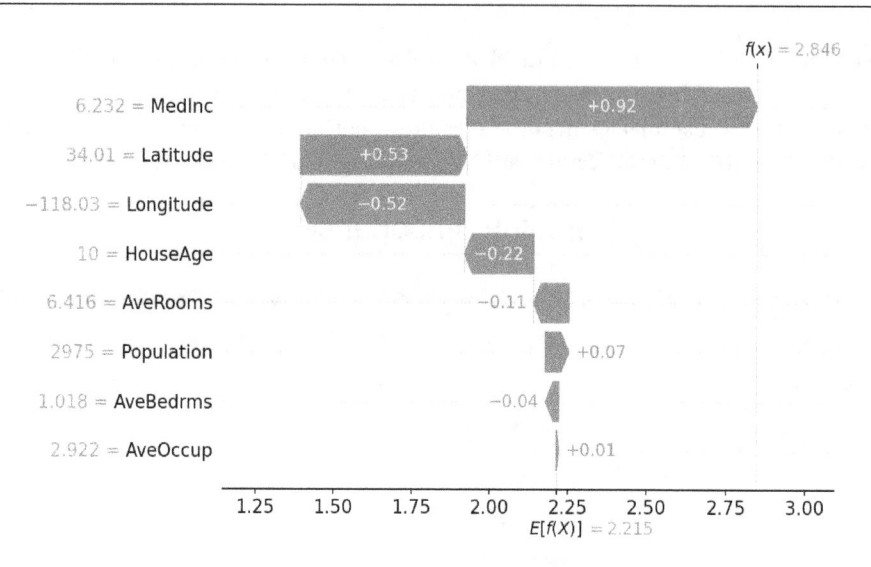

Figure 9.5: SHAP value waterfall plot

For example, in the preceding chart, a SHAP plot for an individual prediction on a house pricing dataset is shown. In this case, you can see the contribution to the prediction from each feature to the final prediction. For example, you can see that the age of the house (HouseAge) had a negative effect on the predicted house price.

This is an incredibly useful tool for explaining individual predictions, particularly for models that are not inherently explainable. You can imagine situations where a model's decisions may need to be audited or explained following, for example, a complaint or investigation, and without tools such as SHAP, this can be a difficult situation for companies to find themselves in.

Summary

This chapter on *Interpreting and Evaluating Machine Learning Models* emphasizes the critical importance of understanding, interpreting, and evaluating **machine learning** (**ML**) models in the context of data science projects. It highlights that the potential of ML systems to make decisions without hardcoded rules presents significant opportunities, yet realizing this potential is complex and requires the careful evaluation of models to ensure accuracy and reliability.

The key takeaways from this chapter include the following:

- The necessity of evaluating ML models on test (holdout) data to get a realistic estimate of their performance in real-world scenarios.
- The importance of various evaluation metrics, such as R-squared, RMSE, and MAE, for regression models, and precision, recall, and F1-score for classification models. These metrics help decision-makers understand a model's accuracy, how well it fits the data, and its predictive power.

The discussion on feature importance and methods such SHAP values for explaining predictions provides tools for understanding how different features influence a model's outcomes. This is crucial for both interpreting complex models and making informed decisions based on their predictions.

The chapter concluded by stressing that effectively evaluating and interpreting ML models is essential for making informed business decisions. By understanding evaluation metrics, using holdout data, and interpreting feature importance, stakeholders can gain confidence in their models' accuracy and usefulness.

As we transition into the next chapter, *Common Pitfalls in Machine Learning*, we build on the foundation laid in evaluating and interpreting models by exploring the common challenges encountered in ML projects. This includes issues such as overfitting, underfitting, data quality, the curse of dimensionality, model complexity, and the trade-offs between model accuracy and interpretability. Understanding these challenges is crucial for developing effective ML solutions that are robust, reliable, and aligned with business objectives.

The next chapter will delve into these challenges, providing insights into navigating the complexities of ML projects and strategies for mitigating common pitfalls, thereby enhancing the success and impact of ML initiatives in real-world applications.

10
Common Pitfalls in Machine Learning

Picture this: a seasoned data science manager just launched a new recommendation engine to boost product sales. The model performed brilliantly in tests, but now, customer interest is lukewarm. The problem? The model had gotten too good at mirroring the training data – niche tastes of early adopters that didn't reflect broader customer preferences.

Machine learning (**ML**) promises incredible things, but it's dangerously easy to stumble. According to a survey of over 500 developers working with ML systems (`https://www.civo.com/newsroom/ai-project-failure`), more than half (53%) of respondents have abandoned between 1% and 25% of ML projects, with an additional 24% having left between 26% and 50% of projects. Only 11% of developers said they have never abandoned a project. The first lesson is this: ML isn't some magic algorithm that just needs data. It's about understanding what kind of model is right for the job, ensuring your data actually teaches the right lessons, and knowing when your model might be getting tripped up.

This chapter covers the following topics:

- Understanding the complexity
- Dirty data, damaged models – how data quantity and quality impacts ML
- Overcoming overfitting and underfitting
- Mastering overfitting and underfitting for optimal model performance
- Training-serving skew and model drift
- Bias and fairness

Understanding the complexity

Firstly, let's acknowledge that ML is a complex field, and it's not just about crunching numbers. It involves intricate algorithms, vast amounts of data, and the ability to interpret and apply the results in a meaningful way.

Imagine you're a marketing executive at a consumer goods company. You have access to a wealth of customer data and want to use ML to predict which customers are most likely to buy your new product.

Sounds straightforward, right? But there are many places where complexity can come in. We will briefly explain some of the key considerations, then go into each one in more detail:

- **Data quality and quantity**: Is your data clean and representative of your target population? Do you have enough high-quality data?
- **Model selection and tuning**: Have you selected the appropriate model for your data? Have you correctly trained or fine-tuned your model?
- **Overfitting and underfitting**: Is your model too complex and just memorizing the training data (overfitting)? Or is it too simple and missing important patterns (underfitting)?
- **Training-serving skew**: Will your model perform as well in the real world as it does on your training data?
- **Model drift**: How will your model perform over time as the underlying data changes?
- **Fairness**: Is your model biased against certain groups? Is it treating different sub-groups based on characteristics such as gender, age, and ethnicity fairly?

These are some of the key considerations to have in mind when training ML models, which can initially sound overwhelming. However, by looking at each of these in turn, with some concrete examples, by the end of this chapter, you should be better equipped to know what to look out for. You will also know the steps you, or your team, can take to mitigate the challenges associated with deploying ML models to production.

Dirty data, damaged models – how data quantity and quality impact ML

When training or using ML and artificial intelligence models, data is not only an asset but also the foundation of success. Without high-quality, representative data, even the most sophisticated ML model is useless. But what happens when you don't have enough data, or when the data you have is biased or inaccurate?

To consider one hypothetical example, many banks use ML to flag potentially fraudulent transactions and block accounts based on information about the transaction. Imagine the model was only trained on a subset of account types, such as current accounts that have more regular, lower-value transactions.

Let's say the bank decides to then also apply the model to savings accounts that may have larger, less frequent transactions. The model may now incorrectly flag most typical savings account transactions as false positives, leading to frustrated customers and stressed customer service teams.

To look at another example, imagine a large language model-based customer service chatbot. Let's say this chatbot was trained primarily on interactions where customers are expressing frustration or dissatisfaction. The chatbot learns to associate most customer inquiries with negativity. A consequence could be that the chatbot becomes overly apologetic or defensive, even in neutral conversations. It may misunderstand simple requests and misinterpret the customers' intent, hindering effective customer support.

In this section, we'll look into the common data considerations around quantity and quality that can affect your ML models and how to address them.

The importance of adequate training data

Imagine you're a coach training a team for a basketball tournament. If you only train it on shooting free throws, it will struggle when faced with other aspects of the game such as defense or three-point shooting. Similarly, an ML model trained on insufficient or unrepresentative data will struggle to make accurate predictions.

In industries such as market research and consumer goods, for instance, if a model is trained only on data from urban consumers, it may not perform well when applied to rural consumers.

For many ML models, particularly deep learning models, the quantity of data is paramount.

Mitigating the challenge

To mitigate this challenge, we must do the following:

- **Collect a sufficient volume of data**: This may seem like a brute-force approach, but in many cases, the best way to improve the accuracy of ML models, and particularly deep learning models, is to increase the volume of data the model is being trained on. One way this may be achieved is via collecting data over a longer period.
- **Collect diverse data**: Ensure your training data covers a wide range of scenarios your model is likely to encounter. This may be achieved by expanding the sources where data is acquired, either internal data sources (first-party data), or external data sources (second- and third-party data). It is important, however, to expand data coverage to include only relevant data that is representative of the data your model will see in production. For example, in the previous chatbot use case, expanding the data to cover all types of customer interactions could benefit the accuracy and reliability of the model. However, adding irrelevant chatbot data, say from a different company or industry, may have the opposite effect and lead to a less reliable model.

- **Use data augmentation techniques**: Data augmentation is the process of adjusting or augmenting data examples you already have. These techniques can artificially expand your dataset by creating variations of existing data points. For example, within image recognition, one common data augmentation approach is to adjust existing images by rotating, zooming, blurring, and cropping them, increasing the volume of the training data.
- **Generate synthetic data**: Synthetic data refers to artificially created data that closely mirrors the characteristics and patterns of real-world data. This can be particularly beneficial when real-world data is scarce, sensitive, or difficult to obtain. In the case of **large language models** (**LLMs**), these can be used to generate realistic synthetic data that can be used for fine-tuning models for specific tasks. LLMs excel at creating text-based data and can be fine-tuned to produce diverse and targeted variations, filling gaps in your original datasets and ensuring your model is better prepared for various real-world scenarios.

Dealing with poor data quality

Poor data quality, such as missing values, inconsistencies, and outright errors, significantly hinders the performance of ML models. Imagine trying to teach someone math with a textbook full of typos and incorrect formulas – they'll struggle to learn the concepts correctly. Similarly, a model trained on flawed data will produce unreliable results.

Consider, for example, an image recognition model within the healthcare technology industry that is trained to detect tumors from MRI scans. If the images this model is trained on are poorly labeled, it could lead to potentially disastrous results, with tumors going undetected and false positives being flagged. For critical applications such as this, having very high data quality is one of the most important considerations, if not the most important.

Take another example. A natural language processing model may be fine-tuned for content moderation on a social media platform. If the training data is poorly labeled (e.g., sarcastic statements flagged as hate speech) or lacks diverse examples, the model will struggle. This could lead to false positives, where legitimate content might be wrongly removed, restricting freedom of expression. Additionally, the poor quality training data could lead to the model producing false negatives, where actual hate speech might slip through, making the platform unsafe for users.

Mitigating the challenge

There are various methods to mitigate the challenge of poor data quality, which we will describe in this section. However, often, the best place data quality can be addressed is at the source.

For example, consider an ML model trained to classify customers in a CRM as likely or unlikely to churn. Have the customers, and all the information about them, been accurately entered into the CRM? Is there any validation on the forms to make sure invalid data has not been entered, or is important data missing for some customers? Are there processes for the business teams to follow when entering data? If there is poor quality or missing data, can this be manually fixed by business teams, or the data science teams themselves?

This is all mundane stuff, but if, by the time data is in the hands of data scientists and ML engineers, it is already of poor quality, there is only so much that can be done with the more automated processes we will explain here. As the well-known expression goes, garbage in, garbage out.

Here are some techniques that data scientists, engineers, and analysts can use to mitigate poor data quality:

- **Data cleaning**: There are several techniques that data scientists can apply to clean data before training ML models, including the following:

  - **Missing values**: Decide whether to remove entries with missing data or replace missing values with estimates (e.g., mean or median)
  - **Duplicates**: Remove redundant entries that can skew results
  - **Inconsistencies**: Correct formatting errors (e.g., date formats), and standardize entries for better model understanding (e.g., convert all addresses to lowercase)

- **Data validation**: Data scientists can apply techniques to validate data and exclude or fix invalid data before training ML models. It is also important that when the model is in production (i.e., after training and during inference), the same processes for data cleaning and validation are applied:

  - **Range checks**: Ensure values fall within an acceptable range (e.g., a person's age can't be negative)
  - **Format checks**: Verify that data adheres to specific formats (e.g., phone numbers, zip codes)
  - **Cross-field checks**: Ensure consistency across related data fields (e.g., if a country is "USA," the state field should match the list of US states)

Conclusion

Bad data will sabotage your ML models, plain and simple. Addressing these issues is essential to success, and we have covered some of the techniques that you can leverage in your next data science project. These techniques include improving data collection by expanding the scope and coverage of the training data, augmenting data, and synthesizing data if appropriate, as well as improving the quality of data through data cleaning and validation. These are the hard yards that will set up your project for success. The importance of data cannot be emphasized enough, to the extent that there is a growing approach called Data-centric AI (`https://datacentricai.org/`), which is the discipline of systematically engineering the data used to build an AI system.

Next, we will explore another key challenge: ensuring your model doesn't just memorize your training data but can also learn to generalize to new situations. That means understanding and avoiding overfitting and underfitting.

As we move to the next section, we'll explore this critical aspect of ML – over- and underfitting. How can we ensure our model performs well, not just on our current data, but also on new, unseen data?

Overcoming overfitting and underfitting

Choosing the right complexity for your model is a delicate balancing act. If your model is too complex, it might overfit the training data, meaning it performs well on the training data but poorly on new, unseen data. On the other hand, if your model is too simple, it might underfit the data, missing important patterns and leading to inaccurate predictions.

Imagine you're a market researcher trying to predict consumer trends. An overfitted model might capture every minor fluctuation in past trends but fail to generalize to future trends. An underfitted model might miss important trends altogether.

Navigating training-serving skew and model drift

In an ideal world, your model would perform just as well in the real world as it does on your training data. But this is rarely the case. This discrepancy is known as **training-serving skew**.

Furthermore, as the underlying data changes over time, your model's performance can degrade. This is known as **model drift**.

Imagine you're developing an ML model to predict customer churn for a telecommunications company. During the model training phase, you use a dataset that includes customer information such as demographics, usage patterns, and customer service interactions. However, when the model is deployed in the production environment (the serving phase), you realize that the data pipeline feeding the model is missing some important features, such as the latest customer service interaction data. This discrepancy between the data used for training and the data available during serving is a classic example of training-serving skew.

In this scenario, the model's performance in production may suffer because it was trained on a more comprehensive dataset than what is available in the serving environment. The missing features during serving can lead to inaccurate predictions and suboptimal decision-making.

To address training-serving skew, it's important to ensure consistency between the data used for training and the data available during serving. This can involve regularizing data pipelines, monitoring data quality, and implementing data validation checks to catch any discrepancies early in the process.

Ensuring fairness

Finally, it's important to ensure that your models are fair and don't discriminate against certain groups. This can be a challenge, especially when the training data itself is biased.

For example, let's say you're an HR manager using ML to screen job applicants. If your training data is biased against certain groups, your model might unfairly reject qualified candidates from these groups.

In this section, we've explored why ML can be hard, touching on challenges such as data quality and quantity, overfitting and underfitting, training-serving skew, model drift, and fairness. But don't be discouraged. In the following sections, we'll dive deeper into these challenges and provide practical strategies to overcome them.

Mastering overfitting and underfitting for optimal model performance

In ML, achieving reliable predictions is often the main goal. Overfitting and underfitting are two common obstacles to this goal. Let's break down these concepts and outline concrete techniques to build better models.

Overfitting – when your model is too specific

Imagine your model as a student preparing for a test. Overfitting occurs when the student memorizes the practice questions perfectly but struggles to answer variations of the same questions on the actual exam. Similarly, an overfitted model gets too focused on the details of the training data, including random noise, and fails to grasp the bigger picture.

Real-world consequences

- **Market research**: A model obsessively tuned to existing customers' data won't be able to predict the behavior of new prospects with different characteristics
- **Retail recommendations**: A system trained exclusively on a loyal customer's purchase history may offer irrelevant suggestions when trying to attract new shoppers

Underfitting – when your model is too simplistic

Picture underfitting as a student who only grasps the most basic concepts of a subject. They'll fail the exam regardless of whether the questions are from practice problems or new material. Similarly, an underfitted model misses important relationships within the data and performs poorly across the board.

Real-world consequences

- **Sales forecasts**: A model that ignores factors such as seasonality or marketing promotions will consistently underestimate or overestimate potential sales

Spotting the problem

- **Red flag**: Excellent performance on training data but terrible results on new data is a classic sign of overfitting

- **Warning sign**: If your model struggles with both training data and new data, it's likely due to underfitting

Solutions for building better models

The following are some solutions for building good models:

- **More data = stronger foundation**: Larger, more diverse datasets help the model identify real trends, not just random fluctuations in the training sample.
- **Feature selection = laser focus**: Carefully choose the most relevant data features. Get rid of those that only add confusion, not insight.
  - **Example – predicting customer churn**: Imagine you're predicting customer churn for a telecom company. Your dataset includes relevant features such as monthly charges and customer service calls, but also an irrelevant feature: favorite ice cream flavor. Including "favorite ice cream flavor" adds noise and makes it harder for the algorithm to identify important patterns. By selecting only relevant features, you create a focused model that zeroes in on key factors driving churn. Remember, more data isn't always better. Quality and relevance matter most.
- **Regularization = the guardrails**: Regularization is a technique that adds penalties to the model during training to prevent it from becoming too complex and too reliant on the peculiarities of the training data.
  - **Example – predicting house prices**: When building a model to predict house prices, regularization acts as a safeguard. It discourages the model from giving too much importance to a few unusual, expensive houses with unique features in the training data. By adding these penalties, regularization helps the model generalize better to new, unseen data, rather than getting stuck on the specifics of the training data.
- **Cross-validation = reality check**: Cross-validation is a method that helps assess how well a model will perform on new, unseen data by simulating real-world conditions.
  - **Example – sentiment analysis of movie reviews**: When building a model to predict the sentiment of movie reviews, cross-validation provides a reality check. Instead of training the model on all the data and assuming it's performing well, you split the data into subsets. You train the model on some subsets and test it on others. By doing this multiple times, you get a more realistic estimate of how the model will perform on new data. This helps you catch whether the model is just memorizing the training data instead of learning to generalize to new reviews.

One way to visualize the trade-off between underfitting and overfitting is by looking at a bias-variance trade-off chart:

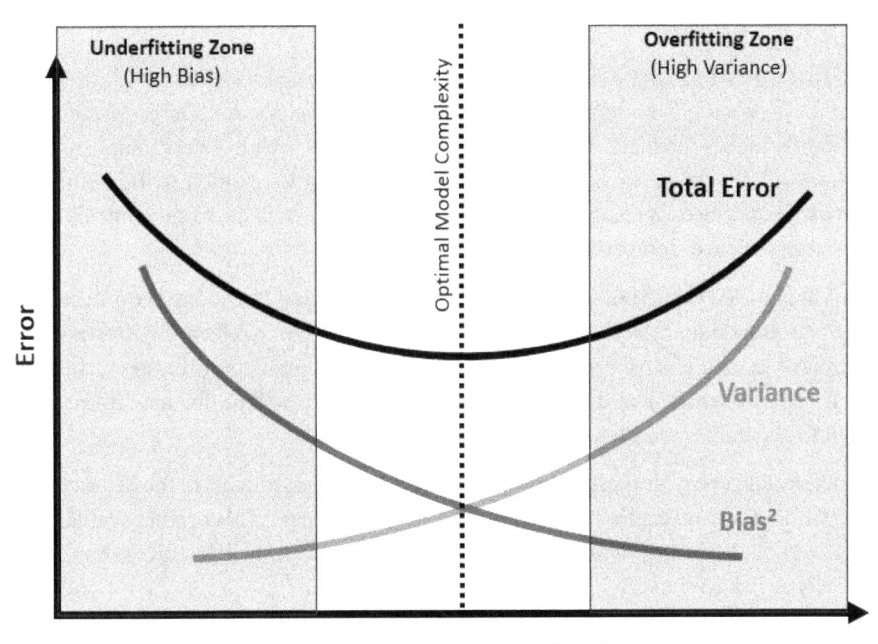

Figure 10.1: Bias-variance trade-off

The chart (*Figure 10.1*) visualizes the relationship between a model's **complexity**, **generalizability**, and **accuracy** on unseen data. This is a very important concept to business-focused decision-makers in data science, ML, and AI because it directly impacts the real-world performance of their models.

Understanding the axes

- **X-axis (model complexity)**: This represents how flexible or complex your model is. Simpler models are on the left, while more complex models are on the right.
- **Y-axis (error)**: This represents the overall error of your model, which is a combination of two key factors: bias and variance.

Key parts of the chart

Let's explore the chart with a real example. Imagine you're building a model to predict which customers are likely to stop using your product or service (churn):

- **Bias**: This refers to the systematic error introduced by the model itself. It's the consistent difference between the model's predictions and the actual values. A high bias means the model consistently misses the mark, regardless of the specific data point. A very simple model might only look at one feature, such as a customer's average purchase amount. This model is likely to have high bias because it ignores a whole host of complex factors that contribute to churn (support experience, competitor offerings).

- **High Variance (Overfitting)**: A very complex model with a huge number of features might fit the training data perfectly. However, it might pick up on irrelevant patterns or random fluctuations in your historical data, leading to inconsistent predictions for new customers (like darts going all over the board). This model would perform well on the data it was trained on but fail to generalize and predict new churn reliably.

- **Optimal Balance**: An ideal model would be complex enough to capture the key factors driving churn without overfitting to the specifics of your training data. This balance would lead to the lowest overall error rate (**Total Error** on the chart), successfully identifying those customers genuinely at risk of churn.

The trade-off

The key takeaway from this chart is the trade-off between bias and variance:

- **Simpler models (left side)**: These tend to have high bias (systematically missing the mark) but low variance (consistent predictions). This is because they are not flexible enough to capture all the complexities in the data.

- **More complex models (right side)**: These tend to have low bias (better fitting the data) but high variance (predictions jumping around for similar data points). This is because they are more flexible and can fit the training data very well, but they also risk memorizing noise or irrelevant patterns in the data, which leads to poor performance on new, unseen data.

Finding the optimal model

The goal is to find the optimal model complexity that balances bias and variance to achieve the lowest total error. This is often achieved through techniques such as regularization, which helps to constrain the model's flexibility and reduce variance without introducing too much bias.

Relevance to business decisions

For business-focused decision-makers, understanding the bias-variance trade-off is useful because it helps you do the following:

- **Evaluate the generalizability of your models**: How well will your model perform on real-world data that it hasn't seen before?
- **Make informed choices about model complexity**: Balance the need for accurate predictions with the risk of overfitting and poor generalizability
- **Avoid common pitfalls**: Knowing the signs of underfitting (high bias) and overfitting (high variance) can help you diagnose and fix issues with your models

By understanding this trade-off, you can make better decisions about your data science projects and ensure that your models are generalizable and impactful for your business.

Conclusion

The best ML models aren't about perfectly mimicking the past. They're about uncovering patterns that help you make accurate predictions for the future. By understanding and tackling overfitting and underfitting, you'll equip your models to deliver the insights that drive better business decisions.

As we move forward, we'll investigate another important aspect of ML: training-serving skew and model drift. These concepts will further equip you to deploy effective and reliable ML models in your business.

Training-serving skew and model drift

As decision-makers, it's important to understand the potential pitfalls in deploying ML models into production. Two of these challenges are training-serving skew and model drift. Let's explore these concepts, understand their implications, and learn how to mitigate their effects.

Training-serving skew

Training-serving skew occurs when the data used to train a model differs from the data used in serving predictions. This can lead to a significant drop in model performance. Imagine you're a retail giant, and you've trained a model to predict customer purchasing behavior based on historical data. If your model is trained on online sales data but used to predict in-store sales, the skew could lead to inaccurate predictions.

Mitigating training-serving skew

How can we address this? Here are some steps to take:

- **Ensure consistency**: Make sure that the data used for training and serving is consistent. This includes aspects such as data sources, feature extraction methods, and data distribution.
- **Monitor performance**: Regularly monitor your model's performance. If there's a sudden drop in performance, it could be due to training-serving skew.
- **Update model regularly**: Update your model with recent data to ensure it remains relevant and accurate.

Model drift

Model drift refers to the change in model performance over time due to changes in the underlying data distribution. Consider a marketing firm that uses a model to predict consumer trends. If there's a sudden shift in consumer behavior, the model's predictions may become less accurate over time.

Mitigating model drift

Addressing model drift involves doing the following:

- **Monitor model performance**: Keep a close eye on your model's performance metrics. If there's a gradual decline, it could be due to model drift.
- **Retrain models**: Regularly retrain your models with fresh data to ensure they stay up-to-date with the latest trends.
- **Use robust models**: Some models are more susceptible to drift than others. Using robust models that can handle changes in data distribution can help mitigate this issue.

Key takeaways

In this section, we've explored two common pitfalls in deploying ML models: training-serving skew and model drift. We've learned how to identify these issues and looked at steps to mitigate their effects. By ensuring consistency in training and serving data, monitoring model performance, and regularly updating our models, we can ensure they remain effective and relevant.

As we move forward, we'll explore another critical aspect of ML models: bias and fairness. This will help us understand how models can be biased against different sub-populations and how to ensure our models are fair.

Bias and fairness

Within ML, bias and fairness are not just ethical considerations but critical factors that can significantly impact the effectiveness of your ML models. We have already encountered bias in how it is related to underfitting and overfitting. We will now explore bias in the context of how the model fully and accurately represents all groups within the data – for example, different demographic groups within a dataset of customers.

Understanding bias

Bias in ML refers to a model's tendency to systematically make errors due to limitations in the training data or the model's design. This could be due to various reasons, including the following:

- **Inadequate or unrepresentative training data**: If your dataset doesn't fully capture the complexities and diversity of the real world, your model might make inaccurate assumptions
- **Inherent prejudices in the data collection process**: If there are historical biases embedded in the way data was gathered, your model may perpetuate those biases

Example – bias in loan approval

Consider a bank that uses an ML model to approve or reject loan applications. If the training data used to build this model includes fewer examples of successful loan repayments from a certain demographic group, the model might learn to reject applications from this group more often, regardless of the applicants' individual creditworthiness. This is an example of bias.

Understanding fairness

Fairness is a broader concept that looks at the impact of a model's decisions. A model is considered unfair if it systematically favors one group over another, even if the bias itself is unintentional.

Example – fairness in advertising

Imagine an online retailer that uses an ML model to decide which customers to target with a promotional offer. If the model systematically excludes certain demographic groups from receiving the offer, it could be considered unfair, leading to missed opportunities and potential customer alienation.

Mitigating bias and ensuring fairness

Here are some key strategies to address these issues:

- **Representative data**: Ensure your training data is as representative of the real-world population as possible. This may involve collecting more data, using techniques such as oversampling for underrepresented groups, and carefully addressing inherent biases in existing datasets.

- **Fairness-aware algorithms**: Explore using algorithms that are specifically designed to consider fairness during the training process.
- **Monitoring and evaluation**: Use evaluation metrics such as disparate impact and equal opportunity difference to measure potential biases and disparities in your model's predictions. Regularly monitor these metrics to identify areas where fairness might be compromised.

Key takeaways

By understanding bias and fairness, you can take steps to build ML models that are both accurate and equitable. This is important not only for ethical reasons but also for ensuring that your models make sound business decisions that benefit all stakeholders.

Summary

In this chapter, we've explored some of the common pitfalls in training and deploying ML models, including inadequate training data, poor data quality, over- and underfitting, training-serving skew, and model drift. We've also explored the concepts of bias and fairness, their impact on business outcomes, and how to mitigate these issues.

As we move forward, remember that data science is not just about building models, but also about ensuring that these models are reliable, fair, and beneficial to all stakeholders.

In the next chapter, we'll explore the different types of data science projects you might encounter and how to approach each of them.

Part 3: Leading Successful Data Science Projects and Teams

This part explores the leadership aspects of data science, including project structure, team composition, management strategies, and the importance of continuous learning and staying current with emerging technologies. This part has the following chapters:

- *Chapter 11, The Structure of a Data Science Project*
- *Chapter 12, The Data Science Team*
- *Chapter 13, Managing the Data Science Team*
- *Chapter 14, Continuing Your Journey as a Data Science Leader*

11
The Structure of a Data Science Project

Data science projects can vary significantly in their scope, objectives, and deliverables. From exploratory data analysis and building reports and dashboards to developing and deploying machine learning and artificial intelligence models to production – the structure and approach to a data science project needs to be tailored accordingly.

In this chapter, we will look at the common types of data science projects and their associated processes and deliverables. This will equip you, as a leader of data science initiatives, with knowledge of how to scope and plan a data science project, and the key steps involved in researching, developing, testing, and deploying a data product.

By the end of this chapter, you will be able to do the following:

- Identify, prioritize, and frame data science use cases
- Distinguish different types of data science projects and deliverables
- Scope and plan a data science project and create useful artifacts such as requirements documents, project plans, and test strategies
- Understand the research and development process associated with data science projects
- Appreciate the importance of thoroughly testing a data product before delivery or deployment
- Safely deploy and monitor a data product in a production environment

Whether you are overseeing a short-term data science project or the development of a machine-learning-powered software application, understanding the key stages and best practices covered in this chapter will help ensure your data science initiatives are set up for success.

The various types of data science projects

Before looking at the structure of a data science project, let's discuss the different types of data science projects you might encounter. The type of data science, machine learning, or artificial intelligence project can radically alter how the project should be structured.

The three broadest categories of data science projects are as follows:

- Data products
- Reports and analytics
- Research and methodology

Within these categories are a wide range of projects, but this is a useful distinction to understand. This is because data products are deployed and maintained over time, whereas a one-off report, analysis, or research has a finite lifespan.

Let's look at these in more detail.

Data products

Data products are software applications or systems that can leverage data, machine learning algorithms, and artificial intelligence techniques to provide valuable features, insights, or automated decision-making capabilities to end users or other systems.

These products are designed to be deployed, maintained, and continuously improved over time.

The following are some of the key characteristics of data products:

- They are driven by data and powered by machine learning or artificial intelligence algorithms
- They provide continued value to users through features, predictions, recommendations, or automation
- They require ongoing maintenance, updates, and monitoring to ensure performance and reliability
- They often involve integration with other systems or APIs
- Scalability and efficiency are important considerations

To give a concrete example, a data product could be, for instance, a delivery time prediction model within a food delivery app. This model could provide, via an API, estimates on how long it would take from ordering to the food being delivered to the user, with this information being provided continuously during delivery based on features such as the distance from the restaurant to the customer's location, the location and availability of drivers, and the traffic levels. You may have seen the outputs from one of these models when using apps such as Uber Eats, DoorDash, or Deliveroo.

As you might well imagine, deploying a scoring model that can serve many thousands of customers in real time would be a huge engineering effort. Most data products aren't as complex; however, the point of this example is to emphasize that data products require a level of design, engineering, testing, and maintenance that reports and pure research do not.

Data products are not "fire and forget"; they must be supported and maintained after deployment. So, plan with the end in mind and think about how and who will maintain a successful product as it serves users.

This chapter will primarily focus on how to plan and deliver data products, which we will cover later in this chapter. But before this, let's look at the two other broad categories of data science projects that you might encounter.

Reports and analytics

Reports and analytics projects focus on analyzing and deriving insights from data to support decision-making or tracking of business performance. These projects typically involve collecting, processing, and visualizing data to provide meaningful and actionable information to stakeholders.

Some of the key characteristics of reporting and analytics are as follows:

- Emphasis on data exploration, analysis, and interpretation
- Utilizes statistical methods, data visualization techniques, and business intelligence tools
- Aims to uncover patterns, trends, and relationships in data
- Supports data-driven decision-making and strategic planning
- Deliverables often include reports, presentations, or interactive visualizations

Many of these deliverables are one-off, ad hoc outputs with a finite lifespan so that you can plan the project accordingly. This may follow the following structure:

1. **Gathering requirements**: Gathering business and data requirements and planning the analysis or modeling approach.
2. **Collecting data**: Collecting all the relevant data from internal or external sources.
3. **Processing data**: Cleaning and wrangling the data so that it's in the required structure for analysis and/or modeling.
4. **Analysis and modeling**: Carrying out data analysis and statistical or machine learning modeling to provide insights and understanding of the data that support the business requirements.
5. **Reporting**: Producing the reporting deliverable, whether it's a report, presentation, or interactive visualization, using data visualization techniques and summarizing the data in a way that it can easily be interpreted by the viewer while providing insights and recommendations that they can act upon.

This structure may not be strictly linear, and there may be iterations of data collection or gathering additional requirements or inputs from the business at each stage before the final deliverable is presented.

The final deliverable should emphasize actionable insights and recommendations and encourage the end user to act upon insights that you are confident about. Often, reports are merely looked at and no further action is taken, which has limited value for the business.

Finally, let's look at the third type of data science/machine learning project: research and methodology. Unless you're working within academia or a research company or lab focused on advancing the field of machine learning or artificial intelligence, you may not come across this type of project. Often, within the industry, companies rely on tried and tested techniques or models to develop their use cases.

Research and methodology

Research and methodology projects focus on advancing the field of artificial intelligence, machine learning, or data science by developing new algorithms, techniques, or approaches. These projects often involve experimenting, benchmarking, and evaluating different methods to push the boundaries of what is possible and improve the state-of-the-art.

Some of the key characteristics of research and methodology projects are as follows:

- Emphasis on innovation, experimentation, and pushing the limits of current techniques
- Involves developing novel algorithms, models, or optimization techniques
- Requires a deep understanding of the underlying mathematical and statistical principles
- Often involves comparative analysis and evaluating different approaches
- Aims to contribute to the scientific community through publications, open source code, or research papers

This type of project could follow an approach with involves the following stages:

1. **Literature review**: Reviewing existing research and identifying gaps or areas for improvement.
2. **Hypothesis formulation**: Developing a clear research question and hypothesis.
3. **Methodology development**: Designing and implementing novel algorithms, models, or techniques.
4. **Experimental setup**: Preparing data, defining evaluation metrics, and setting up experiments.
5. **Evaluation and analysis**: Conducting experiments, analyzing results, and comparing them with state-of-the-art models.
6. **Documentation and dissemination**: Writing research papers, preparing presentations, and sharing code and findings with the company or wider research community.

Now that we have seen the main, broad types of data science projects, let's focus on the structure and stages of a data science project that aims to deliver a data product. This is where companies and teams often trip up since designing and developing a machine learning or artificial intelligence solution comes with a lot of challenges. Planning the project with the right level of expertise and resources is crucial.

The stages of a data product

When leading the development of a new machine learning or artificial-intelligence-based product, there are several stages that you will encounter and are useful to understand. This section will provide you with a framework and tools so that you can work with machine learning and artificial intelligence teams in developing successful data products:

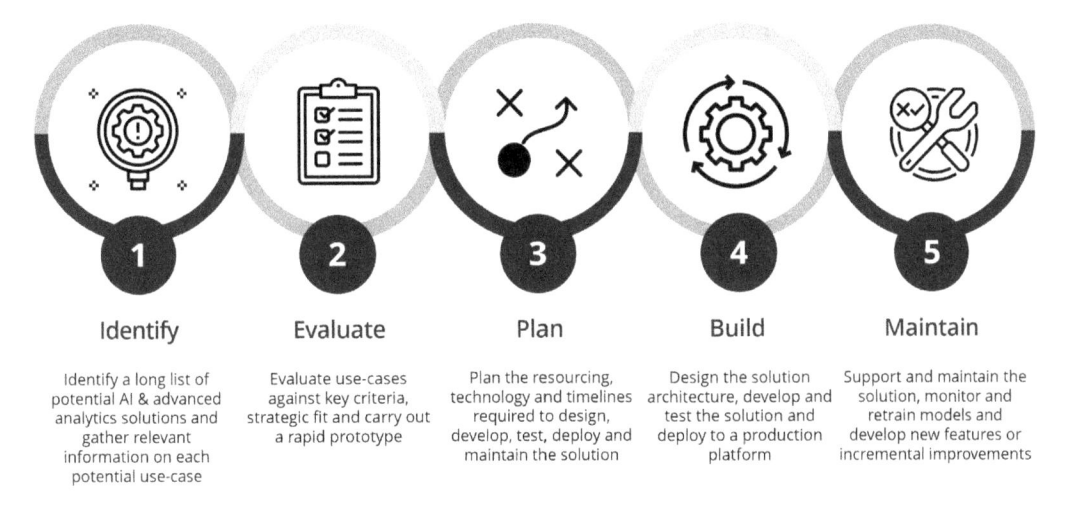

1. Identify
Identify a long list of potential AI & advanced analytics solutions and gather relevant information on each potential use-case

2. Evaluate
Evaluate use-cases against key criteria, strategic fit and carry out a rapid prototype

3. Plan
Plan the resourcing, technology and timelines required to design, develop, test, deploy and maintain the solution

4. Build
Design the solution architecture, develop and test the solution and deploy to a production platform

5. Maintain
Support and maintain the solution, monitor and retrain models and develop new features or incremental improvements

Figure 11.1: The stages of a data science product

While the stages of a data science product can be roughly outlined as Identify, Evaluate, Plan, Build, and Maintain, it's important to note that modern product development typically follows an Agile methodology. In practice, these stages are not strictly sequential, but iterative and interconnected.

Teams often work in short sprints, continuously gathering feedback, re-evaluating priorities, and adapting their plans. This allows for more flexibility, quicker iterations, and the ability to pivot when needed, ultimately leading to a product that better meets user needs and business goals.

So, while this framework provides a helpful overview of the key considerations at each stage, keep in mind that the process is more cyclical than linear, with insights from later stages often informing and refining earlier assumptions and decisions.

Identifying use cases

An often-overlooked stage in the data science project life cycle is taking time to identify the "right" use cases. Many organizations start with the wrong premise, wanting to "do artificial intelligence," "do machine learning" or "do data science" without clear business objectives. These companies end up investing time, effort, and human resources into projects that deliver little to no value.

This may seem obvious; however, many organizations fail to deliver a **return on investment** (**ROI**) through data science, machine learning, or artificial intelligence initiatives. One of the most significant factors that contribute toward this is developing solutions that do not have a material impact on the business's bottom line. This is much easier said than done.

Spending sufficient time and effort identifying the right use cases, and projecting their financial impact, is a foundational step in any data science project. Get it right, and you set your project up for success. Get it wrong, and you risk wasting time and resources on initiatives that fail to deliver real value.

A use case, in this context, is a specific application of data science techniques to solve a business problem or capture an opportunity. However, it's important to recognize that data science isn't always the best solution. In many situations, traditional business intelligence, software engineering, or even simple process improvements can be more effective.

To identify use cases that are both technically feasible and deliver clear business value, it's best to follow a structured approach:

- **Understand the value chain**: Start by understanding the key functions and processes within your organization. Identify areas where data science/machine learning/artificial intelligence could potentially deliver value, whether by reducing costs, increasing revenue, improving efficiency, or mitigating risks. The solution should ultimately contribute to the business's bottom line through one or more of the following, either directly or indirectly:

Increase revenue

Reduce costs

Improve operational efficiency

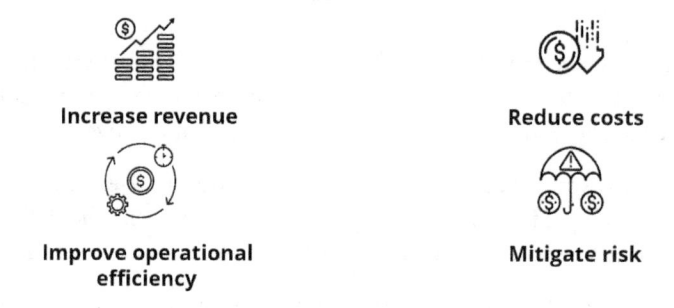

Mitigate risk

Figure 11.2: Data science use case aims

Use this stage to develop a long list of potential data science, machine learning, or artificial intelligence use cases.

Try to estimate the financial value for each use case under different scenarios, such as via a base-level scenario, a more optimistic scenario, and a more pessimistic scenario.

- **Speak to stakeholders**: Conduct workshops and interviews with business stakeholders to gain insights into their challenges, pain points, and opportunities for data science and machine learning/artificial intelligence. Ask about data availability, current analytical capabilities, and decision-making processes:

Conduct interviews & workshops with business stakeholders

Conducting interviews or workshops with business stakeholders will help identify potential use-cases for AI or advanced analytics that can deliver tangible value for the organisation.

Below are some example questions that could be asked, obviously the questions to ask will depend on the specific organisation, department and stakeholder.

EXAMPLE QUESTIONS

What existing data or analytics do you use to perform your role?	Is there data within your organization that you think could be better leveraged?
What do you think are the biggest challenges your department faces in being able to effectively perform its function?	Do you see any opportunities for AI or advanced analytics within your department?
Are the any processes within your department which you think could benefit from automation?	Do you know of AI or advanced analytics use-cases from your industry or competitors?
Where do you think there are gaps in the data or analytics you have access to?	Have there been AI or advanced analytics initiatives or projects within your department?
Where do you think there are gaps in the data or analytics you have access to?	If so, how successful do you think these initiatives were and what were the challenges?

Figure 11.3: Example business questions to identify use cases

- **Frame the data science use cases**: Based on these insights, start framing potential use cases that align with key business objectives. Importantly, these use cases need to be framed as problems that data science, machine learning, or artificial intelligence can realistically solve. Involve data science/machine learning experts to validate the technical feasibility.

Evaluating use cases

Once you have identified a long list of use cases, you can evaluate each to decide where the team should focus their effort with confidence:

- **Prioritize based on value and feasibility**: Gather information on each potential use case, including data requirements, technology needs, and estimates of business value. Use this to prioritize use cases based on their potential impact and likelihood of success.
- **Prototype and test**: Before fully committing to a use case, if there is time, it may be useful to develop a rapid prototype using sample data to test its technical feasibility and potential value. If the prototype shows promise, the use case can be greenlit for full development.

The following is a template use case scorecard for an example use case that you can utilize to evaluate the use cases you have identified:

Use-case Evaluation Scorecard

Name of Use-Case	Supply Chain Demand Forecasting
Type of Use-Case	Time-Series Forecasting

Description	Forecasting supply chain demand using LSTMs on sales, supplier and weather data.	Benefits or Advantages	Improve accuracy of product demand forecasting, to reduce the necessary stock levels and associated costs of storing stock.
Objective	Forecast demand for each product over a 3-month horizon to assist purchasers in ordering the correct quantities of stock.	Risks	Risk that unforeseen rare events (e.g., COVID-19) or outside factors not considered in the model significantly reduce the forecasting accuracy.

Revenue/Cost-Savings Potential: Very High | **High** | Medium | Low | Very Low

Technical Feasibility: Very High | High | **Medium** | Low | Very Low

Data Availability: Very High | High | Medium | **Low** | Very Low

Necessary Investments: Very High | **High** | Medium | Low | Very Low

Conclusion: AI use-case with potentially high cost-savings, which requires significant investment and improved access to internal data.

Overall Evaluation: Very High | **High** | Medium | Low | Very Low

Figure 11.4: Template use case evaluation scorecard

By following this pragmatic approach to use case identification, you can generate a pipeline of data science projects that are closely tied to business objectives and have clear, measurable KPIs. This helps with avoiding common pitfalls, such as pursuing use cases that are a poor fit for data science or that are unlikely to deliver meaningful outcomes.

In the next section, we'll explore best practices for scoping and planning a data science project once you've identified a promising use case.

Planning the data product

When planning a data product, top artificial intelligence/machine learning teams move away from extensive documentation and rigid, long-term plans. Instead, they adopt a more agile, iterative approach that emphasizes collaboration, adaptability, and delivering value incrementally. Here's what that looks like in practice:

- Define clear, measurable objectives:
  - Work with stakeholders to establish specific, achievable goals for the data product
  - Ensure these objectives align with the organization's overall strategy
  - Focus on outcomes, not just outputs

- Build a skilled, cross-functional team:

  - Identify the key skills needed for the project (for example, machine learning/artificial intelligence, data engineering, domain expertise, UX/UI design, and development)
  - Assemble a lean, agile team with a mix of these skills
  - Bring in expertise and insights from outside the team, whether from customers, other business units, or external advisors

- Assess data and technology requirements:

  - Determine the data and infrastructure needed to support the product
  - Plan for data governance, security, and privacy
  - Select tools and platforms that enable rapid experimentation and iteration

- Develop a roadmap:

  - Break the project into manageable sprints, each with clear deliverables
  - Prioritize features and tasks based on their value and feasibility
  - Remain open to adapting plans based on feedback and learnings

- Foster a collaborative working environment:

  - Use tools to facilitate planning and communication, including team documentation spaces such as Notion or communication channels such as Slack
  - Hold meetings as necessary but avoid introducing meetings for their own sake or bureaucracy as this slows the team down without a clear benefit
  - Promote a culture of peer review among team members, such as data scientists, machine learning engineers, and data engineers, to collectively improve the quality of the team's work
  - Encourage open communication, continuous feedback, and a focus on iterative improvement

Practical example – planning a data science project in marketing

Let's consider a practical example of planning a data science project in the marketing industry. A company wants to use data science to optimize its digital advertising strategy:

- The problem is defined as *"How can we use data science to improve the effectiveness of our digital advertising campaigns?"* The stakeholders are the marketing team, the sales team, and the company's leadership.
- The deliverable is a minimum viable product predictive model that can forecast the performance of different advertising strategies. The data required includes historical advertising data, sales data, and customer demographic data.

- Success will be measured by the increase in sales attributable to the optimized advertising strategy. The constraints include a 6-month timeline, a budget for a technical team and testing advertisements, and the need to comply with data privacy regulations.

Think about the team you might need, the data and systems you and your team would need access to, and how the team will deploy and maintain the solution.

By focusing on the core elements of planning and embracing an Agile mindset, artificial intelligence/machine learning teams can effectively plan and execute data product development while remaining responsive to change. The emphasis is on collaboration, flexibility, and delivering value to users and stakeholders consistently.

Developing a data product

When it comes to developing a data product, following best practices can make the difference between a solution that truly delivers value and one that falls short. Since you have some knowledge of data science, you understand the potential of data products to drive business outcomes, but you also know that the development process is not always straightforward.

In this section, we'll cover the key stages of data product development and explore the best practices that top artificial intelligence/machine learning teams rely on to create successful solutions.

Data preparation and exploratory analysis

The first stage of developing a data product involves acquiring and analyzing the data the product will be built upon. We covered many techniques for this stage in *Chapters 2* and *3*.

The following tasks are included within the data preparation and exploratory analysis stage:

- Identify and acquire relevant data sources
- Perform data cleaning, integration, and preprocessing
- Conduct exploratory data analysis to gain insights and inform feature engineering
- Establish data validation and quality control processes
- Develop data pipelines for both training and inference

> **Best practice**
> Invest in building robust, scalable data pipelines that can handle the demands of your data product and ensure data quality and consistency between training and inference.

Model design and development

This second stage often involves the most interesting part for machine learning and artificial intelligence engineers as they have the chance to bring their expertise to the fore in terms of designing and developing (training) the model.

This could include doing the following:

- Selecting appropriate algorithms and modeling techniques based on the problem type and data characteristics
- Designing the model architecture and hyperparameters
- Implementing the model using suitable programming languages and frameworks
- Conducting model training, tuning, and validation

> **Best practice**
> Employ techniques such as cross-validation, regularization, and ensemble methods to improve model performance and generalization.

Evaluation and testing

Before deploying a model to production, ensuring that you thoroughly evaluate and test the model is the most important step.

We covered many evaluation metrics in *Chapter 9*.

Here are some of the steps that could be included within this stage:

- Defining relevant evaluation metrics and testing procedures
- Assessing model performance using appropriate validation techniques (for example, hold-out validation and k-fold cross-validation)
- Conducting thorough testing to verify model behavior and identify potential issues
- Performing sensitivity analysis and stress testing to ensure robustness

> **Best practice**
> Use a combination of quantitative metrics and qualitative analysis to gain a comprehensive understanding of model performance and limitations.

Deploying and monitoring a data product

Finally, your team is at the stage of deploying the model to production. This should be the aim of every successful machine learning or artificial intelligence product project, but it must be done with care. There are several steps and best practices to follow:

- **Integration**: Integrate the model into the broader system architecture. This involves ensuring the model can communicate with other components of the system, such as databases, APIs, and user interfaces.

- **Deployment infrastructure**: Establish deployment processes and infrastructure. This includes setting up the necessary servers, containers, or cloud services to host the model. Automation tools such as Docker, Kubernetes, and cloud-specific services can streamline this process.

- **Online testing**: Alongside offline evaluation and testing, an important process before deploying to production is online testing – that is, testing the system on real, live data before deployment. There are various strategies to achieve this:

    - **A/B testing**: If you want to compare the performance of two or more models, carry out A/B testing by randomly splitting traffic between the different models and measuring key metrics. You should use A/B testing for model selection and iterative improvements.

    - **Canary deployment**: After successful shadow testing, perform a canary deployment by releasing the model to a small subset of users or traffic while keeping the majority on the existing system. Monitor the model's performance and gather feedback from this limited release.

- **Deployment strategies**: Deploying to production is a critical step, and a successful deployment should be the aim of any machine learning or artificial intelligence model development. Following evaluation and testing, you could deploy the model directly to production. However, to add an additional level of safety, blue/green deployment is one strategy you can implement to ensure continuity:

    - **Blue/green deployment**: If the canary deployment proves successful, proceed with a blue/green deployment. Set up two identical production environments (blue and green) and deploy the new model to one environment while keeping the existing system in the other. Switch traffic to the new environment and monitor for any issues. If problems arise, quickly switch back to the previous environment.

- **Monitoring and logging**: Implement comprehensive monitoring and logging for the deployed model. This includes tracking model performance metrics, system health, and user interactions. Set up alerts to notify the team if any issues or anomalies are detected.

- **Feedback loop**: Establish a feedback loop to continually gather data and insights from the production system. This data can be used to retrain and update the model, ensuring it remains accurate and relevant over time.

Creating a good control test is a challenging but crucial part of the deployment process. It requires careful design to ensure the test accurately reflects real-world conditions and provides meaningful insights.

Remember, the specific deployment steps and best practices may vary depending on your organization's infrastructure, requirements, and constraints. It's important to adapt these general guidelines to your specific context.

> **Best practice**
> Adopt DevOps and MLOps practices to streamline the deployment and management of data products in production environments.

General best practices for data product development

To ensure successful outcomes and maintain high standards, top data science, artificial intelligence, and machine learning teams employ the following cross-cutting best practices throughout the development process:

- **Version control and reproducibility:**

    - Implement robust version control systems for code, data, and models. For code version control, Git and Git-based software such as GitHub, GitLab, and Bitbucket are common tools. For data and model version control, software such as **Data Version Control** (**DVC**) and MLflow are also common approaches to tracking data, model artifacts, and model training experiments.

    - Ensure reproducibility by documenting dependencies, configurations, and experimental setups.

    - Use containerization technologies to create reproducible environments for development and deployment.

- **Clear documentation and knowledge management**:

    - Maintain clear and comprehensive documentation for data, code, and models

    - Establish knowledge-sharing practices, such as wikis, tutorials, and internal forums

    - Encourage team members to document their work, insights, and lessons learned

- **Continuous integration and continuous delivery (CI/CD):**

    - Implement CI/CD pipelines to automate build, testing, and deployment processes

    - Ensure code quality through automated testing, code reviews, and static code analysis

    - Enable rapid and reliable deployment of models and applications to production environments

- **Adherence to responsible machine learning/artificial intelligence principles**:
  - Prioritize fairness, transparency, and accountability in machine learning/artificial intelligence development
  - Conduct thorough testing and validation to identify and mitigate biases in models
  - Provide clear explanations of model decisions and ensure interpretability where necessary
  - Establish governance frameworks and ethical guidelines for artificial intelligence development and deployment
- **User-centric approach**:
  - Keep the end user at the center of all development efforts
  - Gather user feedback and incorporate it into the iterative development process
  - Continuously validate solutions with users to ensure they meet their needs and expectations

By adhering to these best practices and tailoring them to specific contexts, you can navigate many of the complexities of data product development. Stay focused on delivering value to users, embrace a culture of continuous learning and improvement, and foster a collaborative environment that encourages innovation and excellence in data science, artificial intelligence, and machine learning initiatives.

Having followed all the processes and best practices for developing and deploying successful solutions, there is an important step that should not be overlooked: evaluating the business impact.

As data science practitioners, our work is only valuable if it delivers tangible benefits to the organizations we serve. The time, effort, cost, and resources invested in developing these solutions must yield real, measurable results; otherwise, the work remains a mere technical exercise.

In the next section, we will explore methods to assess business impact and discuss strategies to expand the influence of a solution.

Evaluating impact

Alongside evaluating model accuracy, it is essential to gauge the business impact of a data product. This involves selecting relevant metrics or **key performance indicators** (**KPIs**) that align with the organization's goals and objectives.

These metrics or KPIs should provide a clear picture of how the solution is affecting the business's bottom line.

Let's look at some concrete business examples of data science, machine learning, and artificial intelligence solutions across different industries, and how business impact could be measured.

Predictive maintenance in manufacturing

- **Use Case**: Implementing machine learning models to predict equipment failures and optimize maintenance schedules within a manufacturing company
- **Metrics/KPIs**: To measure the impact of manufacturing, the following metrics could be tracked:
  - Reduction in unplanned downtime
  - Increase in equipment availability and uptime
  - Reduction in maintenance costs
  - Improvement in **overall equipment effectiveness** (**OEE**)

Fraud detection in banking

- **Use case**: Deploying artificial-intelligence-powered fraud detection systems to identify and prevent fraudulent transactions
- **Metrics/KPIs**: The banking KPIs that could be tracked for the fraud detection model could include the following:
  - Reduction in fraudulent transactions
  - Increase in fraud detection accuracy
  - Reduction in false positives
  - Savings from prevented fraudulent activities

Customer churn prediction in telecom

- **Use case**: Using machine learning models to predict customer churn and implement targeted retention strategies
- **Metrics/KPIs**: The KPIs associated with a custom churn and retention solution could include the following:
  - Reduction in customer churn rate
  - Increase in customer retention
  - Improvement in **customer lifetime value** (**CLV**)
  - Increase in revenue from retained customers

Demand forecasting in retail

- **Use case**: Utilizing machine learning algorithms to forecast product demand and optimize inventory management
- **Metrics/KPIs**: To measure the impact of a demand forecasting model, the following could be tracked:
  - Reduction in inventory holding costs
  - Reduction in stockouts and lost sales
  - Increase in inventory turnover ratio
  - Improvement in forecast accuracy

Personalized recommendations in e-commerce

- **Use case**: Implementing machine-learning-powered recommendation engines to personalize product recommendations for customers
- **Metrics/KPIs**: To track the effectiveness of an e-commerce recommendation engine, you could track the following:
  - Increase in conversion rate
  - Increase in **average order value** (AOV)
  - Improvement in customer engagement and loyalty
  - Increase in cross-sell and upsell opportunities

Predictive maintenance in energy

- **Use case**: Applying machine learning techniques to predict equipment failures and optimize maintenance in energy production facilities
- **Metrics/KPIs**:
  - Reduction in unplanned downtime
  - Increase in energy production efficiency
  - Reduction in maintenance costs
  - Improvement in safety and compliance metrics

Workforce optimization in quick service restaurants

- **Use case**: Utilizing machine learning algorithms to optimize staffing levels and scheduling in restaurants

- **Metrics/KPIs**:

  - Improvement in staff utilization and productivity
  - Reduction in overtime and agency costs
  - Increase in patient satisfaction and care quality
  - Improvement in employee satisfaction and retention

Chatbot-assisted customer support

- **Use case**: Implementing a **large language model** (LLM)-powered chatbot to provide instant customer support and handle common inquiries

- **Metrics/KPIs**:

  - Reduction in customer support costs
  - Improvement in customer response times
  - Increase in customer satisfaction
  - Deflection rate and human agent productivity
  - Expansion of support coverage

These additional examples further illustrate the wide range of data science, machine learning, and artificial intelligence applications across various industries and the specific business metrics and KPIs that can be used to measure their impact.

By aligning data-driven initiatives with key business objectives and tracking relevant metrics, organizations can demonstrate the tangible value and ROI of their data science/machine learning/artificial intelligence investments.

Think about the core business metrics and KPIs within your organization or industry. Which metrics and KPIs relate most closely to the bottom-line profit for the business?

Which of your use cases will have the greatest impact on those KPIs and the overall business performance?

By consistently monitoring and reporting on these business impact metrics, data science teams can demonstrate the value they bring to the organization and justify the investment in their projects. This not only helps secure continued support for ongoing initiatives but also paves the way for expanding the impact of successful solutions across the enterprise.

Summary

In this chapter, we covered the essentials of structuring a data science project, focusing on developing impactful data products.

We discussed three project categories, emphasizing the importance of selecting the right use cases that align with your organization's goals and have the potential to deliver real value.

We provided a framework for evaluating and prioritizing use cases based on feasibility and impact, ensuring that you invest resources in projects that drive your business forward.

We also explored the key stages of data product development, from data preparation to model design, evaluation, and deployment, while adhering to best practices such as responsible AI principles, clear documentation, version control, and CI/CD practices.

Finally, we discussed evaluating the business impact of your data product by selecting relevant metrics and KPIs that align with your company's goals. By demonstrating the tangible value and ROI of your data science initiatives, you can secure ongoing support and expand the influence of your solutions across the organization.

You should now have a much better idea of how to structure and run a data science, machine learning, or artificial intelligence project.

However, nothing beats real-world experience. As you apply these concepts to your projects, you'll encounter unique challenges and opportunities that will further refine your skills. Embrace these experiences, learn from successes and failures, and continuously adapt your approach.

In the next chapter, we'll focus on building and managing a high-performing data science team while exploring key roles, skills, collaboration strategies, and best practices for fostering a culture of innovation and continuous learning.

12
The Data Science Team

As data science has matured from a nascent field to a critical business function, organizations have realized that assembling a dream team is not as simple as hiring a bunch of PhDs and hoping for the best.

> **Note**
> Data science is not an individual effort, but a team sport.

The quality of decisions depends not just on the brilliance of individuals, but on the collective intelligence of the team.

It requires a thoughtful mix of talents, from the technical prowess of data engineers to the business acumen of product managers, all working together to extract insights, build robust solutions, and drive impact.

Through my interactions with data science leaders and practitioners, I've observed that the most effective teams are those that embrace the principles of cognitive diversity and psychological safety. They bring together individuals with different backgrounds, skill sets, and ways of thinking, creating a fertile ground for innovation and problem-solving. They also foster an environment where team members feel empowered to speak up, challenge assumptions, and learn from failures.

In the following sections, we'll take a closer look at the key roles that make up a high-performing data science team, drawing on real-world examples and research-backed insights. We'll explore how each role contributes to the decision-making process, from framing the problem to communicating the results, and how the interactions between these roles can make or break a project.

This chapter covers the following topics:

- Assembling your data science team – key roles and considerations
- The hub and spoke model
- The art of recruitment
- How high-performing data science teams operate

Assembling your data science team – key roles and considerations

Building a successful data science team requires a carefully curated mix of roles and skills. There are many roles that have evolved since companies started to introduce data science, machine learning, and artificial intelligence into their business processes and products.

There are now many different, sometimes overlapping roles, not all of which are essential to every team.

Here's a breakdown of the roles to consider when assembling your team, along with insights from leading tech companies.

Data scientists

Data scientists are at the core of many data science teams, focusing on framing business problems as machine learning tasks, developing predictive models, and extracting valuable insights from data.

Responsibilities

- Frame business problems as machine learning tasks
- Develop predictive models
- Extract valuable insights from data

Skills and knowledge

- Strong foundation in statistics, programming, and domain knowledge
- Deep expertise in one area and a broad understanding of the entire data science pipeline

Industry insights

Google's data science teams emphasize the importance of "T-shaped" skills, each member having deep expertise in one area and a broad understanding of the entire data science pipeline.

Machine learning engineers

Machine learning engineers bridge the gap between data science and software engineering, ensuring that machine learning models are efficiently deployed, scaled, and integrated into production environments.

Responsibilities

- Deploy and scale machine learning models in production environments
- Bridge the gap between data science and software engineering
- Ensure models are efficient, reliable, and integrate seamlessly with existing systems

Skills and knowledge

- Expertise in machine learning and software engineering
- Knowledge of production-grade model deployment and scaling

Industry insights

Netflix has pioneered the concept of "machine learning platform engineers," who build tools and infrastructure to accelerate the deployment of ML models.

Data engineers

Data engineers are responsible for designing, building, and maintaining the data infrastructure that supports the entire data science pipeline, ensuring that data is efficiently collected, stored, and processed.

Responsibilities

- Design, build, and maintain the data infrastructure
- Ensure data is efficiently collected, stored, and processed
- Enable data scientists to focus on analysis and modeling

Skills and knowledge

- Expertise in data pipeline development and management
- Knowledge of data storage, processing, and retrieval technologies

Industry insights

Uber has invested heavily in its data engineering capabilities, building a robust data platform that supports real-time decision-making across the organization.

MLOps engineers

MLOps engineers focus on streamlining the end-to-end life cycle of machine learning models, from experimentation to production deployment and monitoring, ensuring the reliability, scalability, and performance of ML systems.

Responsibilities

- Streamline the end-to-end life cycle of machine learning models
- Build and maintain infrastructure and processes for continuous delivery of ML models
- Ensure the reliability, scalability, and performance of ML systems

Skills and knowledge

- Expertise in machine learning operations and infrastructure
- Knowledge of DevOps practices and tools

Industry insights

Uber has invested heavily in building an MLOps platform called Michelangelo to support its data science efforts.

Analytics engineers

Analytics engineers apply software engineering best practices to the development of data pipelines and analytical models, focusing on building and maintaining the data infrastructure that powers business intelligence and reporting.

Responsibilities

- Apply software engineering best practices to data pipelines and analytical models
- Build and maintain data infrastructure for business intelligence and reporting
- Ensure data reliability, consistency, and accessibility for decision-making

Skills and knowledge

- Expertise in data engineering and data analysis
- Knowledge of software engineering best practices

Industry insights

Airbnb has been a pioneer in developing the analytics engineering role, recognizing the need for a specialized skill set to support its data-driven culture.

Software engineers (full stack, frontend, backend)

Software engineers play an important role in building and maintaining the web application infrastructure that leverages machine learning and artificial intelligence, ensuring smooth performance and personalized, data-driven user experiences.

Responsibilities

- Build and maintain web application infrastructure
- Integrate machine learning models into applications
- Ensure smooth performance and personalized, data-driven user experiences

Skills and knowledge

- Expertise in web development (full stack, frontend, or backend)
- Knowledge of integrating machine learning models into applications

Industry insights

Companies such as Spotify and Netflix have emphasized the importance of close collaboration between software engineering and data science teams to deliver personalized, data-driven user experiences.

Product managers

Product managers define the vision and roadmap for data-driven products, prioritizing features, gathering requirements, and ensuring that the team delivers value to end users.

Responsibilities

- Define the vision and roadmap for data-driven products
- Prioritize features and gather requirements
- Ensure the team delivers value to end users

Skills and knowledge

- Business acumen and customer-centric approach
- Understanding of both technical and business aspects of data-driven products

Industry insights

Meta (Facebook) has emphasized the role of "data product managers," who deeply understand both the technical and business aspects of data-driven products.

Business analysts

Business analysts act as the link between the data science team and the broader organization, translating business needs into analytical requirements, supporting data mapping, and helping stakeholders understand the implications of data-driven insights.

Responsibilities

- Act as the link between the data science team and the broader organization
- Translate business needs into analytical requirements
- Support data mapping and help stakeholders understand the implications of data-driven insights

Skills and knowledge

- Understanding of business processes and requirements
- Ability to communicate effectively with both technical and non-technical stakeholders

Industry insights

Airbnb has pioneered the concept of "data science ambassadors," who are embedded within business units to drive the adoption of data-driven decision-making.

Data storytellers/visualization experts

Data storytellers and visualization experts communicate complex data insights to non-technical stakeholders through compelling narratives and visualizations, ensuring that data-driven recommendations are understood and acted upon.

Responsibilities

- Communicate complex data insights to non-technical stakeholders
- Create compelling narratives and visualizations
- Ensure data-driven recommendations are understood and acted upon

Skills and knowledge

- Expertise in data visualization and storytelling
- Ability to simplify complex concepts for non-technical audiences

Industry insights

Spotify has invested in building a strong data visualization community of practice, recognizing the importance of effective communication in driving a data-driven culture.

Considerations when assembling your team

When building a data science team, consider the following factors to ensure the team is well-equipped to tackle the challenges of data-driven projects:

- **Project requirements**: Assess the specific needs of your data science projects. If the focus is on developing data products, prioritize roles such as machine learning engineers and data engineers. If the goal is to drive strategic decision-making, emphasize roles such as data scientists and business analysts.

- **Business leadership**: Assign a business lead who is responsible for setting priorities based on the needs of the business, end users, and customers. This person should have a clear understanding of the project's objectives and be able to communicate effectively with both the data science team and other stakeholders.

- **Technical leadership**: Appoint an experienced technical lead who is responsible for the overall technical solution. This person should have a deep understanding of the data science pipeline and be able to guide the team in making technical decisions that align with the project's goals.

- **Collaboration and communication**: Foster a culture of collaboration and open communication within the team. Encourage team members to share knowledge, discuss challenges, and work together to find solutions. Regular stand-up meetings, code reviews, and knowledge sharing sessions can help build a strong, cohesive team.

- **Continuous learning**: Data science is a rapidly evolving field, so it's important to support continuous learning and skill development within the team. Encourage team members to attend conferences, workshops, and training sessions to stay up-to-date with the the latest techniques and best practices.

- **Ethical considerations**: As data science and artificial intelligence projects often involve sensitive data and have the potential to impact people's lives, it's essential to prioritize ethical considerations. Ensure that the team is aware of data privacy regulations, fairness in machine learning, and the potential biases in data and algorithms. Foster a culture of responsible and transparent data science practices.

By carefully considering these factors and assembling a diverse, skilled team with strong leadership, you'll be well-positioned to drive successful data science initiatives that deliver meaningful impact to your organization.

Data science teams within larger organizations

Once an organization has grown beyond having one data science team to having many, the question arises about how the teams should be structured and interact.

Perhaps your data science or machine team is the only such team, and this is not relevant, but if you are leading a department where you need to structure several teams, understanding the different operating models can give you some guidance on what to do, based on what you want to achieve.

There are many different operating models for data science and analytics departments, each with its own pros and cons.

These include the following:

- **Centralized**: A large central data science team that serves all parts of the business, usually within an IT, technology, or data department
- **Federated**: Smaller data science teams embedded within business units

The advantages of a centralized department are shared data and technology within the department, more specialized roles, and improved knowledge sharing and internal capability development. However, this comes at the cost of lacking a deep understanding of the business's needs and domain knowledge.

Federated teams are closer to the business units and hence have a better understanding of their needs and more domain-specific knowledge.

There is a third organizational structure that can suit large companies with several data science teams, which is called the **hub and spoke** operating model.

The hub and spoke model

The hub and spoke operating model can offer a compromise between the centralized department, which enables internal capability development and a concentration of skills, and the federated model, which operates closer to the different business departments.

What is the hub and spoke model?

Imagine a bicycle wheel. At the center, you have the hub, and radiating out from it are the spokes, connecting to the outer rim. In the context of data science, the hub represents a centralized data science, machine learning, or artificial intelligence team, while the spokes represent different business units or functions. This model allows for centralized strategy, governance, and capability development, while also providing tailored support to individual business units.

- **The hub**: This is your centralized data science team, made up of data scientists, machine learning engineers, data engineers, and other roles. They are responsible for setting the overall data strategy, maintaining data governance, and providing high-level support and expertise.

- **The spokes**: These are embedded data professionals within various business units. They understand the specific needs and challenges of their units and work closely with the hub to implement data-driven solutions. They may include data scientists, or solely business analysts/data analysts. Their work may involve data science and analytics, or engaging with their departments on what solutions and insights the central team should be providing.

This model offers a balance between centralization and decentralization, providing both strategic alignment and operational flexibility.

Often, organizations start with an initial centralized data science, machine learning, or artificial intelligence team to build a capability, and then expand into serving or operating within different departments.

The following is an example illustration of a hub and spoke model within a large organization with different business departments:

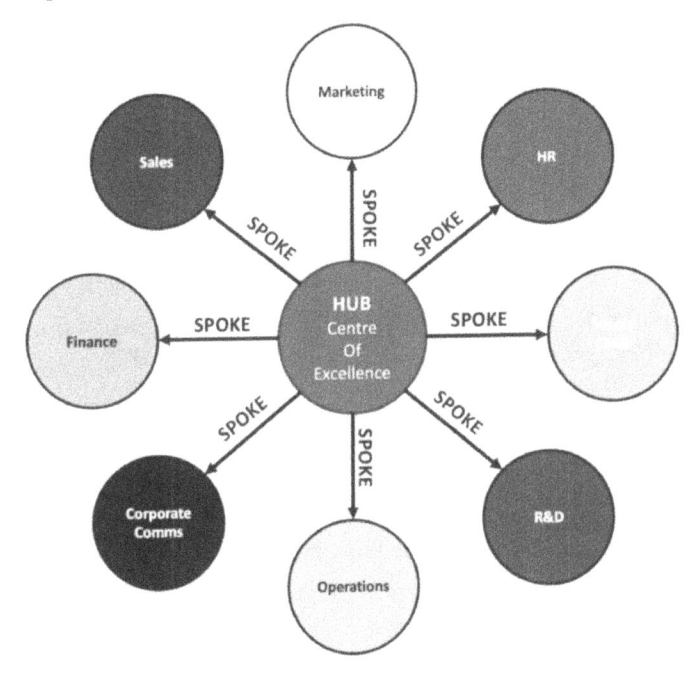

Figure 12.1: Hub and spoke model

Practical applications of the hub and spoke model

Let's look at how this model might play out within different industries:

- **Manufacturing**: A large manufacturing company may build a machine learning team to develop a solution for predictive maintenance (using sensor data to accurately predict when machinery is at risk of becoming faulty or less efficient and requires maintenance or repair). This successful solution may result in interest from other parts of the business for use cases that meet their requirements. For example, the manufacturing company's **supply chain** department may require supply and demand forecasting to reduce the amount of stock it needs to hold at any one time, reduce stock-outs, reduce long lead times, and enhance product availability. Following this, the financial department may also require more accurate financial forecasting to improve the company's balance sheet and know when and where to reduce costs. Over time, a small team serving a specific part of the business can become a core capability within the organization and serve multiple use cases.

- **Consumer goods and retail**: The hub could create a unified consumer insights and customer segmentation solution, while the spokes in marketing, sales, and customer service could apply this model to their specific functions.

Building a hub and spoke model

Creating a successful hub and spoke model involves careful planning and execution. Here are some steps to consider:

1. **Identify the hub**: Start by identifying the roles and skills needed for your centralized data science team. This includes data scientists, machine learning engineers, and data engineers.
2. **Identify the spokes**: Next, identify the business units that could benefit from embedded data professionals. These could be functions such as marketing, sales, finance, and operations.
3. **Recruit the right skills**: For the hub, you'll need a mix of technical skills (such as machine learning and data engineering) and strategic skills (such as data governance and project management). For the spokes, you'll need people who understand both data science and the specific needs of their business units.
4. **Establish governance**: Create clear guidelines for how the hub and spokes will work together. This includes communication protocols, data-sharing policies, and decision-making processes.
5. **Measure success**: Finally, establish metrics to evaluate the success of your hub and spoke model. These could include the number of data-driven projects completed, improvements in decision-making speed and accuracy, and increases in revenue or cost savings.

The hub and spoke model is a powerful way to organize your data science team, providing both strategic alignment and operational flexibility. It's not just about building a team of skilled individuals, but also about creating a cohesive unit that can drive your business forward.

As we move into the next section, we'll look at how to recruit for the roles we have mentioned when building a data science team.

The art of recruitment

Assembling a high-performing data science team is both an art and a science. It requires a deep understanding of the technical skills needed, as well as the ability to identify individuals who can thrive in your organization's unique culture. Top tech companies such as Microsoft, OpenAI, Meta, and Netflix have mastered this art, building data science teams that are not only deeply technically proficient but also highly collaborative and business-savvy.

Jerome Pesenti, previous VP of AI at Meta, stated: "When it comes to hiring for AI and machine learning roles, we look for a strong technical foundation, but also creativity, flexibility, and a drive to have real-world impact. The best candidates are those who cannot only develop powerful algorithms, but who can think critically about how to responsibly deploy AI systems in ways that benefit society."

Finding talent with both deep technical expertise and a drive to have real-world impact is challenging, but necessary to build solutions that will have a material impact on your business.

One key aspect of successful recruitment is looking beyond the resume. While technical skills are undoubtedly important, they are not the only factor to consider. Laszlo Bock, former SVP of people operations at Google, emphasizes the importance of "intellectual humility" in candidates. This means seeking out individuals who are not only smart but also able to admit when they are wrong and learn from others.

Strong problem-solving skills and a motivation to build incredible solutions are also great indicators of a successful candidate. Demis Hassabis, co-founder and CEO of DeepMind, said: "We look for people who are deeply passionate about solving hard problems and building amazing things. AI research is a long-term game, so it's important to hire people who are excited to keep learning and pushing the boundaries of what AI can do."

When building a data science team, it's also important to consider the specific needs of your organization. Are you looking to build data products, drive strategic decision-making, or both? Your first hires will be the most important, and having an excellent, committed technical lead will help steer your future hiring.

Where to find technical talent

When it comes to finding top talent for DS/ML/AI roles, there are more places to find talent than ever, but the competition for top talent is high. Teams that work well generally have a strong core of full-time hires and leverage part-time or contract workers and external consultants as appropriate. Each of these talent pools has its own advantages and trade-offs.

Full-time hires

Full-time hires are essential to building a strong core team with deep institutional knowledge and long-term alignment with company goals. When hiring full-time, companies should look beyond traditional sources such as top computer science programs, and also consider the following:

- Experienced hires from top tech companies or innovative start-ups working on cutting-edge AI
- Candidates with advanced degrees (MS, PhD) in quantitative fields such as physics, applied math, statistics, and so on, who have strong transferable skills
- Domain experts from industries such as healthcare, finance, robotics, and so on, who can bring valuable subject-matter expertise to inform AI applications

Part-time hires

Utilizing contract and part-time hires can be a valuable way to quickly bring in specialized skills for specific projects, handle fluctuating workloads, and test out potential full-time hires. Some good sources of contract DS/ML/AI talent include the following:

- Niche platforms such as Toptal, Upwork, and Arc that focus on matching top tech freelancers with companies
- Alumni networks of top MS/PhD programs in CS, stats, and so on
- Consultant marketplaces such as Catalant and Malt
- Staffing firms that specialize in placing DS/ML/AI talent

Consultants and vendor partners

Consultants and vendor partners can be hugely valuable in providing outside expertise, accelerating key initiatives, and bringing fresh perspectives. Some situations where leveraging consultants makes sense are as follows:

- Embarking on high-stakes "moonshot" AI projects where it's critical to get world-class expertise right from the start
- Implementing major new ML platforms or data infrastructure where hands-on experience with a specific technology is needed
- Providing targeted training and upskilling for the internal DS/ML/AI team
- Conducting objective audits of existing AI systems to assess fairness, robustness, privacy, and so on

Some top DS/ML/AI consulting firms and vendor partners to consider are as follows:

- McKinsey Analytics and QuantumBlack
- QualifAI and Stradigi AI (boutique AI consultancies)

Regardless of the specific mix of talent sources used, it's important to have a clear DS/ML/AI capability-building roadmap, and to ensure that there is strong knowledge transfer and collaboration between full-time teams, contractors, and consultants. A diversity of perspectives and backgrounds is key, but teams must be aligned on shared goals and ways of working.

How high-performing data science teams operate

Very few teams operate at their maximum potential, and even with a team of highly qualified individuals, if there is ineffective collaboration, stifling bureaucracy, or inadequate tooling, the project can break down.

The following are some guidelines on what it takes to run a high-performing data science team.

Cross-functional collaboration is essential

The most impactful DS/ML/AI projects involve close partnerships between data scientists, ML engineers, software developers, product managers, designers, and subject-matter experts. Fostering a culture of collaboration and breaking down silos between these functions is critical.

Diversity of perspectives drives innovation

Top teams bring together people from different backgrounds – not just in terms of demographics, but also academic training, industry experience, and ways of thinking. Cognitive diversity helps teams approach problems more creatively.

Start with the right problem to solve

Highly effective teams don't just dive into the data or algorithms – they first make sure they deeply understand the user needs and business objectives they're trying to address. Involving product, design, and business stakeholders upfront is key.

Invest in tooling, infrastructure, and workflow

With the complexity of modern ML/AI systems, having the right tools for data management, experiment tracking, model versioning, and so on makes a huge difference to productivity. Standardizing the workflow helps teams scale. Often, the additional cost of improved tooling and infrastructure can outweigh the cost of the additional time the team spends on optimizing inadequate tooling to "make it work." Remember, every hour the data science/machine learning team spends on dealing with poorly performing tools and infrastructure has its own cost, and may likely outweigh the cost of better tooling.

Continuous adaption and learning are a must

Given the rapid pace of advancement in DS/ML/AI, high-performing teams carve out dedicated time for learning – through academic papers, conferences, online courses, internal knowledge sharing, and so on. Curiosity is an essential trait.

Focus ruthlessly on outcomes over activity

The most effective DS/ML/AI teams are laser-focused on delivering measurable impact, not just shipping code or publishing papers. This often requires fighting bureaucratic inertia and resisting the temptation to work on intellectually interesting problems that don't drive real value.

As an example, Google Brain founder Andrew Ng has spoken about the importance of a "strategic focus on results, not just research" in building Google's AI capabilities. He notes that many companies make the mistake of treating AI purely as a research activity, when in reality, the most transformative breakthroughs come from close collaboration between research and product teams focused on real-world impact.

Summary

In this chapter, we explored the key roles and considerations for assembling a high-performing data science team, emphasizing that data science is a team sport requiring diverse skills and expertise. We discussed the different roles that make up a data science team, including data scientists, machine learning engineers, data engineers, and others, as well as different models for structuring the team, such as embedded, integrated, and hub and spoke. Building a successful data science team requires careful consideration of the specific needs of your organization, the skills and expertise needed, and the structure that will work best for your projects.

With a strong understanding of these roles and considerations, we're now ready to move on to the next critical step: *Onboarding the Data Science Team*.

13
Managing the Data Science Team

In managing a data science team, you must navigate a terrain quite distinct from traditional leadership contexts. The volatile nature of data science – with its reliance on machine learning and artificial intelligence – demands not just technical acumen but a nuanced approach to leadership. This chapter provides a concise exploration of effective management strategies tailored specifically to the high-stakes and high-innovation environment of data science.

We'll start by examining the day-to-day management of data science teams, emphasizing the creation of a culture that values rapid experimentation and learns constructively from failure.

We will also discuss strategies to manage the inherent uncertainty in data science projects, with examples from Netflix that help in delivering incremental value.

Additionally, this chapter will address the balancing act between research-oriented and production-focused data science work, highlighting collaboration models that are used by organizations such s DeepMind and Google Brain. Ethical considerations, which are crucial in artificial intelligence applications, will also be discussed, alongside best practices in data and model governance, illustrated through case studies from Microsoft and Uber.

The goal is to equip leaders with the understanding and tools necessary for managing data science teams effectively, ensuring both project success and team growth in this complex, rapidly evolving field.

This chapter covers the following topics:

- Day-to-day management of a data science team
- Common challenges in managing a data science team
- Empowering and motivating your data science team

Day-to-day management of a data science team

Leading a data science team is a unique challenge that requires balancing innovation and pragmatism. To drive impactful data science, you must foster a culture of experimentation while ensuring that the team's efforts create business value.

Enabling rapid experimentation and innovation

Successful data science teams embrace rapid experimentation and learn from failures. As a leader, encourage risk-taking and celebrate lessons learned from unsuccessful endeavors. Provide access to powerful tools and platforms, such as cloud computing services, to accelerate the experimentation process. Meta is known for its "move fast" culture, which encourages rapid experimentation and iteration in all aspects of the company, including artificial intelligence and machine learning.

Managing inherent uncertainty

Data science projects are inherently uncertain, with outcomes often unclear at the outset. Manage this ambiguity by structuring projects as a series of experiments and milestones, each yielding new insights. Be transparent with stakeholders about uncertainties and potential risks. Agile methodologies help deliver incremental value and maintain stakeholder engagement. Netflix's personalization algorithms demonstrate how embracing uncertainty and continuous iteration can drive significant gains.

Balancing research and application

Data science teams must balance open-ended research with deploying and maintaining production models. Consider creating dedicated research and applied work streams while fostering cross-pollination between the two. Research breakthroughs should inform applied work, and real-world challenges should guide the research agenda. Organizations such as DeepMind and Google Brain exemplify this symbiotic relationship between research and application.

Communicating effectively in data science and artificial intelligence

Effective communication is crucial for data science leaders. When discussing technical aspects of projects, use precise language and be specific about algorithms, model architectures, and evaluation metrics. Clearly explain the assumptions, limitations, and potential biases of your models. When communicating with non-technical stakeholders, use analogies and visuals to convey complex concepts such as neural networks or reinforcement learning. Highlight the business impact of your team's work, such as improved customer targeting or reduced operational costs. Regularly share updates on project progress, including both successes and challenges encountered. Encourage open dialog within the team to promote collaboration and knowledge-sharing.

Fostering a culture of curiosity and continuous learning

Top tech companies recognize the importance of fostering a culture of curiosity and continuous learning within their data science teams. As Andrew Ng, cofounder and former head of Google Brain and the former Chief Scientist at Baidu states, *"I believe that the ability to innovate and to be creative are teachable processes. There are ways by which people can systematically innovate or systematically become creative."*

To cultivate this culture, encourage your team to stay up to date with the latest research and industry trends. Provide opportunities for attending conferences, workshops, and online courses. Promote knowledge-sharing through regular presentations, brown bag lunches, and internal forums. Encourage team members to pursue side projects and explore new ideas, even if they don't immediately align with current business objectives.

Embracing peer review and collaboration

Establishing a culture of peer review and collaboration is essential for maintaining high-quality work and fostering continuous improvement. Encourage team members to regularly share their code, models, and findings with colleagues for feedback and suggestions. Implement pair programming or code review practices to catch errors, share knowledge, and ensure adherence to best practices. Create a psychologically safe environment where team members feel comfortable giving and receiving constructive criticism, understanding that it is aimed at improving the work rather than targeting individuals. By embracing peer review and collaboration, you can create a culture of excellence and shared ownership within your data science team.

Leading a data science team requires navigating the field's unique challenges. By cultivating experimentation, managing uncertainty, balancing research and application, communicating effectively, fostering a culture of curiosity and continuous learning, and embracing peer review and collaboration, you can position your team for success in this dynamic domain.

In the next section, we will explore some of the common challenges in managing a data science team and how to navigate them.

Common challenges in managing a data science team

Managing a data science team can be a complex task, especially for those new to the field. Data science is a multidisciplinary field that requires a unique blend of skills, and managing such a team can present several challenges. Let's explore some of these challenges and how to overcome them.

Challenge 1 – recruiting and retaining top talent

As we discussed in the previous chapter, hiring and retaining a talented team is the foundation for addressing all the challenges a data science team might encounter.

To quote Google's Chief Decision Scientist, Cassie Kozyrkov, *"Finding and keeping skilled data scientists is a major challenge due to high demand and competition."*

A robust onboarding process is also key to setting new hires up for success by orienting them to the company's tools, processes, and culture.

Overcoming the challenge

There are several approaches you can take to overcome these challenges to recruit and retain excellent talent:

- **Recruitment**:

  - Look beyond candidates from traditional computer science backgrounds to find hires with strong machine learning and domain expertise from technology startups, academia, or big tech companies.
  - Seek out individuals with "intellectual humility" who can learn from others.
  - When interviewing, look to understand what impact the interviewee has had in previous roles. What have they built? What have they achieved? This is more important than the titles they have held or the certifications they have.
  - Build a base of full-time hires and leverage part-time contractors and consultants to scale up the team as needed.

- **Onboarding**:

  - Develop a clear onboarding process and documentation that introduces new hires to your company's culture, tools, and workflows. This will help them integrate into the team more quickly and effectively.
  - Set up meetings between the new joiners and the rest of the team so that they can build the connections they need and gain any important knowledge for their work.
  - Provide an initial, contained project with some supervision from senior members of the team so that they can hit the ground running and quickly build familiarity with the tools and technologies with hands-on experience.

- **Retaining talent**:

  - Give top talent that you trust the autonomy to be creative and innovate. Talented individuals want to take ownership of their work and not be micro-managed. Marissa Mayer, former President and CEO of Yahoo!, outlined the role of a nurturing environment in innovation, mentioning, *"Really in technology, it's about the people, getting the best people, retaining them, nurturing a creative environment, and helping to find a way to innovate."* Steve Jobs, the late CEO of Apple, believed in the autonomy of smart employees: *"It doesn't make sense to hire smart people and tell them what to do; we hire smart people so they can tell us what to do."*

- Show your team a clear mission and exactly what you are trying to achieve. Elon Musk of Tesla and SpaceX promotes challenging work to retain top talent: *"People work better when they know what the goal is and why."*

- Provide your team with opportunities for growth and development. Richard Branson stated, *"Train people well enough so they can leave, treat them well enough so they don't want to."*

• **Letting people go**:

- **Act decisively when it's not working out**: Sam Altman, CEO of OpenAI and former president of Y Combinator, emphasizes the importance of firing fast when it's clear that an employee is not a good fit. In his blog post on hiring and firing, Altman states, *"You will not get 100% of your hires right. When it's obviously not working, it's unlikely to start working. It's better for everyone involved to part ways quickly, instead of hanging on to unrealistic dreams that it's going to get better."* He argues that delaying the inevitable only makes the situation worse for everyone involved.

- **Be compassionate but clear**: While letting someone go is never easy, it's important to handle the situation with compassion and clarity. As Altman advises, *"Having to fire people is one of the worst things a founder has to do, but you have to just get it over with and trust that it will work out better than dragging things out."* When communicating the decision, be direct and honest about the reasons for the termination, and provide the employee with any necessary support, such as severance pay or assistance with job searching. Remember that the way you handle these situations will have an impact on your team's morale and trust in leadership.

By taking a holistic approach to talent management that balances technical skills, soft skills, and team composition, data science leaders can build high-performing teams that deliver transformative business impact. The foundation of recruitment and retention is critical to overcoming the other challenges we'll explore.

Challenge 2 – aligning projects with business goals

One of the key challenges for data science leaders is ensuring that their team's projects are aligned with the company's strategic objectives. Without this alignment, even the most technically impressive projects may fail to deliver meaningful business value.

Overcoming the challenge

To align data science projects with business goals, consider the following strategies:

- **Understand the business**: Take the time to deeply understand your company's business model and strategic priorities. Attend leadership meetings, read company reports, and engage with colleagues from other departments to gain a holistic view of the business.

- **Collaborate with stakeholders**: Work closely with business stakeholders to identify high-impact projects that address their most pressing challenges and opportunities. Involve them in the project planning process to ensure that the project scope and deliverables meet their needs.
- **Prioritize and iterate**: Use a data-driven approach to prioritize projects based on their potential impact, feasibility, and alignment with business goals. Be willing to pivot or sunset projects that are no longer aligned with changing business needs.
- **Communicate value**: Regularly communicate the value that your team's projects are delivering to the business. Use metrics and case studies to demonstrate how your work is driving key outcomes such as revenue growth, cost savings, or improved customer experience.

By aligning data science projects with business goals, leaders can ensure that their teams are delivering high-impact work that drives meaningful outcomes for the organization.

Challenge 3 – managing inherent uncertainty

Data science projects often involve a high degree of uncertainty as the outcomes of experiments and models can be difficult to predict. Managing this uncertainty is a key challenge for data science leaders, who must balance the need for exploration and innovation with the realities of limited resources and timelines.

Overcoming the challenge

To manage the inherent uncertainty of data science projects, consider the following approaches:

- **Embrace risk-taking**:
  - Encourage your team to take calculated risks and run experiments to test new ideas and approaches. Create a culture that values learning and rapid iteration over perfection.
  - Elon Musk, CEO of Tesla and SpaceX, emphasizes the importance of managing risk: *"When something is important enough, you do it even if the odds are not in your favor."*
- **Rapidly prototype**:
  - Create a system to rapidly create experiments and prototype features. For machine learning, the ability of data scientists and machine engineers to quickly run experiments, train, evaluate, and iterate upon machine learning models is essential. Aim to reduce the cycle time for training and evaluating models as much as possible. Reducing this cycle time will enable machine learning engineers to train performant models and get them into production quickly, thereon the models can be rapidly iterated on and improved:
    - Investing time in creating reusable pipelines to train, evaluate, compare, and deploy your machine learning models can save time in the long run

- Open source software such as MLflow and cloud platforms such as Azure AI Studio, AWS SageMaker, AWS Bedrock, and Google Vertex AI contain features to train and fine-tune machine learning models while tracking these experiments

- Jeff Bezos, founder, and CEO of Amazon, emphasizes the importance of experimentation: *"If you double the number of experiments you do per year, you're going to double your inventiveness"*

• **Fail fast**: Recognize that failures are a natural part of the innovation process. The important thing is not to let failing projects drag on. Once it has become clear that an experiment will not deliver results, or that a project is failing, you must cut the cord quickly. Too often projects continue long past this point, using valuable time and resources, when it has long become clear that they will not deliver value. Sometimes, this can be ambiguous, and it is not clear whether to persist or pivot. Gather any data you can on whether the project is going to deliver clear, tangible value, and act decisively. Go with your gut if necessary.

By embracing uncertainty and using strategies to manage risk, data science leaders can create an environment that fosters innovation and drives breakthrough results.

Challenge 4 – scaling and operationalizing models

Once a data science team has developed a successful model, the next challenge is to scale and operationalize it for real-world use. This involves not only technical considerations around infrastructure and deployment but also organizational challenges around integrating the model into existing business processes and ensuring its long-term sustainability.

Overcoming the challenge

To scale and operationalize models effectively, consider the following strategies:

- **Plan for production**: From the outset of a project, plan for how the model will be deployed and maintained in production. This includes considering factors such as data pipelines, infrastructure requirements, and monitoring and maintenance needs.

- **Remove the gap between machine learning and operations**:

    - Within traditional software engineering, there has been a revolution with the concept of DevOps. This concept has removed the silos between the team developing software and the team deploying and operating it, into one team responsible for the product end-to-end.

    - This concept has now extended to machine-learning-based software, with **machine learning operations** (**MLOps**) providing a framework around how teams can see their machine learning models into production and maintain, iterate, and improve them over time. As illustrated in *Figure 13.1*, the MLOps cycle encompasses the key stages of developing, testing, deploying, and monitoring machine learning models.

- Roles such as machine learning engineer, artificial intelligence engineer, and MLOps engineer have emerged alongside data scientist and now it has become an expectation that anyone working in these roles has the engineering skills to be able to deploy and monitor reliable, robust models in production:

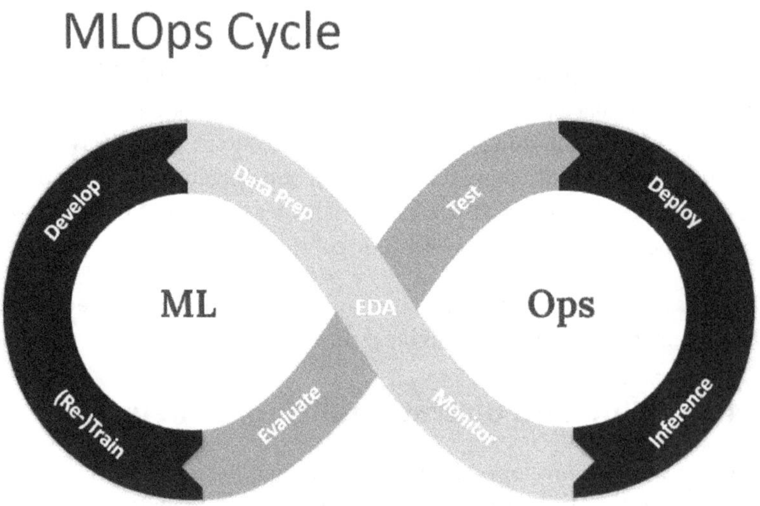

Figure 13.1: Example MLOps life cycle of machine learning models

- **Establish governance**: Put in place clear governance processes around model deployment, monitoring, and maintenance in place. This includes establishing roles and responsibilities, setting performance metrics and thresholds, and creating processes for model updates and retraining.
- **Continuously monitor and improve**: Once a model is in production, continuously monitor its performance and look for opportunities to improve it over time. This may involve retraining the model on new data, tuning its hyperparameters, or exploring new architectures or techniques.

By planning for production, collaborating with engineering, establishing governance processes, and continuously monitoring and improving models, data science leaders can ensure that their team's work has a lasting impact on the business.

Challenge 5 – deploying robust, reliable, fair models ethically

As data science models become increasingly integrated into critical business processes and decision-making, ensuring that they are robust, reliable, and fair becomes a key challenge. Models that are biased, brittle, or opaque can lead to unintended consequences and erode trust in the organization.

Overcoming the challenge

To deploy models that are robust, reliable, and fair, consider the following strategies:

- **Prioritize model explainability:** Develop models that are interpretable and explainable so that their decision-making processes can be understood and audited. Use techniques such as feature importance analysis, decision trees, or SHAP values to provide visibility into how the model arrives at its predictions.
- **Test for fairness and bias**: Rigorously test models for bias and fairness issues using techniques such as demographic parity, equalized odds, or counterfactual fairness. Be proactive in identifying and mitigating any disparate impacts on protected groups.
- **Establish ethical guidelines**: Develop clear ethical guidelines and principles for the development and deployment of artificial intelligence models. This may include considerations around data privacy, informed consent, human oversight, and accountability.
- **Foster interdisciplinary collaboration**: Bring together experts from diverse disciplines – including not only data science and engineering but also social science, law, and ethics – to inform the development and deployment of artificial intelligence models. Foster a culture of interdisciplinary collaboration and dialog.

By prioritizing model explainability, testing for fairness and bias, establishing ethical guidelines, and fostering interdisciplinary collaboration, data science leaders can ensure that their team's models are deployed in a responsible and trustworthy manner.

Empowering and motivating your data science team

Effectively empowering and motivating a data science team requires tapping into their intrinsic drive. As Daniel Pink discusses in his book *Drive*, the key motivators for knowledge workers are autonomy, mastery, and purpose.

By empowering your data science team by providing autonomy to make decisions, enabling mastery of their field, and connecting their work to a larger purpose, you can tap into the deepest wells of intrinsic motivation. An empowered and motivated team will not only deliver better results but will find fulfillment and meaning in their work, fueling long-term engagement and innovation.

In the next section, we will explore how data science teams engage with other teams and stakeholders and how they can empower other teams to use data. This will further enhance your ability to lead a data-driven organization.

Working with other teams and external stakeholders and empowering them to use data

As a data science leader, the impact of your team's work must extend beyond yourselves. The machine learning models you train, the statistical insights you identify, or the artificial intelligence applications you develop need to have an impact either within other parts of your organization or on your company's customers directly.

To truly drive data-driven decision-making, you must effectively collaborate with other teams and empower them to leverage data in their work. This requires a blend of technical translation, relationship-building, and evangelism.

Driving adoption and the impact of data science work

Ultimately, the value of data science is realized when solutions are adopted and drive business impact. To achieve this, data science leaders must work closely with engineering, product, and business teams to integrate solutions into production workflows.

Start by clearly defining success metrics and aligning them with the desired outcome. Involve stakeholders early and often, soliciting requirements and feedback. As solutions are developed, provide regular demos and pilot results to build buy-in and trust.

When transitioning to production, don't just hand off models to engineering. Work closely with the team to ensure proper deployment, monitoring, and maintenance. Provide documentation and training to enable long-term ownership.

After deployment, measure and communicate the impact of your solutions. Share success stories widely and celebrate wins with stakeholders. Airbnb attributes much of its data science success to this focus on quantifying and communicating impact.

An excellent example of a machine learning team that delivers impactful models to production is the Uber Engineering team.

This team has developed an internal platform called Michaelangelo that has enabled the deployment of machine learning models for security and login authentication, search auto-completion and result ranking, pickup ETA and map routing, pricing, trip ETA, product personalization, rider/driver matching, safe dispatch, payment fraud detection, chargeback prevention, and customer support:

You can check out Uber's real-time machine learning applications at `https://www.uber.com/en-GB/blog/from-predictive-to-generative-ai`. Almost every customer touchpoint within Uber's rider app incorporates some aspect of machine learning. As a technology-first company, Uber has the advantage of a strong engineering team, but the most successful companies of the future, whether a bank, a retailer, or an insurance company, will also be deploying machine learning and artificial intelligence features into their core offerings.

Empowering other teams to leverage data

Beyond delivering solutions directly, data science leaders can amplify their impact by empowering other teams to work with data effectively. This involves providing the right tools, training, and support to enable a self-service model for common data tasks.

Provide training and resources to upskill teams in data basics. Create a community of practice where people can learn from each other and share best practices.

By empowering other teams to work with data directly, you can scale the impact of data science across the organization. This enables a virtuous cycle where more people are asking questions about data, uncovering new opportunities, and driving a culture of data-driven decision-making.

Collaborating effectively with other teams and empowering them to use data is a key aspect of data science leadership. By partnering with SMEs, driving the adoption of solutions, and enabling self-service for other teams, you can amplify the impact of data science and accelerate your organization's data maturity.

Summary

In this chapter, we explored the unique challenges and opportunities in managing a data science team, including fostering a culture of rapid experimentation, managing inherent uncertainty, balancing research and production work, communicating effectively, cultivating curiosity and continuous learning, implementing peer review and collaboration, empowering the team, aligning projects with business goals, scaling and operationalizing models, deploying robust, reliable, fair, and ethical artificial intelligence, driving adoption of data science work, and empowering other teams to leverage data. While tactical excellence in managing data science teams is crucial, realizing the full potential of data science requires leaders who can navigate the strategic challenges involved in driving data-driven transformation.

In the next chapter, we will explore how, as a data science leader, you can grow and learn beyond what you have learned in this book, how you can stay up to date with developments in machine learning and artificial intelligence without feeling overwhelmed, and how you can use the skills you have gained as a data science leader to lead teams who are developing and deploying the solutions of the future, whether in generative artificial intelligence or beyond.

14
Continuing Your Journey as a Data Science Leader

Embarking on a new career as a data science leader, or continuing your established one, can be both daunting and exciting. This book has given you a broad toolkit for data science. The field, however, is constantly evolving. Machine learning and artificial intelligence are advancing rapidly.

This final chapter aims to guide you. You'll learn how to stay current with emerging technologies. You could specialize and become a thought leader in specific industries. Alternatively, you could become an expert in different fields of data science, machine learning, or AI.

We will discuss networking and promoting data-driven thinking within and outside your organization. We'll explore resources to keep you updated with trends and learn continuously throughout your career.

The progress in data science, machine learning, and AI can be overwhelming. In this chapter, we'll provide tips to stay up to date on important developments. You'll learn how to stay focused and filter out the noise.

Navigating the landscape of emerging technologies

The rate of progress within data science, machine learning, and artificial intelligence is incredibly fast. Groundbreaking research papers come out weekly, state-of-the-art large language models come out every month, and deep learning frameworks are released every month. It can feel hard to keep up. The landscape is vast and varied. Understanding it all is impossible.

Look at the visualization of tools and technologies within machine learning, artificial intelligence, and data for 2024 that follows. Attempting to learn about all of these technologies would be a mammoth task.

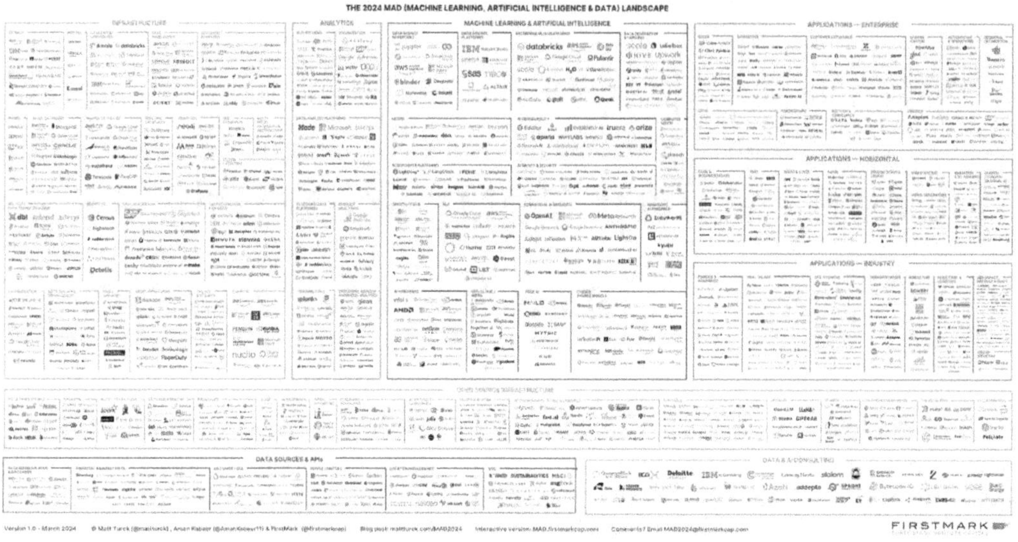

Figure 14.1: The 2024 machine learning, artificial intelligence, and data landscape

Staying up to date is a huge challenge. How can you stay current? How can you work on your career?

First, remember this: You don't need to know everything. You don't need to master every tool. Focus on what's relevant to you. Focus on your work and interests.

In the next sections, we will discuss how you can narrow down your focus to the industries and fields of DS/ML/AI that are relevant to you and most helpful to your career.

Specializing in an industry

The fields of data science, machine learning, and artificial intelligence, are progressing at an exponential rate. New breakthroughs and discoveries are made every day. Yet, despite these rapid advancements, the adoption of these cutting-edge technologies across industries often lags behind the pace of the advancements. There are several reasons for this, including regulation, data privacy concerns, and compliance requirements.

However, one of the most significant factors holding back the adoption of machine learning and artificial intelligence across different industries is a shortage of skills and knowledge of where to apply them. Unless you are working on artificial general intelligence in a frontier lab, it is likely that you will focus on the applications of data science, machine learning, or artificial intelligence within a specific sector.

As a data science leader, you can set yourself apart by having a solid understanding of techniques and developments within DS/ML/AI, while simultaneously possessing the domain expertise of a particular industry. This combination of skills will allow you to identify the best use cases where DS/ML/AI can be applied to drive value and innovation.

Figuring out which industries or sectors to focus on can be a difficult task. You may have worked across different industries throughout your career and might be unsure which ones you would or would not be happy working in. To help guide your decision, consider the following factors:

- **Experience**: In which industries have you worked? Are there particular industries that you preferred working in, and why was that? Your experience can provide valuable insights into which industries align best with your skills and interests.

- **Interests**: Are there particular industries that you are passionate about, whether you have already worked in them or not? For example, are you passionate about the automotive industry, education, or healthcare, and would you be motivated to work in one of those sectors? Following your passions can lead to a more fulfilling and engaging career.

- **Skillset**: Is your skillset best aligned with a particular industry? For example, if you have a deep understanding of forecasting and time series analysis, then working within the finance sector may provide ample opportunities to use those skills. Or, if you have a solid understanding of natural language processing and large language models, an industry that deals with large volumes of text, such as law or publishing and media, may be of interest. If you have extensive experience with computer vision, working within medical imaging may be a good use of your knowledge. Try to align your technical interests and expertise with specific sectors to maximize your impact and value.

- **Location**: Your geographic location may influence the opportunities available to you. For example, if you work in London, a global center for finance, you may find many opportunities within financial services. Similarly, if you live near Washington D.C., you may find numerous opportunities within legal and government sectors. Although remote work and the digital nature of DS/ML/AI have made location less of a constraint, it is still worth considering the local opportunities available in your area.

- **Ethics**: Finally, your ethical principles may encourage or dissuade you from working within certain sectors. For example, if you disagree with gambling, you may want to avoid working in the betting industry, which employs data scientists. Or, if you are a pacifist, you may choose to avoid working within the defense sector. Conversely, if you feel an ethical drive to work within industries that benefit society, you may gravitate toward sectors such as renewable energy, healthcare, or education. Aligning your work with your values can lead to a greater sense of purpose and fulfillment in your career, such as renewable energy, healthcare, or education if you feel an ethical drive to work within industries that benefit society.

Just as specializing in an industry can set you apart as a data science leader, so too can specializing in a specific field within the broad realm of data science, machine learning, and artificial intelligence. In the next section, we will look at some of the subfields within DS/ML/AI so you can think about where you might like to focus.

Specializing in a field

When the term "data science" was relatively new, and companies started hiring data scientists, the breadth of fields a data scientist might have been expected to know about was a lot more limited. Having strong theoretical and applied knowledge of statistics and supervised and unsupervised machine learning – topics we have covered in this book – may have covered most applied data science projects.

In academia, there was a different story, rapid progress was being made within deep learning, and fields such as natural language processing, computer vision, and reinforcement learning were making huge strides. Part of this progress was due to theoretical breakthroughs, particularly around neural network architectures, and part of this progress was due to the massive increases in compute and data available to researchers.

This academic progress has opened up a much broader range of fields within data science, machine learning, and artificial intelligence that can be applied within industries.

Each subfield of data science, machine learning, and artificial intelligence could be the topic of a PhD or an entire academic career in its own right, so for practitioners within the industry, it is impossible to gain more than a surface-level understanding of each.

With this breadth of fields within DS/ML/AI in mind, it makes a lot of sense to specialize your knowledge and focus on the topics that will be most applicable to your work.

Let's explore some of these subfields and how they are applied in real-world scenarios. Think about your industry, and the potential applications of each field, so that you can plan where to focus your attention in your career:

- **Natural language processing (NLP) and large language models (LLMs)**: NLP and LLMs have revolutionized the way we interact with text data. Companies such as OpenAI and Anthropic have developed powerful language models such as GPT-3 and Claude, which can generate human-like text, answer questions, and even write code. These models are used in a wide range of applications, from chatbots and virtual assistants to content creation and language translation. For example, Duolingo, the popular language learning app, uses NLP to provide personalized learning experiences and to assess users' speaking skills.

- **Computer vision**: Computer vision has transformed the way machines perceive and interpret visual data. It has applications in autonomous vehicles, facial recognition, medical imaging, and more. Tesla, for instance, relies heavily on computer vision for its Autopilot feature, which enables its cars to navigate roads and avoid obstacles. In healthcare, companies such as Zebra

Medical Vision use computer vision to analyze medical images and detect signs of diseases such as cancer and osteoporosis.

- **Reinforcement learning**: Reinforcement learning is a subfield of machine learning where agents learn how to make decisions in an environment to maximize a reward signal. It has been applied in robotics, game playing, and even in optimizing complex systems such as data centers. DeepMind, the AI research company owned by Alphabet, has used reinforcement learning to train agents that can play games such as Go and StarCraft II at superhuman levels. In the energy sector, Google has used reinforcement learning to optimize the cooling of its data centers, reducing energy consumption by up to 40%.

- **Time series analysis and forecasting**: Time series analysis and forecasting are important in fields such as finance, economics, and supply chain management. Companies use these techniques to predict stock prices, forecast demand, and optimize inventory levels. Facebook (now Meta) uses time series analysis to predict user engagement and to detect anomalies in its platform. In the retail industry, companies such as Walmart and Amazon use time series forecasting to predict demand and optimize their supply chains.

- **Recommender systems**: Recommender systems are used to provide personalized recommendations to users based on their preferences and behavior. They are ubiquitous in e-commerce, streaming services, and social media. Netflix, for example, uses recommender systems to suggest movies and TV shows to its users based on their viewing history. Spotify uses similar techniques to create personalized playlists and to recommend new artists to its users. In e-commerce, Amazon's recommender system is responsible for a significant portion of its sales, by suggesting products to users based on their browsing and purchase history.

- **Graph analytics and graph neural networks**: Graph analytics and graph neural networks are used to analyze and learn from data that is represented as graphs or networks. They have applications in social network analysis, fraud detection, and drug discovery. LinkedIn uses graph analytics to provide insights into users' professional networks and to recommend potential connections. In the pharmaceutical industry, companies such as Novartis and Pfizer use graph neural networks to discover new drugs and to predict their efficacy and safety.

- **Geospatial analysis**: Geospatial analysis involves analyzing and visualizing data that has a geographic component. It has applications in urban planning, environmental monitoring, and logistics. Uber uses geospatial analysis to optimize its ride-sharing services, by predicting demand and routing drivers efficiently. In agriculture, companies such as Bayer and Monsanto use geospatial analysis to monitor crop health and optimize fertilizer and pesticide application.

- **Edge computing and edge AI**: Edge computing and edge AI involve processing data and running machine learning models on devices at the edge of the network, rather than in the cloud. This has applications in IoT, autonomous vehicles, and industrial automation. Tesla uses edge computing and edge AI to enable its cars to make real-time decisions based on data from cameras and sensors. In manufacturing, companies such as Siemens and Bosch use edge AI to monitor equipment health and to predict maintenance needs.

- **MLOps**: MLOps, or machine learning operations, is an emerging field that focuses on the deployment, monitoring, and management of machine learning models in production environments. It borrows principles from DevOps and applies them to the machine learning lifecycle. Companies such as Uber and Netflix have invested heavily in MLOps to ensure that their machine learning models are reliable, scalable, and maintainable. Tools such as Kubeflow and MLflow have emerged to help organizations streamline their MLOps workflows.

Specializing in one of these fields can make you a valuable asset to organizations looking to harness the power of DS/ML/AI. By developing deep expertise in a specific area, you can position yourself as a go-to resource for companies looking to innovate and stay ahead of the curve. Whether you choose to focus on NLP, computer vision, reinforcement learning, or any of the other exciting subfields, you'll find no shortage of opportunities to apply your skills and make a real impact in the world.

In the rapidly evolving field of data science, machine learning, and artificial intelligence, continuous learning is not just beneficial – it's essential. In the next section, we'll explore effective methods to continue learning without getting overwhelmed, while still focusing on your career growth.

Embracing continuous learning

As a data science leader, learning about the latest advancements, techniques, and tools is important to drive innovation and maintain a competitive edge. However, with the exponential progress in DS/ML/AI, it can be overwhelming to keep pace.

Here are some methods to effectively continue learning without getting overwhelmed, while still focusing on your career growth.

Online courses

Online courses are a great way to learn new skills or deepen your understanding of specific topics. Platforms such as Coursera, edX, and Udacity offer a wide range of DS/ML/AI courses from top universities and industry leaders. Some notable courses include the following:

- **Data science courses**:
  - **Data Science Specialization by Johns Hopkins University (Coursera)**: This comprehensive series covers everything from data manipulation to creating data products. It's ideal for beginners.
  - **Applied Data Science with Python by the University of Michigan (Coursera)**: This specialization covers data analysis, visualization, and machine learning using Python libraries such as pandas, Matplotlib, and scikit-learn.
  - **Data Science MicroMasters by UC San Diego (edX)**: This program is great for those looking to understand the core concepts of data science, including data wrangling, analysis, and machine learning.

- **Machine learning courses**:

  - **Machine Learning by Stanford University (Coursera)**: Taught by Andrew Ng, this is one of the most popular and well-regarded introductory courses to machine learning.

  - **Deep Learning Specialization by deeplearning.ai (Coursera)**: Also led by Andrew Ng, this series dives deep into neural networks and deep learning techniques.

  - **Advanced Machine Learning Specialization by National Research University Higher School of Economics (Coursera)**: This course is designed for those with a strong foundation in ML and covers advanced topics such as Bayesian methods and reinforcement learning.

- **AI courses**:

  - **Artificial Intelligence: A Modern Approach by Peter Norvig and Sebastian Thrun (Udacity)**: This course offers a broad overview of AI techniques, including search algorithms, game playing, and optimization.

  - **CS50's Introduction to Artificial Intelligence with Python by Harvard (edX)**: Part of the professional certificate program, this course is an excellent blend of theoretical and practical AI knowledge.

  - **Deep Learning Specialization by deeplearning.ai (Coursera)**: Focuses on the fundamentals and advanced concepts of deep learning, covering neural networks, optimization, and hyperparameter tuning.

- **Generative AI courses**:

  - **Introduction to Generative AI by Google Cloud**: This course covers the basics of generative AI, including LLMs and ethical considerations, making it great for beginners.

  - **Generative AI Developer Kit by AWS**: Provides hands-on training with AWS products, ideal for those already working within the AWS ecosystem and looking to expand their skills.

Cloud certifications

Certifications provided by major cloud service providers can help you understand how to build DS/ML/AI solutions on cloud platforms and demonstrate your expertise to employers. Here are some respected certifications relevant to data science, machine learning, and AI:

AWS (Amazon Web Services)

- **AWS Certified Machine Learning – Specialty**:

  - **Overview**: This certification validates your ability to design, implement, deploy, and maintain ML solutions. It covers the best practices for model training, tuning, and deployment using AWS services.

- **Skills covered**: Data engineering, exploratory data analysis, modeling, machine learning implementation, and operations.

Azure (Microsoft Azure)

- **Microsoft Certified: Azure AI Engineer Associate**:

  - **Overview**: This certification focuses on implementing AI solutions that leverage Azure Cognitive Services, Azure Machine Learning, and knowledge mining.
  - **Skills covered**: Analyzing solution requirements, designing AI solutions, integrating AI models into solutions, and deploying and maintaining AI solutions.

- **Microsoft Certified: Azure Data Scientist Associate**:

  - **Overview**: Validates expertise in applying data science and machine learning to implement and run machine learning workloads on Azure.
  - **Skills covered**: Data preparation, feature engineering, modeling, and model management.

GCP (Google Cloud Platform)

- **Google Cloud Professional Machine Learning Engineer**:

  - **Overview**: This certification demonstrates the ability to design, build, and productionize ML models to solve business challenges using GCP.
  - **Skills covered**: ML model design, development and deployment, scaling, automation, and monitoring.

If you know that you are going to be working with one of these cloud providers, these certifications can help you or your team learn the relevant skills to start developing cloud-based data science, machine learning, and AI applications.

Technical tutorials and documentation

Hands-on tutorials and official documentation are invaluable resources when learning new tools or frameworks. Often, when working with a new technology, framework, or library, the best source of information is the official docs or tutorials.

Learning plan framework

The following checklist can be used as a simple framework for learning about and applying a new topic, learning the theory, and gaining hands-on experience.

Step	Description	Example	Status
1. Set Clear Goals	Define what you want to achieve in your learning journey.	Goal: Gain proficiency in using Large Language Models for Question-Answering.	[Not Started/In Progress/Complete]
2. Identify Key Topics	List the specific topics or skills you need to learn to reach your goals.	NLP Basics, Text Embeddings, Large Language Models, Retrieval Augmented Generation (RAG).	[Not Started/In Progress/Complete]
3. Choose Learning Resources	Select the best resources to learn each topic (online courses, books, tutorials).	Courses: Natural Language Processing Specialization (Coursera); Generative AI with Large Language Models (Coursera); Tutorial: RAG from Scratch (Learn by Building AI).	[Not Started/In Progress/Complete]
4. Create a Schedule	Plan when and how much time you will dedicate to learning each topic.	Weekdays: 1 hour/day; Weekends: 3 hours on projects.	[Not Started/In Progress/Complete]
5. Set Milestones	Define intermediate goals.	Complete NLP specialization by July; Complete Generative AI course by August; Build a demo RAG application by September.	[Not Started/In Progress/Complete]
6. Apply Learning	Implement what you've learned through projects, experiments, or work tasks.	Project: Create a customer service chatbot.	[Not Started/In Progress/Complete]
7. Seek Feedback	Get feedback from peers, mentors, or online communities to improve.	Join NLP/LLM study groups; Ask mentors/peers for advice.	[Not Started/In Progress/Complete]
8. Review and Adjust	Regularly review your progress and adjust your plan as needed.	Adjust schedule and goals as needed.	[Not Started/In Progress/Complete]

Figure 14.2: Learning plan checklist

Alongside formal learning of key topics, it is useful to keep an eye on emerging developments, news, and trends within data science, machine learning, and artificial intelligence. In this next section, we will look at some channels you can use to stay up to date in a field that is constantly changing and evolving.

Staying up to date with current DS/ML/AI news and trends

In addition to continuous learning through online courses and certifications, staying informed about the latest developments, trends, and news in the world of data science, machine learning, and artificial intelligence is important for data science leaders.

Here are some effective ways to stay up to date:

Industry blogs and publications

Follow reputable blogs and publications that cover DS/ML/AI topics, such as the following:

- *Towards Data Science*
- *KDnuggets*
- *Machine Learning Mastery*
- *Google AI Blog*
- *OpenAI Blog*

These resources provide insights, tutorials, and news on the latest advancements and applications in the field.

Podcasts

Listen to podcasts and YouTube channels that provide AI news, interview experts, and discuss current trends in DS/ML/AI, such as the following:

- *Two Minute Papers*
- *Data Skeptic*
- *Matthew Berman*
- *The AI Podcast by Lex Fridman*
- *Matt Wolfe*
- *Hard Fork*
- *AI Explained*

Podcasts are a great way to learn while commuting or during downtime.

Conferences and webinars

Attend or watch recordings of major conferences and webinars, such as the following:

- NeurIPS (Neural Information Processing Systems)
- ICML (International Conference on Machine Learning)
- KDD (Knowledge Discovery and Data Mining)
- AI Summit

These events showcase the latest research, technologies, and best practices in the field.

AI influencers

Follow thought leaders, researchers, and influencers on social media platforms such as Twitter and LinkedIn. Here are some leading influencers to follow:

- *Andrew Ng (@AndrewYNg):* AI pioneer, cofounder of Coursera, and founder of Landing AI
- *Fei-Fei Li (@drfeifei)*: Professor at Stanford, co-director of the Stanford Institute for Human-Centered AI
- *Yann LeCun (@ylecun)*: Chief AI scientist at Meta, professor at NYU
- *Cassie Kozyrkov (@quaesita)*: Chief decision scientist at Google
- *Andrej Karpathy (@karpathy)*: Former director of AI at Tesla, influential researcher
- *Demis Hassabis (@demishassabis)*: CEO and cofounder of DeepMind
- *Jeff Dean (@JeffDean)*: Senior fellow and SVP of Google Research and Health
- *Sam Altman (@sama)*: CEO of OpenAI, cofounder of OpenAI
- *Ian Goodfellow (@goodfellow_ian)*: Director of machine learning at Apple, inventor of GANs
- *Ilya Sutskever (@ilyasut)*: Former cofounder and former chief scientist at OpenAI

By incorporating these methods into your routine, you can effectively stay up to date with the rapidly evolving landscape of data science, machine learning, and artificial intelligence. Remember to be selective in the content you consume, focusing on high-quality, relevant information that aligns with your goals and interests as a data science leader.

In the next section, we will look at how you can become an advocate for data science, machine learning, and artificial intelligence within your organization, and increase their adoption and impact.

Promoting data-driven thinking within your organization

As a data science leader, your role extends beyond just staying up to date with the latest trends and technologies. You also have the opportunity and responsibility to promote a data-driven culture within your organization. By evangelizing the value of data science, machine learning, and artificial intelligence, you can help your colleagues and decision-makers understand the potential of these technologies and inspire them to embrace data-driven thinking. Here are some practical ways to achieve this:

Host internal learning sessions

- Organize regular lunch-and-learn sessions or workshops to introduce your colleagues to DS/ML/AI concepts, tools, and case studies

- Invite guest speakers from other departments or external experts to share their experiences and insights
- Encourage open discussions and Q&A sessions to foster engagement and address any concerns or misconceptions

Collaborate on cross-functional projects

- Actively seek out opportunities to collaborate with other teams, such as marketing, operations, or product development
- Demonstrate how DS/ML/AI can be applied to solve real-world problems and drive business value within these domains
- By working closely with colleagues from different backgrounds, you can help demystify data science and showcase its practical applications

Share success stories and lessons learned

- Regularly communicate the successes and lessons learned from your data science projects to a wider audience within your organization
- Use internal newsletters, company blogs, or team meetings to share how DS/ML/AI has contributed to improving processes, making better decisions, or driving innovation
- Be transparent about the challenges faced and the solutions implemented to build trust and credibility around data-driven approaches

Mentor and upskill colleagues

- Offer mentorship and guidance to colleagues who are interested in learning more about data science and its applications
- Help them develop basic data literacy skills and provide resources for further learning, such as online courses or recommended reading materials
- Encourage a culture of continuous learning and experimentation, where everyone feels empowered to explore and apply data-driven techniques in their work

Establish a data science community of practice

- Create an internal community of practice for data science enthusiasts, including data scientists, analysts, engineers, and business stakeholders
- Organize regular meetups, discussion forums, or hackathons to foster collaboration, knowledge sharing, and idea generation

- Use this platform to discuss the latest industry trends, share best practices, and brainstorm potential applications of DS/ML/AI within your organization

By actively promoting data-driven thinking and evangelizing the value of DS/ML/AI within your organization, you can help create a culture that embraces innovation, continuous learning, and evidence-based decision making. Your passion and expertise can be a catalyst for transforming how your colleagues approach problems and drive business success in the age of data and AI.

While promoting data-driven thinking within your organization is important, it's equally important to expand your network beyond your company's walls. In the next section, we'll explore how you can build a network outside of your organization, which can support you throughout your career, and unlock new, unforeseen opportunities along the way.

Networking beyond your organization

Building strong connections with professionals in data science, machine learning, and artificial intelligence communities can lead to valuable opportunities for learning, collaboration, and career growth.

Here are some ways to network effectively outside your organization:

Attend industry conferences and events

- Participate in major DS/ML/AI conferences, such as Big Data LDN, or AI Summit, to stay updated on the latest research and trends
- Attend workshops, presentations, and networking sessions to connect with experts and practitioners from various industries and backgrounds
- Engage in meaningful conversations, exchange ideas, and follow up with valuable contacts after the event

Join online communities and forums

- Become an active member of online communities on LinkedIn, Reddit, or Kaggle, where data science professionals gather to share knowledge and collaborate on projects
- Participate in discussions, offer insights, and contribute to open source projects to establish your expertise and build relationships with like-minded individuals
- Join relevant groups or forums focused on specific DS/ML/AI topics or industries to expand your network and stay informed about emerging trends and opportunities

Engage with local meetups and user groups

- Attend local meetups and user groups focused on data science, machine learning, or artificial intelligence in your area
- These gatherings provide an excellent opportunity to connect with professionals from various companies, share experiences, and learn from each other's successes and challenges
- Consider presenting your work or hosting a session to showcase your expertise and contribute to the community

Collaborate on side projects or research

- Identify opportunities to collaborate with professionals outside your organization on side projects, open source initiatives, or research papers
- Reach out to potential collaborators with complementary skills or expertise, and work together to solve interesting problems or explore new ideas
- These collaborations can lead to valuable learning experiences, expanded networks, and potential career opportunities in the future

Offer mentorship or seek mentors

- As you gain experience and expertise in the field, consider offering mentorship to aspiring data science professionals or students
- Share your knowledge, provide guidance, and help them navigate the challenges of building a successful career in DS/ML/AI
- Alternatively, seek out experienced mentors who can provide valuable advice, support, and connections to help you grow in your career

By actively networking outside your organization, you can tap into a wealth of knowledge, opportunities, and relationships that can significantly contribute to your growth as a data science leader. Building a strong professional network takes time and effort, but the benefits of connecting with diverse talent, staying up to date on industry trends, and discovering new opportunities are well worth the investment.

Summary

Congratulations on reaching the end of this book and your journey toward becoming a data science leader. You should now have a solid grasp of key concepts within statistics and machine learning and the techniques and best practices needed to succeed as a data science leader.

We've covered a wide range of topics, from the basics to advanced applications. We've also explored the practical aspects of building teams, promoting a data-driven culture, and staying up to date with the latest developments.

As you transition into your new role, keep learning continuously, collaborate with skilled, like-minded people, and foster innovation as a team.

Don't forget the human factor. Wield these powerful tools responsibly and ethically for the benefit of society.

Move forward with confidence and a curious mindset, never stop learning, and apply your expertise to make a real impact.

The future of data science, machine learning, and artificial intelligence is promising, and we need strong leaders to make this promise a reality. Become a leader with integrity, passion, and drive – I am sure you will go on to build great things.

Index

A

accuracy 104, 105
alternative hypothesis (H_1) 61
   examples 62
   formulating 61
analytics engineers 194
   industry insights 194
   responsibilities 194
   skills and knowledge 194
application programming interfaces (APIs) 30
applications, computer vision
   autonomous vehicles 109
   image recognition 109
   medical imaging 109
applications, deep learning
   image recognition 110
   Natural Language Processing (NLP) 110
   speech recognition 110
applications, Natural Language Processing (NLP)
   automated summarization 108
   chatbots 108
   sentiment analysis 108
applications, supervised learning
   consumer goods 122
   manufacturing industry 123
   retail industry 122

Apriori algorithm 133
   using 133
Area Under the ROC (AUC-ROC) 106, 122
artificial intelligence (AI) 91, 109
   General AI 109
   Narrow AI 109
   versus machine learning (ML) 4
association rule learning 133
   Apriori algorithm 133
   evaluation metrics 134
automated summarization 108
autonomous vehicles 109
average order value (AOV) 188
AWS Certified Machine Learning-Specialty 223

B

Bernoulli distribution 18
bias 107, 169
   example 169
   key feature 170
   mitigating 169
binomial distribution 18
boxplots 50

business analysts 195
  industry insights 196
  responsibilities 195
  skills and knowledge 196

C

causation 17
chatbots 108
chi-squared distribution 20
chi-squared test 68
classification
  examples 113
classification algorithms 119
  decision trees 120
  k-NN 119
  random forests 121
  SVM 119
classification metrics 116
  accuracy 104
  precision 104
  recall 104
classification models
  evaluating 145, 146
  evaluation metrics 147
  F1-Score 150
  precision 147
  recall 149
click-through rate (CTR) 67
cloud certifications
  AWS (Amazon Web Services) 223
  Azure (Microsoft Azure) 224
  GCP (Google Cloud Platform) 224
cloud computing solutions 36
clustering 128, 132
  evaluation metrics 132
  k-means clustering 130
  practical applications 131
  working 129, 130

cluster sampling 10
coefficient of determination
  (R-squared) 86, 139
  example 86
complexity 158
computer vision 27, 108, 220
  applications 109
conditional probability 12, 13
continuous learning
  cloud certifications 223
  embracing 222
  online courses 222, 223
  plan framework 225
  technical tutorials and documentation 224
continuous probability distributions 19
  chi-squared distribution 20
  exponential distribution 20
  F-distribution 20
  gamma distribution 19
  normal distribution 19
  standard normal distribution 19
  student's t-distribution 19
convenience sampling 9
correlation 16
correlation analysis 53, 54
covariance 17
customer churn model 145
customer lifetime value (CLV) 187
customer relationship management
  (CRM) system 45

D

data
  trend lines, fitting to 77-79
Data-centric AI
  reference link 161
data cleaning 161

Index   235

data collection
   methods 29, 30
data-driven thinking promotion 227
   cross-functional projects, collaborating on 228
   data science community of practice, establishing 228
   internal learning sessions, hosting 227
   mentorship, offering 228
   success stories and lessons learned, sharing 228
data engineers 193
   industry insights 193
   responsibilities 193
   skills and knowledge 193
data processing 30, 31, 38
data product 174, 175
   characteristics 174
   deploying 184, 185
   monitoring 184, 185
data product, business impact 186
   chatbot-assisted customer support 189
   customer churn prediction in telecom 187
   demand forecasting in retail 188
   fraud detection in banking 187
   personalized recommendations in e-commerce 188
   predictive maintenance in energy 188
   predictive maintenance in manufacturing 187
   workforce optimization, in quick service restaurants 189
data product development 182
   best practices 185, 186
   data preparation and exploratory analysis 182
   evaluation and testing 183
   model design and development 183

data product stages 177
   example 181, 182
   planning 180, 181
   use cases, evaluating 179, 180
   use cases, identifying 178, 179
data quality 23, 158
   accuracy 23
   completeness 23
   consistency 23
   data training 159
   poor data quality, dealing with 160
   timeliness 23
   uniqueness 23
   validity 24
data quantity 22, 158
   challenge, mitigating 160
   data training 159
data science 3, 6
   mathematical and statistical underpinnings 5, 6
   versus artificial intelligence (AI) 4, 5
data science leader
   landscape of emerging technologies, navigating 217
   specializing in 218, 219
data science projects, types 174
   data products 174
   reports and analytics projects 175, 176
   research and methodology 176, 177
data science team
   assembling 192
   assembling, considerations 196, 197
   data science work, impact and adoption 214
   empowering 213
   key roles and considerations 192-196
   motivating 213
   other teams, empowering to work 215

Index

teams and external stakeholders, working with 214
within larger organizations 197, 198
data science team management 206
  challenges 207
  culture of curiosity and continuous learning 207
  effective communication 206
  inherent uncertainty, managing 206
  peer review and collaboration, embracing 207
  rapid experimentation and innovation, enabling 206
  research and application, balancing 206
data science team management, challenges
  inherent uncertainty, managing 210, 211
  models, deploying 212, 213
  models, scaling and operationalizing 211, 212
  projects, aligning with business goals 209, 210
  top talent, recruiting 207, 208
  top talent, retaining 208, 209
data science teams, within larger organizations
  centralized 197
  federated 197
data scientists 192
  industry insights 192
  responsibilities 192
  skills and knowledge 192
datasets evaluation 22
  data quality 23
  data quantity 22
  data variety 23
  data velocity 22

data storing 30, 31
  data warehouses 35
  document databases 33
  graph databases 34
  key-value databases 34
  object storage 32
  relational databases 31
  vector databases 35
data storytellers/visualization experts 196
  industry insights 196
  responsibilities 196
  skills and knowledge 196
data training
  challenge, mitigating 159
data validation 161
data variety 23
data velocity 22
Data Version Control (DVC) 185
data visualization 45
  code example 46-48
data warehouses 35
Davies-Bouldin Index (DBI) 128
decision trees 99, 120, 121
deep learning 109
  applications 110
degrees of freedom 16
Density-Based Spatial Clustering of Applications with Noise (DBSCAN) 127
density curve 49
descriptive statistics 7, 8, 43
  code example 43-45
dimensionality reduction 52
discrete probability distributions 18
  Bernoulli distribution 18
  binomial distribution 18
  geometric distribution 19
  negative binomial distribution 18
  poisson distribution 19

document databases 33
Dunn index (DI) 129, 132

E

EDA, techniques and tools
  boxplots 50
  correlation analysis 53, 54
  data visualization 45
  density curve 49
  descriptive statistics 43
  dimensionality reduction 52
  heatmaps 51
  histograms 48
  outlier detection 55
edge computing and edge AI 221
equation of line of best fit
  calculating 79-82
error 78
errors, hypothesis testing 63
  balancing 64, 65
  Type I error 63
  Type II error 64
evaluation metrics 121, 138
  classification metrics 121
  mean absolute error 142
  regression metrics 121
  regression models 145
  regression models, evaluating 138
  root mean squared error 140
  R-squared 139
  strategies 144
  using 143
exploratory data analysis (EDA) 7, 41, 131
  data, storing and collecting 43
  techniques and tools 43
exponential distribution 20

F

F1-Score 106, 151
  defining 150
  formula 151
  practical implications 151, 152
  using 151
fairness 158, 169
  example 169
  key feature 170
  mitigating 169
False Negative (FN) 106
False Positive (FP) 106
F-distribution 20
first-party data 24, 25
first quartile (Q1) 50

G

gamma distribution 19
General AI 109
geometric distribution 19
geospatial analysis 221
goodness of fit, in least-squares regression
  evaluating 86
Google Cloud Professional Machine Learning Engineer 224
Google Colab 42
  step-by-step guide, to setting up 42
  working with 41, 42
graph analytics and graph neural networks 221
graph databases 34

H

heatmaps 51
high-performing data science
   teams operation 202
   continuous adaption and learning 203
   investment 203
   outcomes, focusing on 204
   perspectives drives innovation, diversity 203
   problem, solving 203
   ross-functional collaboration 203
histograms 48
hub 198
hub and spoke model 198
   application 199
   building 200
hybrid solutions 37, 38
hypotheses testing 60
   alternative hypothesis, formulating 61, 62
   case study 72-74
   errors 63
   hypotheses, selecting 62
   null hypothesis, formulating 61
   p-values 65
   significance level, determining 62
   working 60, 61

I

image recognition 109, 110
inferential statistics 7, 8
intercept of regression line
   interpreting 83, 84
interquartile range (IQR) 15, 50
IQR method 55

K

key performance indicators (KPIs) 186
key-value databases 34
kilowatt-hours (kWh) 83
k-means clustering 130
   steps 131
k-nearest neighbors (k-NN) 101, 115, 119

L

large language models
   (LLMs) 27, 160, 189, 220
learning model
   accuracy 137
   test (holdout) data, evaluating 138
least absolute shrinkage and selection
   operator (Lasso) regression 118
least squares method 77, 79
linear regression 97
line of best fit
   estimating 79
logistic regression 98

M

machine learning 92, 157
   customer personalization and
      segmentation 93
   fraud detection and security 93
   healthcare diagnostics and treatment 94
   on unstructured data 108
   predictive maintenance 94
   process 103
   reinforcement learning 95
   relation, to statistics 92
   risks and limitations 106
   semi-supervised learning 95
   significance 93

supervised learning 95
supply chain and inventory optimization 93
transfer learning 96
types 94
unsupervised learning 95
versus AI 4
machine learning algorithms 97
  decision trees 99
  k-Nearest Neighbors (k-NN) 101
  linear regression 97
  logistic regression 98
  neural networks 102
  random forests 99
  Support Vector Machines (SVMs) 100
machine learning engineers 192
  industry insights 193
  responsibilities 192
  skills and knowledge 193
machine learning models
  classification metrics 104-106
  evaluating 104
  methods 152
  regression metrics 106
  test set 104
  training set 104
  universal insights, with SHAP values 153
  used, for decoding classification models 152, 153
  using, for regression models 152
  validation set 104
machine learning operations (MLOps) 211, 222
mean absolute error (MAE) 106, 142
  calculation example 142
  formula 142
  interpreting tips 143
  using 144
  values 143

mean squared error (MSE) 106
measures of central tendency 13, 14
measures of dispersion 14
  interquartile range (IQR) 15
  range 14
  variance and standard deviation 14, 15
medical imaging 109
Microsoft Certified
  Azure AI Engineer Associate 224
  Azure Data Scientist Associate 224
MLOps engineers 193
  industry insights 194
  responsibilities 193
  skills and knowledge 194
model drift 158, 162-168
  key feature 168
  mitigating 168
model inference (execution) 7
model selection 158
model training 7
model tuning 158
multicollinearity 118

N

Narrow AI 109
natural language processing (NLP) 27, 108, 110, 220
  applications 108
negative binomial distribution 18
networking, outside organization
  industry conferences and events, attending 229
  local meetups and user groups, engaging with 230
  mentorship 230
  online communities and forums, joining 229
  side projects or research collaboration 230

240 Index

neural networks 102
nonresponse bias 30
normal distribution 19
null hypothesis (H_0) 61
   examples 61
   formulating 61

O

object storage 32
one-tailed test 72
online courses
   AI courses 223
   data science courses 222
   generative AI courses 223
   machine learning courses 223
online transaction processing (OLTP) 35
on-premises solutions 37
outlier detection 55
   IQR method 55
   other techniques 56
   Z-score method 55
overall equipment effectiveness (OEE) 187
overfitting 107, 158, 162
   fairness, ensuring 162, 163
   model drift, navigating 162
   training-serving skew, navigating 162
overfitting, for optimal model performance 163
   consequences 163
   model solutions, building 165
   problem 163
overfitting, for optimal model performance, problem
   axes 165
   business decisions 167
   chart 166
   model solutions, building 164

   optimal model, finding 166
   trade-off 166

P

poisson distribution 19
polynomial regression 117
poor data quality
   challenge, mitigating 160
poor data quality, techniques
   data cleaning 161
   data validation 161
precision 104, 105, 148
   calculating 148
   using 148
principal component analysis (PCA) 52
probability 11
probability density function 11
probability distributions 11, 12, 18
   continuous probability distributions 19
   discrete probability distributions 18
probability mass function (PMF) 11
product managers 195
   industry insights 195
   responsibilities 195
   skills and knowledge 195
p-values 65
   as measure of evidence 65
   example 65, 66
   versus significance level 65

R

random forests 99
random sampling 9
random variables 11
range 14

recall 104, 105, 149
  formula 149
  practical implications 150
  using 150
recommender systems 221
recruitment 200, 201
  technical talent, finding 201
regression 75, 113
  examples 113
  use cases, in business context 75, 76
regression algorithms 117
  Lasso regression 118
  polynomial regression 117
  ridge regression 118
regression metrics 116
  mean absolute error (MAE) 106
  mean squared error (MSE) 106
  R-squared (coefficient of determination) 106
regression models
  evaluating 138, 145
regularization 117
reinforcement learning 95, 103, 221
relational databases 31
reporting and analytics
  characteristics 175
research and methodology 176
  characteristics 176
residuals 78, 84
  example 85
  patterns and causes 85
retrieval-augmented generation (RAG) 35
return on investment (ROI) 178
ridge regression 118
risks and limitations, machine learning 106
  approximations of reality 108
  balanced dataset 107
  bias 107
  overfitting 107

underfitting 107
variance 107
root mean squared error (RMSE) 86, 140
  calculation example 141
  example 86
  formula 140, 141
  interpreting 141
  using 144
  values 141
R-squared 139
  calculation example 139, 140
  formula 139
  using 143
R-squared (coefficient of determination) 106

S

sampling strategies 9
  cluster sampling 10
  convenience sampling 9
  probability distribution 11
  random sampling 9
  random variables 11
  stratified sampling 9
second-party data 24, 25
self-selection bias 30
semi-structured data 28, 29
semi-supervised learning 95
sensitivity 149
sentiment analysis 108
serving-skew 158
shape of data 18
significance level
  common significance levels 62
  determining 62
  example 63
  selecting 63

significance testing 59
significance tests, for population average (mean) 70
   hypotheses, writing 71
   one-tailed test 72
   p-value estimation, from t-statistic using table 72
   p-value, versus significance level 72
   t-statistic, calculating 71
   t-statistic, using 71
   t-test conditions 71
   two-tailed test 72
   z-statistic, using 71
significance tests, for population proportion 66
   example 67
   z-test 68
   z-test example 70
   z-test, performing 68-70
Silhouette Score 132
slope of regression line
   interpreting 82, 83
software engineers (full stack, frontend, backend) 194
   industry insights 195
   responsibilities 194
   skills and knowledge 195
speech recognition 110
spokes 198
standard deviation 15
standard normal distribution 19
statistics 6, 91
   using 6, 7
stratified sampling 9
structured data 26
student's t-distribution 19

supervised learning 95, 103
   algorithm selection 115
   applications 112, 122
   bias-variance trade-off 114
   classification 113
   data preparation 115
   defining 111, 112
   key considerations 121
   key factors 113
   model evaluation 116
   model training 116
   number of input variables 114
   prediction and deployment 116
   regression 113
   steps 115
   target data quality 114
   training data, quantity 114
   types 112
supervised machine learning model
   testing 104
   training 103
   validation 103
support vector machines (SVMs) 100, 115, 119

T

third-party data 24-26
third quartile (Q3) 50
time series analysis and forecasting 221
training-serving skew 162, 167
   key feature 168
   mitigating 168
training-skew 158
transfer learning 96, 103
trend lines 76, 77
   fitting, to data 77-79

True Negative (TN) 105
true positive rate 149
True Positive (TP) 105
two-tailed test 72
Type I error 63
Type II error 64

U

UL applications
   anomaly detection 134
   feature extraction 135
   market segmentation 134
underfitting 107, 158, 162
   fairness, ensuring 162, 163
   model drift, navigating 162
   training-serving skew, navigating 162
underfitting, for optimal model performance 163
   consequences 163
   problem 163
underfitting, for optimal model performance, problem
   axes 165
   business decisions 167
   chart 166
   model solutions, building 164, 165
   optimal model, finding 166
   trade-off 166
unstructured data 27, 28
unsupervised learning (UL) 95, 103
   applications 134
   data collection 127
   data preprocessing 127
   defining 125
   evaluation 128
   examples 126

   interpretation 128
   model, training 128
   right model, selecting 127
   steps 126-128

V

variance 15, 107
vector databases 35

W

ways, for staying up to date
   AI influencers 227
   conferences and webinars 226, 227
   industry blogs and publications 226
   podcasts 226

Z

Z-score method 55
z-test 68
   alternative hypothesis 68
   example 70
   null hypothesis 68
   performing 68, 70
   p-value 68
   z-score 68

packt

packtpub.com

Subscribe to our online digital library for full access to over 7,000 books and videos, as well as industry leading tools to help you plan your personal development and advance your career. For more information, please visit our website.

Why subscribe?

- Spend less time learning and more time coding with practical eBooks and Videos from over 4,000 industry professionals
- Improve your learning with Skill Plans built especially for you
- Get a free eBook or video every month
- Fully searchable for easy access to vital information
- Copy and paste, print, and bookmark content

Did you know that Packt offers eBook versions of every book published, with PDF and ePub files available? You can upgrade to the eBook version at packtpub.com and as a print book customer, you are entitled to a discount on the eBook copy. Get in touch with us at customercare@packtpub.com for more details.

At www.packtpub.com, you can also read a collection of free technical articles, sign up for a range of free newsletters, and receive exclusive discounts and offers on Packt books and eBooks.

Other Books You May Enjoy

If you enjoyed this book, you may be interested in these other books by Packt:

Modern Generative AI with ChatGPT and OpenAI Models

Valentina Alto

ISBN: 978-1-80512-333-0

- Understand generative AI concepts from basic to intermediate level
- Focus on the GPT architecture for generative AI models
- Maximize ChatGPT's value with an effective prompt design
- Explore applications and use cases of ChatGPT
- Use OpenAI models and features via API calls
- Build and deploy generative AI systems with Python
- Leverage Azure infrastructure for enterprise-level use cases
- Ensure responsible AI and ethics in generative AI systems

The AI Product Manager's Handbook

Irene Bratsis

ISBN: 978-1-80461-293-4

- Build AI products for the future using minimal resources
- Identify opportunities where AI can be leveraged to meet business needs
- Collaborate with cross-functional teams to develop and deploy AI products
- Analyze the benefits and costs of developing products using ML and DL
- Explore the role of ethics and responsibility in dealing with sensitive data
- Understand performance and efficacy across verticals

Packt is searching for authors like you

If you're interested in becoming an author for Packt, please visit `authors.packtpub.com` and apply today. We have worked with thousands of developers and tech professionals, just like you, to help them share their insight with the global tech community. You can make a general application, apply for a specific hot topic that we are recruiting an author for, or submit your own idea.

Share Your Thoughts

Now you've finished *Data Science for Decision Makers*, we'd love to hear your thoughts! Scan the QR code below to go straight to the Amazon review page for this book and share your feedback or leave a review on the site that you purchased it from.

`https://packt.link/r/1-837-63729-6`

Your review is important to us and the tech community and will help us make sure we're delivering excellent quality content.

Download a free PDF copy of this book

Thanks for purchasing this book!

Do you like to read on the go but are unable to carry your print books everywhere?

Is your eBook purchase not compatible with the device of your choice?

Don't worry, now with every Packt book you get a DRM-free PDF version of that book at no cost.

Read anywhere, any place, on any device. Search, copy, and paste code from your favorite technical books directly into your application.

The perks don't stop there, you can get exclusive access to discounts, newsletters, and great free content in your inbox daily

Follow these simple steps to get the benefits:

1. Scan the QR code or visit the link below

    `https://packt.link/free-ebook/9781837637294`

2. Submit your proof of purchase
3. That's it! We'll send your free PDF and other benefits to your email directly

Printed in the USA
CPSIA information can be obtained
at www.ICGtesting.com
LVHW080557170824
788485LV00006B/709

9 781837 637294